North of Quabbin

Saw-whet owl

Wild turkey

North of Quabbin

By Allen Young

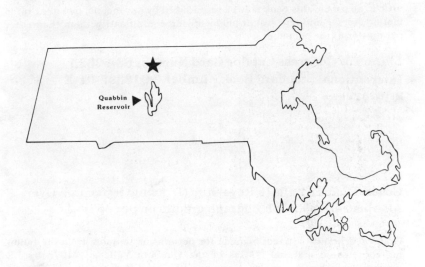

A Guide to Nine Massachusetts Towns

Athol	**Orange**	**Royalston**
Erving	**Petersham**	**Warwick**
New Salem	**Phillipston**	**Wendell**

Library of Congress Catalog Card Number 83-62325
International Standard Book Number 0-912395-01-X
Revised Edition

Cover: Doane's Falls in Royalston (Drawing by George Dyer)
All illustration and photograph credits on pp. 251-52.

Grateful acknowledgement is made for permission to quote from the following copyrighted material: "Atlas of the Quabbin Valley," ©1975 by J.R. Greene; "Quabbin Reservoir," a poem ©1976 by J.R. Greene; and "Enfield, Massachusetts," a poem © by Brendan Galvin. Additional acknowledgements appear on pp. 252-54.

Published by Millers River Publishing Co.
P.O. Box 159
Athol, Massachusetts 01331

Manufactured in the United States of America

Copies of this book may be ordered directly from the publisher at the above address for $6.95 plus $1 for shipping. Add 5% sales tax for books shipped within Massachusetts.

Please note: All telephone numbers listed in this book are in Area Code 617 unless otherwise indicated.

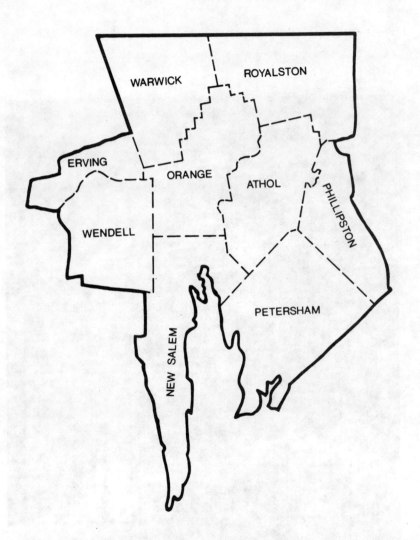

For D.M.

Raccoon

Table of Contents

Ring-necked pheasant

About This Book

The natural and human resources of the Central Massachusetts towns north of the Quabbin Reservoir – as well as the huge reservoir itself – are deserving of more appreciation and attention than they usually receive.

Populated by hard-working and friendly men and women, these nine towns offer a pleasant and eminently practical mixture of commerce and industry, farmland and forest, countryside serenity and smalltown bustle. A nature-lover's paradise, the area has numerous sparkling ponds and streams and tens of thousands of acres of public lands.

This guide has been written and compiled as a kind of tribute to a unique region. Its purpose is to share the "secrets" and the long-standing traditions of this special place, with the dual purpose of introducing the area to visitors and potential newcomers while providing a handy and informative reference for residents. Even people native to the area may not be aware of much of the history and points of interest detailed in this volume.

These nine towns – Athol, Erving, New Salem, Orange, Petersham, Phillipston, Royalston, Warwick and Wendell – often seem to be the forgotten cousins of larger or better-publicized Massachusetts communities. This is not a resort area as such, and few who live here would want tourism to predominate, but there is much here to interest the visitor.

Winter scene in Wendell

11

Cape Cod and the Berkshires are Massachusetts' major vacation attractions, but those looking for an unusual out-of-the-way place to enjoy a day trip or a full-length vacation will find this "North of Quabbin" area free of crowds and trashy commercialism. Its beauty and points of interest may be less obvious but they are no less rewarding than those found in more established resort areas.

The Quabbin Reservoir – a man-made lake of 39 square miles plus a watershed of 80,000 acres – is intentionally given little publicity by its owner, the Metropolitan District Commission, whose main job is to provide clean water to its customers. Those who know about the Quabbin's lands and waters, however, can use them with endless pleasure and still obey all of the MDC's long list of rules and regulations.

Several large state forests are found in these region, as are numerous properties owned by conservation groups such as the Trustees of Reservations. This is a place for people who love trees – the largest living things on earth – as they cover most of the craggy hills. Of these hundreds of hills, the highest is Mt. Grace in Warwick, 1,617 feet above sea level, with an old tower offering hikers a great view. In homage to this peak, the nine-town area is sometimes called the Mt. Grace Region – a name promoted by Edward T. Fairchild, former publisher of the Athol Daily News.

Some of these lands are wildlife sanctuaries, while others are open to hunting, fishing and trapping. There are many trails and roadways for hiking, snowshoeing, cross-country skiing, and travel by recreational vehicles.

The agencies who own these lands and the people who use them with respect and love are greatly concerned, however, with their abuse by those who are prone to spoil the countryside by making excess noise, failing to obey regulations and leaving behind litter. No welcome mat is set out for the polluters, the litterers and the other spoilers!

Who makes up the approximately 24,000 people who live in these hills and valleys? For more than a century, the most important economic activity here has been manufacturing. These industries, primarily in Athol and Orange, provide employment for most of the people. Some of their products – in particular the measuring tools of the L.S. Starrett Co. in Athol and the water-treatment equipment made by the Rodney Hunt Corp. in Orange – are internationally known for their outstanding quality.

The remaining seven towns can be termed "bedroom communities," since their inhabitants travel for employment to

Region's rivers and lakes stand out in this satellite photo

Monarch butterfly

Athol and Orange and places more distant. Especially in the 1970s and 1980s, as the United States experiences a population shift from urban toward rural areas, newcomers are moving gradually into these communities. They come from throughout New England, as well as New York, New Jersey and more distant places, seeking the pleasures of traditional New England country living – and by and large they are not disappointed.

Prior to the more recent influx, the area's population consisted of a mixture of traditional Yankees, French-speaking immigrants from Canada and some Europeans. Residents of area towns anticipate continued growth in population, and most hope for some new industries to locate here. However, only gradual, limited growth is seen as desirable and there is wariness of too much change. In general, newcomers are welcomed and easily integrated into community life, though there can be resentment of "outsiders" who move here with an attitude of superiority. The drama of the interaction between established residents and newcomers to an area is an ancient American one being replayed here in the 1970s and 1980s.

One aspect of these communities that appears to have universal respect is the tradition of New England democracy. Despite considerable erosion of local autonomy by federal and state government, town meetings here make decisions affecting the lives of the people. And despite some apathy, civic pride and participation in community affairs are substantial.

Area towns have direct town meeting government with the exception of Athol which has a representative town meeting. Each town elects three citizens to its board of selectmen, the highest body of government. There are various other elected and appointed town officials. The town clerk of each town can provide detailed information about the various boards, their members and functions. New residents especially will find that town

Taking an autumn stroll in a North Orange meadow

clerks are equipped to provide information about the rights and duties of residents and taxpayers.

Five of these towns (Erving, New Salem, Orange, Warwick and Wendell) are in Franklin County; the remaining four (Athol, Petersham, Phillipston and Royalston) are in Worcester County – yet the county line does not seem relevant to many residents, especially those in the two largest towns, Athol and Orange. The centers of Athol and Orange – which serve the region's needs for commerce and banking – are only five miles apart and the people of the two towns frequently interact.

The isolation of these nine towns is both a curse and a blessing. The towns have been "left alone" to their benefit, as the beauty of the villages and countryside attests, but sometimes to their detriment especially when economic stagnation is considered.

So near and yet so far, the state's three largest cities – Boston, Worcester and Springfield – cannot claim any of these nine towns as "suburbs." Yet these cities are close enough – two hours or less to Boston, an hour or less to Springfield and Worcester – so that they can be visited regularly for shopping, cultural and sporting events and big city night life.

A similar dynamic exists in relation to several other communities, including Northampton, Amherst, Gardner, Greenfield, Fitchburg and Leominster; Brattleboro, Vt.; and Keene and Peterborough, N.H. All of these communities are less than an hour away, and they offer opportunities for employment, shopping, entertainment and education that are sometimes

Old wagon wheel and barn wall on New Boston Road in Royalston

not available in the immediate area. They are distant enough, however, so that this region cannot be characterized as a satellite of any other place.

Residents of this area have easy access not only to the major cities of New England and New York but to all the spectacular outdoors of the Northeast U.S. – Mt. Monadnock in Jaffrey Center, N.H., the Northeast's most popular climbing mountain, about an hour from here; the Berkshires and Cape Cod; Nantucket and Martha's Vineyard, the seacoast north of Boston in Massachusetts, Maine and New Hampshire (approximately two hours' drive, for example, to resorts such as Hampton Beach and Ogunquit); the White Mountains and Lakes Region of New Hampshire, the Green Mountains of Vermont, and the Adirondacks and Catskills of New York.

This guidebook is organized in an alphabetical format, its contents offering an integrated regional view rather than listing everything town by town. In its proper place in the text, each of the nine towns is presented in a separate "portrait" giving a geographical and topographical description, some history, facts and figures, "local color" and a little sociology. The unique character of each community thereby emerges along with common regional threads. (As the reader encounters these portraits, which include ranking of the various towns in the state for size and population density, it should be kept in mind that there are 351 cities and towns in Massachusetts.)

In preparing this book, the author has stressed some things at the expense of others. (Isn't it always that way?) Information is provided on industry, commerce, history and services, but there is a special accent on natural and scenic attractions and on local agriculture. The reasons for this emphasis are partly personal, perhaps, but the emphasis results in great measure from a belief that the natural beauty of the area is one of its most neglected resources while local agriculture deserves all the help it can get. Two sayings, "You are what you eat!" and "Massachusetts grown – and fresher!" are worth repeating here. Preservation and development of farmland and support by non-farmers of those who are growing food go hand in hand. For the overall benefit of the people of this region, its ecology and its economy, a healthy mixture of industry, commerce, forestry and agriculture are essential. An appreciation of local history and of the area's natural resources – stressed throughout this guidebook – is the foundation upon which all of this may most successfully be built. Happy reading!

Airpark

The Orange Airpark might be characterized as the great white hope of economic progress in the region. With considerable financial assistance from various federal and state agencies, a 75-acre tract adjacent to the municipal airport has been developed for use by industry. Included in the development, undertaken with the cooperation of the Orange-Athol Industrial Development District (IDD), were paved roadways into the airpark, water mains, and underground electrical and telephone lines. The site is covered by evergreen forest, so that tenants will be able to enjoy a park-like atmosphere rather than the wasteland effect that characterizes so many industrial parks.

A preliminary division of the park shows 14 lots, ranging from three to 12 acres in size. Many of these have direct access to the taxiway of the municipal airport, and officials are especially seeking tenants who will be able to take advantage of the aviation angle.

The town of Orange has complete flexibility in the size and location of lots within the airpark, and parcels are available for purchase or long-term lease. Exclusive marketing rights to the airpark have been granted by selectmen to Arthur H. Platt of Countryside Realty, 253 East Main St., Orange MA 01364, Tel. 544-7406.

In mid-1983, the airpark's first occupants broke ground for an industrial rolls plant, an tangible indicator of the promise of cooperative efforts between the public and private sectors to provide employment for area residents and contribute to the community's econonic growth. See also AIRPORT.

Airport

The Orange Municipal Airport, best known for the private sport parachuting center located there, is a public facility developed initially by townspeople from Athol and Orange fascinated by the development of aviation in the 1920s. Originally called the Orange-Athol Airport, the facility began to be planned when members of the Orange Post American Legion made initial inquiries about the availability of a tract of land on the south side of Millers River.

The Kiwanis Club of Orange, the Exchange Club of Athol and the Rotary Club of Athol all got involved, and officials from the state Department of Aeronautics came to the area and inspected all possible fields in both towns. The current site was decided upon, and an option on about 125 acres was secured. A corporation was formed and stock was sold with the agreement half of the money should come from residents of each town. The company was incorporated for $25,000; it recruited 443 stockholders.

Ground was broken on June 24, 1929. Two runways were constructed, one 2,000 feet long by 175 feet wide, the other 3,000 feet long by 250 feet wide. Warren O. "Bud" Russell became "resident flyer," serving as associate agent for the Curtiss Flying Service at the field along with C.M. Taft, president of the airport (who died in a plane crash). The first air meet was held Sept. 13-15, 1929; in a harbinger of things to come in Orange, this first event included a parachute demonstration.

During the depression years, income from the field fell off and it was not possible to retain the service of a resident flyer. The airport was leased jointly to the towns of Athol and Orange in order that development work might be done through the New Deal's Works Progress Administration (WPA). Approximately $100,000 was expended for such improvements and later the airport was leased to various parties, including Millard F. Estey and the Athol-Orange Aero Club.

In 1939 Arthur Starrett of the L.S. Starrett Co. became president and initiated a series of conferences with state and federal aeronautical officials concerning the future of the port. As federal funds were available for development if the facility were municipally owned, the board moved in this direction. In 1941 articles were placed in the town warrants of Athol and Orange to see if the towns would purchase the airport jointly. Athol voted against the plan. Orange voters agreed to buy the airport for $5,000, providing federal funds were available for development.

World War II had arrived and the U.S. government was increasingly interested in airports for national defense, so an elaborate program for developing the field was set up. The stockholders of the corporation accepted the offer of the town, and Orange-Athol Airport, Inc., was liquidated. The town took over the airport in the spring of 1942 under an agreement with the U.S. government that assured town ownership but obliged the town to lease the facility to the War or Navy Departments during any national emergency.

During the war years, approximately $1,000,000 was spent to expand the two runways to 5,000 feet and build a third one of the same length. These funds were provided by the U.S.

19

Civil Aeronautics Administration (CAA), and the Orange airport is the largest in New England constructed exclusively with CAA funds. The airport was envisioned as an emergency alternative to Westover Air Force base in Chicopee, but the war ended soon after the expansion was completed.

In any case, hopes for the airport were great at the Oct. 14-15, 1944, dedication, where a souvenir program announced Norseman Air Transport service to Worcester and Providence, Montreal and Quebec, "truly placing Orange on the new global air map," and a schematic map showed "Orange Airport is hub in circle of 20 air minutes to important centers in New England and New York." Norseman's service did not last long but a Norseman aircraft was used for years by Parachutes Inc. Northeast Airlines offered scheduled service in the 1950s out of Orange but this did not continue due to lack of passengers.

The airport's importance to the community was revived in the 1960s when Parachutes Inc. attracted sport parachutists to the area and an international competition was held, but relations between PI and the town were not cordial and a civil suit resulted in the 1970s; the court determined that the PI lease expires in 1985 and it seems unlikely it will be renewed as there is widespread feeling locally that PI has exploited the town.

The future of the airport now seems linked to the possibility of new specialized industries with an interest in air transport being installed in the adjacent Orange Airpark. Plans have long existed to further upgrade the facilities by installing lights and instrument landing equipment.

As for the present airport facilities, two of the three runways (designated 0119 and 3214) are maintained under the supervision of the Orange Airport Commission, whose members are appointed by selectmen. (The third runway is not maintained due to budgetary constraints.) The airport now covers more than 700 acres and includes an administrative building (partly leased to PI), taxiways, and tie-down areas with capacity for hundreds of aircraft. The Athol-Orange Aero Club has its own building and four planes for use by members. Fuel service is handled by PI. A new "fixed base operator," City Engines, Inc., was scheduled to begin operations in the airport in late 1983 with the construction of a hangar for engine repairs. Flight instruction and expanded aviation services will also be provided. The airport is accessible via East River Street in Orange and from Daniel Shays Highway in Athol. See also AIRPARK, PARACHUTING.

Angel Gabriel

A tale of Royalston folklore concerns a small but beautifully carved statue of the angel Gabriel. The statue was made of a block of "first pine" around 1799 when parishioners found $65 left over after the expenses of building the church had been met. In 1840, when the parish replaced this building, Deacon Seth Holman was shocked to find Gabriel on a pile of rubbish. He carried the statue home for safekeeping.

Years later, the Holman family moved to Fitchburg. In 1903, Royalston held its first Old Home Day. Everybody had forgotten about Angel Gabriel by then, but a Holman descendant returned the carving. It remains today in the sanctuary of the First Congregational Church in the center of town.

Antiques

Hunting for antiques in the small towns of New England is a favorite pastime of visitor and resident alike. There are several antique shops in the region and "attic treasures" are often sold at flea markets, village fairs and tag sales. Among the established shops are the following:

Orange Trading Co., 13 South Main St., Orange, Tel. 544-6683; used furniture; specializes in coin-operated amusement machines and juke boxes.

Haley's Antiques, 488 South Main St., Athol, Tel. 249-9400; housewares, picture frames, bric-a-brac.

Ray Sault, 325 East Main St., Orange, Tel. 544-2826.

Sawyer's, 156 East Main St., Orange, Tel. 544-6024.

Edgar Stockwell, 80 New Athol Rd., Orange, Tel. 249-6541; specializing in Oriental porcelains.

Apples

Apples may be one of the few agricultural products in which Massachusetts is self-sufficient. Apples also are the stuff of American and New England legends. There's the saying, "An apple a day keeps the doctor away"; the famous Johnny Appleseed tale with its roots, according to one version, in nearby Leominster; and who is there that can turn down a portion of warm apple pie (with or without vanilla ice cream)? An orchard at blossom time (late April and early May) is a treat for the senses of sight and smell.

While McIntosh is by far the most popular Massachusetts apple, the area's orchards offer other varieties, some of which are favored for pie-making (Cortland early in the season and Spy later on), and all of which are worth giving a try – for variety if nothing else. Donald R. Schlicke, manager of Red Apple Farm in Phillipston, has prepared an information sheet on the 23 varieties of apples grown in the Red Apple orchards. He explains that most of the apple varieties planted in this country originated here, but the history of many is obscure. With the exception of recent varieties, few came into existence as the result of a plant breeder's efforts; most originated as chance seedlings. A typical chance seedling apple is the McIntosh, originated on the McIntosh homestead, Matilda Township, Dundas County, Ontario. Propagation was begun by Allan McIntosh about 1870, and strains have been improved through discovery and propagation of "bud sports," especially to produce fruit of brighter red color.

Fruit in local orchards is not organically-grown; fruit-growers claim there is no commercial orchard operation that does not use frequent sprays of pesticides.

The following orchards serve the public in the region:

Haley's Orchard, Main Street, North Orange; proprietor, Ronald Hurlburt, 25 Fairman Rd., Orange MA 01364, Tel. 544-2218; orchard manager, Fay Whipple; Apple Store during the fall season on Route 2A near WCAT; McIntosh, Red Delicious and Cortlands; old orchard being revived under new management.

Hamilton Orchards and Apple Barn, West Street, New Salem 01364; proprietors, William and Barbara Hamilton; Tel. 544-6867; marked by ubiquitous road signs on Route 202; pick-your-own apples and raspberries, both in fall season; open weekends beginning with maple syrup season, daily beginning Labor Day weekend; snacks on sale in Apple Barn include home-made apple squares and turnovers baked by Mrs. Hamilton; fresh cider and apples also on sale, including McIntosh, Cortland, Macoun, Delicious and Red Spy; Nature Trail (20-30 minute hike with explanations of natural features); groups welcome; children welcome; nice view of surrounding countryside; being expanded.

Red Apple Farm, Highland Avenue, Phillipston MA 01331, Tel. 249-6763; proprietor, Mrs. Spaulding Rose; orchard manager, Donald R. Schlicke; located one mile north of Route 2A; beautiful colonial home with adjacent retail store selling apples, pears and peaches (no pick-your-own); gift boxes of apples shipped anywhere; fresh cider pressed here; apples from this orchard available in some area retail outlets year round; varieties grown (listed in their approximate order of ripening) are Yellow Transparent, Puritan, Early Mac (not an early McIntosh but a cross between Yellow Transparent and McIntosh), Dutchess, Paula Red, Red Gravenstein, Wealthy, McIntosh, King, Macoun, Cortland, Empire, R.I. Greening, Spartan, Spencer, Delicious, Winter Banana, Baldwin, Senator, Northern Spy, Golden Delicious, Wagner and Newtown Pippin or Yellow Newtown; scions of the varieties listed are available to home orchardists who would like to try grafting these on their own trees.

Architecture

Throughout the towns and cities of Massachusetts are thousands of masterpieces of residential architecture; the nine-town region covered by this book has some of the best though it is often ignored by residents and visitors alike.

From the grand houses built by merchants to the modest capes of struggling farmers, colonial houses can be seen at the edge of busy streets and tucked away in backwoods glens. They remain standing more than 200 years after their hand-hewn timbers were first set in place. Their simple style has a strong appeal, as evidenced by the modern colonial-style houses in suburban developments; there are also lovingly made timber-

The Ballard Tavern, a Wendell landmark

A Victorian house on North Main Street in Orange

frame reproductions of colonial houses recently built in area towns by contemporary crafstmen.

In the early decades of the American republic, sometimes known as the Federal Period, numerous fine houses were built, exhibiting the classic symmetry of the period. Later structures often incorporated classical columns in an architectural style called Greek Revival. Fine local examples of Federal and Greek Revival homes can be found throughout the region; clusters of them are located on the commons in Petersham and Royalston.

The Victorian period of the late 1800s has also produced structures of extreme grace and beauty. Following the style of the period, these houses are characterized by embellishments such as octagonal cupolas and "gingerbread" wood trim, often quite ornate. Some have handsome hand-carved woodwork in their interiors. Fine Victorian homes are scattered throughout Athol and Orange, where the industrial revolution helped create the wealth that made them possible. Some of these fine buildings, including some old hotels, have been demolished to make way for new construction, especially as taxes and maintenance costs soared. Occasionally, Victorian architecture had its expression in more rural settings, such as the beautiful mansard a couple of miles north of Orange center on North Main Street.

Public and religious buildings, including churches and town halls, offer fine examples of New England architecture from the 1700s and 1800s. The Royalston town hall is a handsome mansard, designed and built in the 1860s by Chauncey

Chase who lived next door and gave the land. The Petersham Town Hall was rebuilt in 1960 following a fire as a replica of the original 1850 design. The New Salem Unitarian Church in the town center was judged at the time of its construction in 1794 to be one of the best examples of church architecture in the area. The Congregational Church on Royalston Common, another traditional church, has the quintessential tall church steeple – though it had to be rebuilt after it was blown over in the 1938 hurricane. The Community Church of North Orange and Tully, built in 1781, is a handsome building set in the village of North Orange. Located nearby this historic stagecoach stopover are several colonial homes, painstakingly restored by Mrs. Betty Kimball and other preservation enthusiasts.

While most of the industrial buildings in the area are plain brick structures of no special interest, there is one – a brick building located behind the Athol-Clinton Cooperative Bank – which has unusual ornate brickwork worthy of attention. This building is currently a warehouse for Plotkin Furniture Co.

Listed in the National Registry of Historic Places, the Pequoig Hotel of Athol is of some architectural note, if only because it is the grandest structure on the town's Main Street – the "centerpiece" of downtown Athol, as a Daily News editorial once noted when the building was in danger of demolition. As a result of a community effort spearheaded by concerned citizens and town officials, the old four-story brick hotel was sold to a developer for conversion to more than 50 units of housing for the elderly and some commercial space.

Pequoig Hotel on Athol's Main Street as seen on an old post card

25

The White Drum (now Pearl Island), art deco creation in West Orange

For several years prior to the reconstruction plan, which involves state and federal financing, the building had been boarded up.

Contemporary architecture has not been outstanding in Massachusetts' rural communities, though there are some exceptions. Some of the owner-built homes created as a result of the back-to-the-land movement are aesthetically pleasing. In addition, two twentieth century buildings, both in Orange, merit special attention. One is the Eastern Star Home, 75 East Main St., the mansion that once served as the opulent home of John W. Wheeler, president and treasurer of the New Home Sewing Machine Co. This striking edifice was completed in 1903 at a cost of $200,000. Interior finish in the house included ornaments finished with gold, hand-painted brocade wallpaper, and birchwood and mahogany paneling. Wheeler died only seven years after the house was completed, and in 1925 it was taken over by the Masonic order as a shelter for elderly women, all members of the Order of the Eastern Star. At the intersection of Routes 2A and 78 in Orange stands the former White Drum restaurant, one of the few interesting examples of Art Deco architecture in western and central Massachusetts. The building, designed by Alfred Glass of Greenfield, was erected in the early 1930s. Pearl Island, a Chinese and Polynesian restaurant, was opened in late 1982. For a few years prior to that, the building was owned by the Knights of Columbus of Orange. The K of C has a new home and community center on Daniel Shays Highway.

Armory

Members of the Massachusetts National Guard, formerly housed in the Orange Armory, trace their origins to volunteer militias in the early years of the American colony. Men of Orange participated in various conflicts – for example, a unit serving in 1916 on the Mexican border against Pancho Villa's raids under the command of Gen. John J. Pershing and a 150-man unit of men from Orange fighting in France against Germany during World War I.

The Guard's first quarters were upstairs in the old town hall, but when these became inadequate, a brick and stone armory was constructed at 135 East Main St. at a cost of $60,000. It was dedicated Nov. 14, 1913.

Company F, the last guard unit located here, ceased to exist in 1959, but there are many in Orange who can remember the drills, classroom work and other training activities in the armory as well as the summer encampments at Camp Drum, N.Y.

Eventually, the building was turned over to the town which rehabilitated it with the help of a grant. The armory has become home for a meal program and other senior citizen activities, roller-skating for youths and adults under the sponsorship of the private Orange Roller Skating Association, bingo games and other events.

Arts and Crafts

Creative energies flow throughout the region, inspiring artists and craftsmen whose efforts range from part-time hobbies to full-time businesses.

An accomplished artist named James Franklin Gilman (1850-1929) lived and worked in New Salem, Orange and especially Athol in the latter part of his life. His work – in oil paints, pastels, charcoal and pencil – depicted farm life, scenery, and industrial and public buildings. He moved from place to place, sometimes residing at the farms that were the subject of his canvases. When not painting, Gilman dedicated himself to spreading the message of Christian Science and he gained some renown as a close friend of the religion's founder, Mary Baker Eddy, illustrating her "Christ and Christmas" and publishing a calendar for the Mother Church. Gilman originals are owned by several local historic societies and by individuals in the area. Some of them were reproduced on postcards which

Painting by J.F. Gilman portrays Uptown Common in Athol

can occasionally be found at flea markets. Gilman's life and work are chronicled in an informative book, "James Franklin Gilman: Nineteenth Century Painter," by Adele Godchaux Dawson (Phoenix Press, 1975).

Many amateur and a few professional artists live today in the towns of the region. When a group of artists organized an art show in 1981, more than 75 individual artists were represented. Several of the towns have arts councils in conjunction with the state lottery program but these have not been active due to lack of funding. The New Salem-Wendell Rural Arts Program is a non-profit group formed in 1977 to bring arts activities to the area. It has sponsored children's workshops, performances, contra-dances, films and evening courses. The Franklin County Arts Council, based in Greenfield, has promoted and supported various arts programs. The Arts Extension Service at the University of Massachusetts, Amherst, promotes the arts by means of publications and expositions. Banks and libraries in area communities frequently arrange displays of artwork. Retired banker William K. Durfee has donated more than 100 paintings to the Athol Public Library for circulation to library patrons. Barbara Ellis of Athol, well-known for local landscapes, has had many displays of her work throughout New England. Sculptor Gene Cauthen of Royalston, who teaches art at Mt. Wachusett Community College, Gardner, is preparing a statue he hopes will be accepted for permanent display on the Royalston Common.

The best established institution for area crafts is the Petersham Craft Center, which has its own building on North

Street in Petersham, just off Route 122. The center is a non-profit organization offering classes, exhibitions, workshops and educational events. These programs are supported by annual memberships, donations and shop sales. The sales room and gallery are open Tuesday through Saturday, 1:30-5 p.m. (Tel. 724-3415). Products available include quilts, pottery, baskets, greeting cards and prints, sachets, toys, candles, stained glass, herbal wreaths, jewelry, wood products and other items.

The Petersham Craft Center has its roots in the town's Women's Exchange, which was established in 1912 to provide a market for the handwork of the neighborhood women. It was located on West Street. In 1917, Mrs. James J. Higginson gave the Exchange a building on Athol Road and land on North Street where the Center is now located. She also met the expense of moving the building to North Street and refurbishing it.

During the 1930s, the Rev. Earl Davis, a skilled woodworker, formed a group called the Petersham Handicrafts. Many of the town's best craftsmen learned their skills with this group. Prominent were Mr. and Mrs. Basil Coolidge, who worked in metals. Mrs. Coolidge also became an outstanding rug maker. Working with this group was Laura Amsden who taught art and metalcraft.

In 1955, the Women's Exchange and Petersham Handicrafts united to form the Petersham Craft Center. Clay, metal, wood, textiles and needlework were included initially in the program of the center. In 1958, Mrs. Earle Marsh offered crewel embroidery for the first time and this involved a new group of members. Mrs. C. Edward Rowe taught permanent wreath-making and in 1960 the Center sponsored its first large crafts exhibit, which has become an annual event.

Course and workshop offerings in 1982 included stained glass, refinishing and restoration of furniture, basic sign language, stenciling on tin and wood, introduction to silk screening and graphic design, straw ornaments, dough decorations, herbal gifts and three varieties of specialized needlework.

The Phillipston Parent-Teacher Group sponsors an annual October crafts show at Narragansett Regional High School, with proceeds used to provide scholarships, field trips and equipment for children from Phillipston. Information is available from Jeannine Batchelor, Tel. 249-8979, or Sam Kaczmarczyk at the Phillipston Memorial School, Tel. 249-4969.

There is an annual arts and crafts show at the Mahar Regional School, Orange, usually in early December in time for Christmas shopping. Booths and tables are set up throughout the building, creating a showcase for more than 80 craftsmen from several dozen towns in the tri-state area. Special features include a drawing for a faculty quilt, as each year teachers at the school cooperate in the production of an "heirloom quality" quilt. Proceeds are used to provide scholarships for past graduates and graduating seniors from the school. Information about the show can be obtained from Mahar Regional School, Orange MA 01364, Tel. 544-2542.

Among the many accomplished artists and craftsmen in the region are the following who requested a listing in this guidebook. Future editions will include others who request a listing, available free of charge from Millers River Publishing Co., Box 159, Athol MA:

Peggy Allen, 2117 Chestnut Hill Ave., Athol, Tel. 249-8209; copper foil stained glass.

Carol Brouillet, 84 Wallingford Ave., Athol, Tel. 249-3188; decorative art of all types; samples on display.

The Country Ell, Ellie Voutselas, proprietor, Elm St., New Salem, Tel. 544-7535; handwoven items including scarves, placemats, baby blankets, sachets and shawls; dried flowers and herbs for flower bouquets, potpourris, insect repellants

Table of native cherry handcrafted by Michael Humphries of Warwick

Artwork from herbal calendar by Petersham Calligraphers

and herb wreaths; plus selected work of other craftsmen and natural wool yarns from Victor's Farm.

Ann Forrester, 15 Athol Rd., Tully, Tel. 249-6903; patchwork and other hand sewing.

Michael Humphries Woodworking, HCR W130 White Road, Warwick MA 01364, Tel. 544-2694; custom furniture, cabinetmaking, interior architectural work.

Linda Teresa Kurkoski, LTK Originals, P.O. Box 68, Wendell Depot MA 01380, Tel. 544-3021; hand-painted T-shirts, card, greetings, posters, pastel drawings.

Knotty Pine Gift Shop, John Cameron, proprietor, RFD 2, South Athol MA 01331, Tel. 249-9642, handmade small wooden articles, mostly of pine, including candlesticks, shelves, paper towel holders and similar items.

Lupine Meadow Glass, Pam Bailey, proprietor, Lupine Meadow Farm, Star Route, New Salem MA 01355; stained glass.

Virginia MacDonald, 39 Meadow St. Athol, Tel 249-8468,

home-knitted apparel and blankets by hand and machine.

George Patriquin Scrimshaw, Spring Street, Petersham, Tel. 724-3444; etchings in ivory, whale teeth and whale bone.

Paw Print Pottery, Elizabeth W. Ringus, proprietor, 50 Glen St., Athol, Tel. 249-2270; wheel and handbuilt creations.

Petersham Calligraphers, Janet Palin and Ken Levine, proprietors, West Road, Petersham, Tel. 724-3394; graphic design; certificates; framing; herbal calendar.

Specialty Signs, Anneke Corbett, proprietor, 192 West Main St., Orange, Tel. 544-6404; general graphic design; signs.

Athol

Nicknamed "Tooltown USA," Athol is the largest community in the nine-town North Quabbin area and is its major commercial center.

The visitor who comes to Athol from the east first enters the historic Highlands section, now called "uptown," location of the Uptown Common and a small shopping district. Downhill on Route 2A toward the town center, several expansive red brick factory complexes, each adorned with large U.S. flags, come into view. The Main Street shopping district is just below that. The factory buildings, identified by large signs, house the town's two largest industries, the L.S. Starrett Co. and Union Butterfield Division of Litton Industries, both tool-manufacturing concerns. The third-largest company is the N.D. Cass Co., toymaker.

On the basis of these factories, and several smaller ones, Athol is a community predominantly of working people. People call the factories "shops," and the town is sometimes called a "mill town," a somewhat outdated reference to the original use of water power as the source of the industrial growth here in the 19th century. Each weekday, Main Street fills up with factory workers on their noon hour lunch break. The fire horn sounds at ten minutes before seven in the morning and ten minutes before one in the afternoon – familiar reminders to workers who have time clocks to punch.

In 1979, the last year for which figures are available, 224 Athol businesses large and small reported to the Massachusetts Division of Employment Security. These firms employed 4,424 persons, and had an annual payroll of $55,630,700. Manufacturing is by far the leading source of employment, with 62 percent of the total employed population

Aerial view of downtown

and 70.1 percent of the total annual payroll. Second in importance was wholesale and retail trade, with 17.1 percent of the total number of employees in the town. During recent hard times, some plants have laid off workers. A large shoe manufacturing operating, the J.F. McElwain Co., went out of business in 1981.

Located in Worcester County, the town is bordered on the west by New Salem and Orange, on the north by Royalston, on the east by Phillipston and the southeast by Petersham.

The town's area is 32.34 square miles, ranking it 68th in the state. Athol is the only town in the region to experience a population decline in the past decade, from 11,185 in 1970 to 10,634 in 1980. The population density is 327 persons per square mile. Athol's population is a friendly, diverse mixture, predominantly of Yankees, French-Canadians and Lithuanians, with smaller numbers of Italians, Irish, Jews and Asians, and the usual combinations present in the proverbial American melting pot.

The terrain is wooded and hilly, with elevations ranging from 500 at the edge of Miller's River – the town's most significant waterway, flowing from northeast to west – to 1,282 at the top of Pratt Hill near the Bearsden Woods. That heavily forested and scenic area includes approximately 1,000 acres controlled by the town's Conservation Commission. In addition to Bearsden Woods, other lands open to the public and controlled by the Commission, which undertook a land-acquisition program in the 1960s, include the Cass Meadow, the Rowe Half Acre, Neale Area, Millers River Northwest Area and Minnie French Area. (The Commission's publication entitled "Lands and Waters" provides detailed information and may be obtained free of charge from the town clerk.)

Athol was first settled in 1735 and named "Pequoiag," after an Indian grouping that inhabited the area. Athol acquired its present name when it was incorporated in 1762. John Murray, one of the proprietors of the land, chose the name because the area reminded him of his ancestral home among the hills of Blair-Atholl, Scotland. (In a recent attempt to preserve the link between Massachusetts' Athol and Scotland's Blair-Atholl, Roderick McColl, president of the Athol Savings Bank, paid a call on the Duke of Atholl while on a visit to the United Kingdom.) Local residents rightfully tend to ignore with disdain the occasional sophomoric jesting one hears about the town's name.

Like most of the early white settlers in Massachusetts, Athol's pioneers engaged in agriculture as well as hunting to survive, and found it necessary to protect their newly-acquired lands from raids by the Indians who had been forced off. By 1791, Athol had four grist mills, six sawmills, a fulling mill, and a shop with a trip hammer, all of which were operated by water power. The Athol Cotton Factory, built in 1811, was one of the first industries to serve a market beyond the local one,

Youthful gardener waters seedlings at Old Keene Road farmstead

Aerial view of Fish Park neighborhood

and further along into the 1800s, industries were built up in connection with leather, textiles, wood and metals. A scythe factory was started in 1800, and a shop to make shoe pegs was built in 1825. Charles M. Lee made shoes here and amassed a considerable fortune in the business. The construction of the Vermont and Massachusetts Railroad in the 1840s (now the Boston and Maine, or B&M) was an important factor in the growth of the town's industries as it improved communication with the outside world.

The Athol Machine Co., organized in 1868, made iron, hardware specialties, vises, meat cutters and machinists' tools. The Millers River Manufacturing Co. was incorporated in 1863 and made satinets and blankets. A steam box mill was set up in 1852 and in 1870 a woodturning business was launched. The Athol Carriage Works was set up in 1876. Other products manufactured in town were kegs and half-barrels, doors and blinds, cribs, cradles, towel racks and boxes.

Most of the population is found in the downtown and uptown areas, but there is scattered housing in the Daniel Shays Highway area, where the Fleetwood Nursing Home and the new Silver Spirit adult mobile home community are located; in South Athol, a village with its own community activities and site of a Morgan Memorial summer camp; and on rural byways such as Old Keene Road, New Sherborn Road, Conant Road and South Athol Road. Approximately one-third of Athol's residents are tenants. The remainder live in owner-occupied

"Bicycle Bill" of Athol beats the oil crunch

homes. Throughout the town there are many beautiful homes, and most homeowners put considerable amounts of energy into making their places comfortable and attractive. Indeed, this is a home-oriented community. Flowers, shrubs and lawns, and freshly-painted houses give an impression of a community that takes pride in itself. The town has a taxpayer-supported shade tree commission to promote planting of new trees every year.

Town government is located in Memorial Building, erected in the 1920s as a memorial to veterans, whose names are inscribed on the walls in the rotunda. Professional town employees, including efficient police and fire departments, meet the needs of townspeople for government services. The department of public works attends not only to roadways, but to water works, sewage treatment, parks and cemeteries. There are several town-operated tennis courts and two public beaches supervised by lifeguards.

Aside from being an industrial and commercial center, Athol has several small farms. Many Athol residents also maintain backyard gardens and raise small amounts of livestock, without being full-time farmers.

Several individuals who have lived in Athol have gained national fame as entertainers. Among them are Busby Berkeley, choreographer of Hollywood extravaganzas; Charles Starrett, who portrayed the Durango Kid in westerns; Dave Bargeron, brass player with the 1960s rock group Blood, Sweat and Tears; Neil Hamilton, an actor who played Commissioner Gordon in the "Batman" TV series; and Jack Burns of the Burns and Shriver comedy team, who had his first broadcasting job at radio station WCAT, then in Athol.

Athol's contemporary problems include unemployment, empty stores and abandoned buildings, high rates of alcoholism and teen-age pregnancy, and a tendency for young people to leave the area due to lack of opportunity. Nonetheless, community life is rich with the activities of social, civic, fraternal and religious organizations. Popular events include weekly bingo, the annual Minstrel Show, and the River Rat Spectacular canoe race. While the community is sometimes described as "depressed," there is a long-range view that the many skilled, hard-working residents will pull together toward a brighter future. See also ATHOL HISTORICAL SOCIETY, BEARSDEN WOODS, FRENCH-CANADIANS, HATCHET HUNT, HISTORY TRAIL, LITHUANIANS, STARRETT'S, UNION TWIST DRILL, YMCA.

Athol Historical Society

The Athol Historical Society was founded July 27, 1953, when a small gathering of residents met in the director's room of the Athol Cooperative Bank to form a group to serve as "guardian and keeper of Athol historical records and relics."

The society now has several hundred members and its own building, used for meetings and to house its museum of antiques and memorabilia. The residence of Eida W. Limbach at 1477 Main St. was the society's first home, but in the fall of 1957, the town voted to turn over the old town hall on upper Main Street to the society. Only one dollar was paid for the

Athol artist Barbara Ellis' rendition of Athol Historical Society

building, but the society has put some $25,000 into renovations and repairs, paid for by membership fees and donations.

Hundreds of articles and thousands of photographs are on display in the second-floor museum depicting the life of the town from its earliest days to the middle of this century.

Among the oldest items is a pewter communion service of the First Church, which dates from 1776. The society has files of Athol's first newspaper, the Freedom Sentinel, published in 1827-28; the original list of Minutemen drawn up in 1775 just before they left for Lexington; the hammer used by Charles M. Lee when making his first pair of shoes at home before starting the Lee Shoe Factory which grew into one of the town's leading industries (the recently defunct J.F. McElwain Co.); the old meat chopper designed by Laroy S. Starrett which led to the formation of the tool-manufacturing company that bears his name, now the town's largest industry. Photographs owned by the society include portraits of town fathers and ordinary citizens in days gone by, views of buildings (including many that no longer stand), and local scenery including views of the famous flood of 1938.

The museum, at 1307 Main St., is open regularly in the summertime and by special arrangement at other times. The person to contact about museum hours and access is M. Dexter Gleason, the curator, at home (249-6598) or at the museum (249-4115).

Bear's Den (New Salem)

Legendary and beautiful, Bears's Den is a natural scenic attraction located south of Lake Mattawa on the north side of Neilson Road in North New Salem, approximately one-half mile west of Elm Street.

Here, the middle branch of the Swift River, which rises in Wendell and flows south, emptying into the Quabbin, has carved a small gorge through the hills creating a sparkling waterful adjacent to granite cliffs almost 100 foot high.

According to Mrs. Carolyn Chouinard, a local historian, the Bear's Den was a meeting place for Indian tribes. The story goes that during the summer of 1675, the Indian chieftain Metacomet, called King Philip by the white settlers, camped at Bear's Den to consult neighboring leaders and obtain their assistance during his campaign against white settlements in the Connecticut River valley and environs. The Swift River Valley Historical Society, however, has been unable to confirm the tradition of King Philip's visit, although the Native American leader is known to have been part of an encampment in the area. Over the years, Indian artifacts have been found within the North New Salem area, although reportedly none at the side of Bear's Den itself.

As for the locale's name, it is said that one of the first settlers of the area shot and killed a black bear here and called the place

Swift River (middle branch) flows through Bear's Den

"bear's den."

The Bear's Den is preserved as a public place through the generosity of Mrs. Grais Poole Burrage, who died in 1968 leaving the property to the Trustees of Reservations. Mrs. Burrage, a New Salem native, served as town treasurer and tax collector. She was also treasurer of the Swift River Valley Historical Society.

She acquired the Bear's Den in 1925 and continued the tradition of allowing free access to the area. She constantly refused lucrative offers for the property, fearing it would be exploited and its natural beauty destroyed. It was her lifelong wish to have the Bear's Den remain, as it had throughout history, a natural area to be enjoyed by all.

The land owned by the Trustees includes the waterfall and 3.4 acres. Access is by means of a footpath, not too steep, and it takes only a few minutes to get from the roadside to the falls.

Bearsden Woods

The Bearsden Woods, a tract of land of some 1,000 acres controlled and maintained by the Athol Conservation Commission, is a hilly wooded wildnerness between the Millers River and the old Highlands or uptown section of Athol. Access is by means of Bearsden Road, near Athol Memorial Hospital. A roadside sign points the way.

Bear sightings in past years gave origin to the name, and although there are stories of bears' caves in the hills, no one can point them out with authority.

Pratt Hill, Athol's highest peak, at 1,282 feet above sea level, looms off Templeton Road (Route 2A) near South Royalston Road, though it is not within the conservation area. The town's second-highest peak, Round Top, at an elevation of 1,278 feet, is within the conservation land and offers one of the best scenic views of the area. The view is aided by the dearth of trees at the top, caused by a 1957 fire. Approximately 1,000 feet to the northeast is a high plateau known as Warren's Vista, named in 1967 by the commission for Commissioner M. Addison Warren who brought attention to the fine view during an exploration hike. (To the south of Round Top is the 1,244-ft. peak – officially unnamed – upon which the cable television antenna tower was erected in 1954. It is sometimes referred to as Bearsden Mountain because the tower is seen from all points in town and easily locates the area.) The rounded summit of the various hills in Bearsden were caused by centuries of erosion by glaciers, rain and wind.

Bearsden Road is mostly paved to a parking lot at the conservation area. A dirt road continues northward toward Millers River, however, leading to a site that has been documented by historians as a major Indian crossing. What was the continuation of Bearsden Road crossed Millers River over Lewis Bridge, later rebuilt as Red Bridge. The Lewis Bridge collapsed in April 1907 and its successor was washed away in the 1936 flood. Only the stone abutments remain, but many Athol residents still cite the bridge as a destination, as in, "Let's hike to Red Bridge!" This bridge crossing once provided a direct route between Athol and South Royalston through the section known as The Gulf.

One landmark in the area is Lawton's Barway. In olden times, farmers sometimes built bar-ways instead of swinging gates at gaps in their stone walls. The bars, which were removable long wood poles, were easily socketed into the stone or wood pedestals. Lawton's Bar-Way is on the Bearsden Road extension beyond the Round Top trails, about half the distance between the end of the paved road and Millers River.

Ox Bow, a W-shaped curvature of the Millers River in the remotest area of Bearsden, was so named because it resembles an ox yoke. It has been popular as a hikers' goal and picnic area for decades. The Ox Bow peninsula is located on the north side of the river, just north of where the Buckman Brook empties into the river. Through this area a crew of immigrant Irish laborers began in 1845 to clear Athol's first railroad bed.

Other interesting features of Bearsden include the remains of the "mud hut colony" once inhabited by immigrant Italian workers who built the Newton Reservoir, abandoned stone quarries, Sheep Rock which offers a view of the Millers River far below, Duck Pond (directly north of Sheep Rock), the narrow 300-foot canyon called "the cut" blasted in 1907 to facilitate passage of water pipe from Newton Reservoir, the so-called Indian cellarhole and many miles of fieldstone walls built by the town's hardy pioneers.

A network of hiking trails and fire roads, well marked and cleared, has been constructed in the area – 13 routes totaling 10 miles. Various sections are appropriate for horseback riders and hikers.

A log cabin, donated to the town in 1967 by Timothy Paige of Longmeadow, a former Athol resident, was refurbished for use as the field quarters of the Conservation Commission. The 30-ft. by 20-ft. cabin off Bearsden Road extension was built during World War II with hemlock planks and covered with horizontal hemlock slabs. It is available for overnight outings by any adult-supervised groups provided the commissioners are notified in advance.

Bearsden Woods was acquired through purchase and easement by the Commission, mostly 1965-70, under the leadership of its first chairman, Robert Lawton. An excellent description of Bearsden's history and features (plus a detailed map, adapted and revised by J.R. Greene from a map by R. Thompson) is contained in the Conservation Commission's booklet, "Lands and Waters," available free of charge at the office of the Town Clerk, Memorial Building, 584 Main St., Athol. See also HATCHET HUNT, LAKES AND PONDS, MILLERS RIVER.

Bicentennial Park

To celebrate the nation's 200th birthday, the Orange Kiwanis Club donated $5,000 and combined the funds with $5,000 from the state to create a woodland park off Holtshire Road. Named Bicentennial Park, the area provides for picnicking and hiking with nature trails heading toward nearby Beaver Pond through water department land. There is a barbecue pit and a covered picnic area.

Birch Hill Dam

Following the devastation of the flood of 1938, the U.S. Army Corps of Engineers moved to construct flood control dams in the Millers River watershed.

The Birch Hill Dam on the Millers is located in South Royalston and the flood control land covers 4,600 acres, some in Royalston but most in Winchendon. The Winchendon community of New Boston was located in this area; some houses were moved but 25 were razed including the former Baptist church that was once the focus of New Boston's village life. There is a sadness about the "lost" village of New Boston, less well known than the sadness surrounding the inundated Quabbin towns, but just as meaningful to those who lived on and loved that land.

The damage from the flood of 1938 was so traumatic to the people of Athol and Orange that when work on Birch Hill was delayed in the early 1940s, local officials became concern-

44

ed and pressed for the dam to be completed. In all 174 parcels of land were taken to create the flood protection zone, to an elevation of 852 feet above sea level. This included 4,394 acres taken for fee and 253 by easement.

Work was begun in 1940 and completed in 1942. Total cost of the project was $4,576,600. An original plan to excavate a tunnel from Birch Hill under Royalston Center to the Tully basin was dropped.

The dam is made of rolled earth fill, with rock slope protection and an impervious core, with a total volume of 359,000 cubic yards. It is 1,400 feet long with a top width of 25 feet. Its height is 56 feet above the level of the river, 864 feet above sea level. The drainage area is 175 square miles. Spillway crest covers 3,200 acres. The spillway is located about 1,900-2,400 feet northwest of the dam. The outlet consists of four rectangular conduits, with an electrically operated gear-driven slide service gate and a crane-operated slide emergency gate.

Birch Hill, for which the area is named, is located nearby in the Otter River State Forest. The hill that abuts the dam is called Buck Hill. See also BIRCH HILL WILDLIFE AREA, MILLERS RIVER, TULLY DAM AND LAKE.

Birch Hill Wildlife Area

A sportsmen's and nature-lovers' mecca, the Birch Hill Wildlife Management Area offers residents of the area convenient access to hunting, fishing, trapping, target shooting, canoeing, snowshoeing and hiking. The scenic aspects of this large area, however, are marred by accumulations of "slash" (piles of limbs) from logging operations and broken glass from littering.

The area consists of approximately 8,500 acres, half of it U.S. government land under the jurisdiction of the U.S. Army Corps of Engineers in conjunction with its Birch Hill Dam. This flood control acreage is leased to the Massachusetts Department of Environmental Management and is subject to inundation during flood operations. The remaining acreage is controlled outright by the state, with the entire area managed by the state's Division of Fisheries and Wildlife. The administration building is on Dennison Road just off Route 202, Baldwinville.

Winston Neale of South Royalston is Birch Hill's supervisor and Arthur Myers of Ashburnham is his assistant. The two men constitute the entire staff of this place, and it's a big job to keep watch over so much territory and protect this vast natural resource from spoilers who litter the land with trash and who cannot obey simple regulations regarding hunting, fishing, trapping and general land use.

Approximately 1,000 acres of the area lies in Royalston, including Beaver Pond and stretches of Stockwell Brook and Millers River. The remaining acreage is mostly in Winchendon, with some in Templeton. The target range is in Winchendon, off Goodnow Road, just east of the Royalston line.

Camping is prohibited here, with the exception of scout groups who can gain full access by obtaining prior permission. (There are public campgrounds and other recreational facilities nearby in Otter River and Lake Dennison state forests.)

Among the animals hunted at Birch Hill are cottontail rabbit, snowshoe hare, coyote, deer, woodcock, partridge and pheasant (stocked from state farms). Species that are trapped include beaver, fox, fisher cat, muskrat, mink and weasel. The Millers River is stocked with rainbow trout and brook trout throughout the spring.

The area includes pine and birch forest of recent growth as well as mature forest, fields and wetlands. Much of the acreage here was acquired by the state in the 1970s from a single large landholder, the Landvest Co., which retained logging rights for five years. Loggers recently completed their work, according to Neale.

Birds

Many species of birds inhabit the region year-round or seasonally, or pass through it during migration each fall and spring. With its varied habitat – woodlands, brushy areas, swamps, fields, lakes and rivers – the area is a birdwatcher's paradise. Some birds are hunted and there is stocking of pheasants by the state in several area locales. New Salem's Prescott Peninsula, within the Quabbin wilderness, has been the site of an attempt by state scientists to reintroduce the bald eagle to Massachusetts and to encourage the naturalization of wild turkeys. The sound of the honking of a flock of Canada geese and the sight of their amazing "V" formation is a traditional local harbinger of fall and spring.

The Athol Bird and Nature Club, headquartered in the Athol Junior High School is a focal point for bird-watching enthusiasts. Robert Coyle, science teacher at the school, has

46

Chickadee, the state bird of Massachusetts

several stuffed birds on display in the school's nature museum, and is singlehandedly responsible for teaching bird-watching techniques to many area residents.

The club sponsors a variety of events, include bird walks, the annual Christmas bird count, an autumn hawk count from Round Top Mountain in Athol's Bearsden Woods conservation area, trips to the Plum Island wildlife reservation on Boston's North Shore and other outings.

The Christmas count has been an annual event here for two decades. The junior high school is the hub of the count circle which is 15 miles in diameter. This event is held in conjunction with national bird groups, which receive reports from local birders. In one recent count, the most common birds were, in order of frequency: starling, evening grosbeak, dark-eyed junco, black-capped chickadee (the state bird), house sparrow, blue jay, mourning dove and rock dove (Athol's "city pigeon"). A total of 43 species were observed; more than 80 species have been observed on at least one Christmas count census.

Many area residents successfully attract an amazing array of birds to feeders. Many area residents belong to the Massachusetts Audubon Society (South Great Road, Lincoln MA 01773), which provides nature-lovers in general and bird-watchers in particular with publications and programs of special interest to them. Information about bird-watching is available from Robert Coyle, 1978 Chestnut Hill Ave., Athol, Tel. 249-6083. See also QUABBIN WILDLIFE.

Bread

Everyone likes fresh-baked bread. Its smell is irresistible, the taste all the more so.

The Athol Bake Shop, 524 Main St., features a variety of bread and pastries. Especially appealing are their Vienna and French loaves and dinner rolls, including custom orders for special occasions, and their hot cross buns are a traditional Eastertime treat.

The Orange Bake Shop, 1 South Main St., includes a restaurant and snack bar. Its baked goods range from white and whole wheat bread to assorted donuts, cupcakes, pastries and cookies.

Connoisseurs who like home-made bread and pies with their meals can't go wrong at the New Salem Restaurant on Route 202, which has a different kind of fresh bread every day and fresh pies with an emphasis on seasonal local ingredients. They serve breakfast and lunch only.

A traditional European sourdough bread, baked on a wood-fired brick hearth oven for distribution throughout New York and New England, is produced by the Baldwin Hill Bakery, Baldwin Hill Road, Phillipston. With a weekly output of nearly 10,000 loaves and its sanctification by various authorities for individuals following macrobiotic and kosher dietary laws, the bakery is one of the more unusual institutions of the region.

Baldwin Hill Bread, as it is called, is sold in health food stores, food cooperatives and specialty shops as well as some supermarkets.

Dr. Hy Lerner of Pelham and Paul Petrofsky started the bakery in 1974 after being inspired by the LIMA bakery in Belgium. Baldwin Hill Bread contains 100 percent stone-ground whole wheat flour, well water and sea salt – nothing else. Other varieties now marketed include salt-free, rye, sesame and cinnamon raisin.

The bread rises due to fermentation caused by a natural sourdough culture, the same one that has been retained since the bakery started producing its product. Part of the baker's job is to "feed" the culture by giving it flour, water and salt. The bread rises for several hours before being baked in the oven for about 45 minutes at 450-550 degrees.

The oven was constructed of red brick by Petersham stonemason James Dowd. Its walls are two feet thick. The baking chamber is about 80 square feet, lined with firebrick, with a capacity of almost 100 loaves.

The bread is shipped from Phillipston by truck to New York and New England outlets and to places throughout the United States via United Parcel Service. Locally, the bread has a small following, and the proprietor and staff welcome visitors to come and buy the bread when it is still warm, fresh out of the oven.

"Ideally," Lerner said, "people should come to a bakery to get their bread." He said the best time for visitors is Sunday in the daytime; the bakery is open to the public Sunday through Thursday, 10 a.m. to 6 p.m. Visitors are advised to call first (Tel. 249-4691) to find out the best time to visit – when the baker on duty has a few free minutes to play host.

The Baldwin Hill Bakery is seen by its founders as part of a "revival" of interest in "high quality, whole natural foods, untained by chemicals of any kind." Lerner, who abandoned his medical practice to promote "health and longevity" through the bakery's products, points out that over the past 50 years there has been a gradual replacement of small, neighborhood bread bakeries. In their place has come highly mechanized bread factories, and as a consequence bread flour is no longer wholesome but is highly refined with "additives put in to maintain an illusion of freshness and flavor."

Baldwin Hill uses a blend of winter and spring wheat grown on fields that are compost fertilized. No chemicals are used in its cultivation, harvesting or shipping, which is unusual.

The wheat used comes from a single farm in Bloomfield, Montana, owned by the Whitmer family. Lerner said the Whitmers grow "the best organic wheat in the country." He said they plant thousands of acres in wheat, with about 300-400 acres needed annually to grow the wheat that is eventually stoneground to flour here in Phillipston. Nothing is added to or removed from the whole grain at any time; it contains all of its natural fiber, bran, protein, carbohydrates, germ, vitamins and minerals.

By today's standards, Baldwin Hill Bread might be characterized as heavy, but Lerner points out that it is the "kind of bread which was once the mainstay of most families."

Brooks Woodland Preserve

Entrance to trails penetrating the Brooks Woodland Preserve in Petersham are located on the south side of East Street at Shaw Road and Brown Pond, approximately one mile from the Petersham Common. The Trustees of Reservations owns the land, including some 405 acres, with extensive stands of old-growth trees, pond and wetlands.

The James W. Brooks Woodland Preserve is named for a Harvard Forest benefactor and was given to the Trustees by Mr. and Mrs. John Fiske of Petersham and John Fiske Jr. of West Hartford, Conn., acting as trustees of the Brooks Wildlife Sanctuary. In addition to preserving beautiful forestlands, the site protects portions of the Swift River watershed and includes old Indian grinding stones, several cellar holes and a bridge abutment.

A program is underway to recreate a forest typical of central New England at the time of the region's first settlements and to use the forest to train foresters in woodland management. A campaign to raise $332,000 to fund the program is underway.

This land is part of an environmental protection plan including ownership as well as conservation restrictions or easements along the Swift River. This greenway assures a protected wooded area extending for more than three miles along both sides of the stream shortly before it enters the Quabbin Reservoir.

The Brooks Preserve is traversed by a portion of Roaring Brook which passes through a ten-acre swamp that was once a storage pond in colonial times. It has more recently become a beaver pond. The southerly part of the land, or Swift River tract, is divided by the Swift River which, for a mile, flows through it among marshes and abandoned ponds and between the abutments of an old timber bridge and sluiceway.

The westerly slope is mostly hardwoods, whereas white pines dominate the easterly slopes which rise at one point to form a considerable hill. There are outcrops of cliff formations and a cascade of giant boulders. It is a prime geological exhibit of glacial, frost and root action at work.

There are porcupine caves with trails radiating in every direction, winding their way through maidenhair ferns, trillium and Jack-in-the-pulpit. Through the preserve there are numerous species of wildflowers, animals and both migrating and nesting birds that can readily be observed from the more than five miles of roads and trails.

Remains of the Charles Dudley farmstead are located within the preserve. The Dudley farmhouse was built in 1811 and was abandoned early in this century. Cellar walls, doorsteps and central chimney remain with miles of stone walls that enclosed the barnyards and lanes leading to pastures.

Nearby are the "Indian grinding stones," a group of large boulders, split and separated by frost, in which small hollows connected by troughs were apparently carved by members of the Nipmuck tribe. Kernels of corn were stripped from the cobs, pounded with a stone pestle in the hollows, and the Indian meal produced as a result was pushed along the troughs to waiting baskets.

Camping

There are three public and five private camping areas in the region:

Federated Women's Club State Forest, off Route 122, Petersham, information from Otter River State Forest, 939-8962; four wilderness sites.

Laurel Lake Recreation Area, Erving State Forest, State Road, Warwick, and Laurel Lake Road, Erving; 544-3939 or 544-6933; 32 sites; tents and trailers; public swimming area with lifeguard; May-October.

Tully Lake Recreation Area, Doane's Hill Road, Royalston, 249-8193; leased by U.S. Army Corps of Engineers to Massachusetts Department of Environmental Management; 21 tenting sites (accessible by backpack or canoe only); full bathroom including facilities for handicapped persons; canoe launch access to Tully Lake and nearby Long Pond; swimming prohibited; Memorial Day to Labor Day.

Hidden Haven Campground, Royalston Road, Phillipston, 249-6169 or 249-8401; 45 sites; tents and trailers; recreation hall and safari area; April 15 to October 15.

Lakeridge Campground, 300 Daniel Shays Highway, Orange, 544-7111; 180 sites, tents and trailers; April-December.

Pineridge Campgrounds, Mountain Road, Erving, 544-6056; 30 sites, tents and trailers; swimming pool; May-October.

The Ranch, East River Street, Orange, 544-6270.

Wagon Wheel Camping Area, Wendell Road, Warwick, 544-3425; 110 sites, tents and trailers; live musical entertainment, including annual Labor Day Weekend benefit for Muscular Dystrophy Foundation; activities program for adults and children; swimming on premises; state-owned Laurel Lake Recreation Area nearby; May 1 to Columbus Day.

Camping is explicitly illegal in the Quabbin area; the law is enforced by Metropolitan District Commission police.

Cemeteries

There are several cemeteries in each of the area towns; many of them contain tombstones put in place 150-250 years ago.

The cemetery on Route 78 in Warwick just south of the town center is particularly evocative of local history; even from the roadside, one can sense the inexorable march of time by observing the old stones at the north end of the cemetery yielding gradually to the newest ones at the south end.

The Locks Village Cemetery on Jennison Road in Wendell is a particularly scenic old cemetery. Athol's oldest burial grounds are on Mt. Pleasant Street and Hapgood Street. In Orange, the burial ground at North Orange is the oldest, with 15 Minutemen buried there; the Jones Road cemetery contains early settlers' tombstones.

Some cemeteries are completely forgotten on backwoods roads; others are used annually as a gathering place for patriotic orders, veterans' groups, scouts and bands on Memorial Day. War memorials honoring those who died in the nation's various conflicts are found at many cemeteries.

Most cemeteries are maintained by town cemetery commissions or departments. These cemeteries are interesting places to visit for meditative or historical purposes and gravestone rubbing is permitted but those pursuing such interests are urged to show proper respect. Unfortunately van-

Locks Village cemetery in southern part of Wendell

dalism in local cemeteries has been a growing problem.

All cemeteries are indicated on topographical maps. See also PEACE STATUE.

Chase Memorial

The Chase Memorial is a 114-acre forested tract of land off Route 68 between Royalston Center and South Royalston. The woods are open to the public.

The land is owned by the New England Forest Foundation, which received it as a donation from Alice E. (Chase) Glassett of Needham. The woodland was originally a farm owned by Mrs. Glassett's forebears since colonial times.

Most of the land lies on the west side of Route 68, where it is marked by a sign. A 35-acre parcel lies on the other side. Much of the land has been logged for timber and cordwood.

Local forester for the foundation is James E. Bailey of Orange, whose forestry and woodlot management services are available to private landowners. The late Harris A. Reynolds, former secretary of the Massachusetts Forest and Parks Association, was the founder of the NEFF. The foundation was conceived of as a means to aid the New England economy and protect its natural beauty. The organization has an annual budget of about $700,000, and about eighty percent of this comes from services provided by foresters.

Churches

Approximately three dozen churches offer weekly services and other regular activities, such as Sunday schools and organ and choir programs, in area towns. Most major denominations as well as several smaller ones are represented here, while houses of worship representing other faiths and teachings can be found in nearby communities.

A complete listing of churches and their clergy and programs is published each Saturday in the Athol Daily News. Visitors are always welcome.

Although churches are important in the life of the community, many residents tend to their spiritual needs without being affiliated with organized religion; the area has its share of agnostics and atheists, too. In these matters, the diversity seems accompanied by an atmosphere of mutual respect, tolerance and understanding.

Churches on New Salem common at time of town's bicentennial (1953)

Many of the church buildings in the area are beautiful and well-maintained architectural masterpieces; much of the rural New England charm of area towns is due to these buildings and to such traditional features as their towers and steeples – many of which have chimes, clocks and weather vanes. See also ANGEL GABRIEL, ARCHITECTURE, FRENCH-CANADIANS, LITHUANIANS; SYNAGOGUE, WAYSIDE CROSS.

Clubs

From the I Wunder What club, a 55-year-old sewing club in Athol, to the Jumptown Twirlers, a square dance group that fills the Orange town hall regularly to the call of "allemande left" and "do-si-do," dozens of clubs and organizations occupy the evenings and weekends of residents of the nine-town region.

Virtually every area of interest is covered by these voluntary organizations, whose purposes range from politics to charity, but which have a profoundly social function.

There are numerous veterans' groups, senior citizens' clubs, the Margery Morton Chapter of the Daughters of the American Revolution, the Athol Bird and Nature Club, Overeaters Anonymous and many sporting groups.

Some of these clubs, such as Masons, Rotary, Odd Fellows, Grange, Kiwanis, Lions, Elks, Exchange, Quota and

Business & Professional Women, are affiliated with state, national and international organizations. Among these national affiliates are those, such as the Knights of Columbus and B'nai Brith, with a religious basis. Local churches also sponsor their own fraternal organizations. Most area towns have their own Democratic and Republican committees. Some organizations are for women only, others for men only. For youths, there are various scouting organizations under the sponsorship of diverse groups.

A directory of area clubs is published by the Athol Public Library. Information about clubs is readily available in each area town from librarians, town clerks and clergymen. See also SPORTS.

Communes

In the late 1960s and early 1970s there were numerous experiments with communal living in area towns. Most famous of these was the "Brotherhood of the Spirit," led by Michael Metelica, a commune with hundreds of members. The Brotherhood owned property on Shepardson Road in Warwick; members came from all over the United States and a dormitory was constructed near an old farmhouse. The commune received widespread publicity but eventually many members became disillusioned and drifted away. In recent years, Metelica changed his named to Michael Rapunzel and the group changed its name to the Renaissance Church of Beauty and moved to Turners Falls and Gill. The Warwick property was sold and the dormitory dismantled.

Experimental living arrangements were plentiful. Social and economic focal points for the area's counter-culture in those days included the Our Daily Bread Food Cooperative in Orange (now defunct) and the Warwick Inn (where weekend rock and roll boogie sessions were held regularly). A group of people constructing ferro-cement boats rented an old farm in South Royalston. There was a gay commune in New Salem. In Wendell, members of several rock and roll bands lived communally. Some of the communal households attracted the attention of local and state police and there were some arrests for marijuana cultivation. By the beginning of the 1980s, few if any of the communes survived though many of the people restructured their lives and continued to deepen their new roots in area towns.

Connecticut River

On the western edge of the North Quabbin region flows the Connecticut River, New England's longest river, traversed between Erving and Gill along Route 2 by the French King Bridge.

The Connecticut is one of the most impressive features of the area's rural landscape, and most of the land in the nine towns covered by this book are located in the Connecticut River watershed (more specifically, in the watershed of a major tributary, the Millers River).

The Connecticut's beginnings are in New Hampshire near the Canadian border where a series of mountain peaks create a sharp watershed dividing line. The rain and snow that fall in those northern mountains are thus destined to fall and drain into either the St. Francis River and thence to the St. Lawrence, or, falling on the other watershed, to the Connecticut River and thence to the Long Island sound.

For 201 miles the river flows through New Hampshire and Vermont – or 236 miles if you follow the curves. Within these first 201 miles of the course of the river, the land drops from 2,551 feet above sea level (at the headwaters) to 206 feet above sea level – just above the Massachuetts-New Hampshire line. From this point the terrain is flatter, the floor for the most part wider, and only occasionally is it interrupted by rapids and falls. Thus, entering Massachusetts, the mature river meanders in graceful curves through Northfield, then angles through the confines of the French King Gorge (at the western edge of Erving), rounding a bend and flowing northwest (for the only time in its 409-mile course). This area of rapid flow was likened to a horse-race by the old settlers and so they nicknamed this section of the river "the horse race."

The river's watershed provides drainage to large parts of four New England states (Vermont, New Hampshire, Massachusetts and Connecticut). Its four major Massachusetts tributaries are the Deerfield, Westfield, Chicopee and Millers rivers. See also FRENCH KING BRIDGE, MILLERS RIVER, NORTHFIELD MOUNTAIN, POWERHOUSE.

Curling

The Petersham Curling Club on Route 32 is the only facility in west-central Massachusetts where the sport of curling is enjoyed on a regular basis. This unusual sport incorporates elements of shuffleboard, billiards, horseshoes, quoits and darts. It is played on ice and rubber-soled shoes are worn by players. The aim of the game is to accurately slide the curling stone, a 42½-lb. rounded piece of polished granite, along the ice to a 12-ft. diameter goal area known as the house.

A team or rink consists of four players with two stones per player. Two rinks compete in an inning or "end," playing 16 stones. Normally, eight ends are played in about two hours.

The team's captain, the skip, assists members of his team in determining the action of each stone. Crucial to successful placing of the stones is sweeping the ice by two teammates using corn brooms or lightweight plastic push brooms. A stone can be made to travel as much as 6-10 feet further by vigorous sweeping. The action of the broom removes particles of ice and slickens the surface. The sweeping may seem comical but it is in earnest and is a vital part of the game.

Curlers are committed to a code of etiquette or politeness. There is a commitment to maintaining curling as an amateur sport.

Spectators are welcome to visit the Petersham Curling Club, where the season is from November through mid-April.

The origins of curling are obscure. A version of curling was played on frozen ponds and rivers in Europe but the game is often considered Scottish in origin and old curling clubs are found in Scotland. Members of Scottish regiments assigned to Quebec in the 19th century introduced the sport in Canada and it found its way southward across the border. The U.S. Curling Association was formed in 1958. Scottish traditions have made their way to Petersham; members can be seen wearing tam-o-shanters and bagpipe music is played on occasion.

The Petersham Curling Club was founded in 1960 when Stanley Holland, former president of Union Twist Drill, came to the Athol UTD plant from the company's affiliate in Derby Line, Vt. Members of the Holland family were curling enthusiasts who zealously promoted the sport here.

Dana

Dana, one of the four "lost" Quabbin towns, was formed from parts of Petersham, Hardwick and Greenwich. The area was first settled around 1735. Petitions for the creation of the town were filed as early as 1798, but were met with opposition at first. Differences were settled and the town was incorporated on Feb. 18, 1801, as Dana. It was named after Judge

Francis Dana of the Massachusetts Supreme Court.

Dana's population peaked at 876 in 1860. The population in 1925 was 657, about the same number of people as lived there in 1810.

The town was about four and a half miles wide by five and a half miles long. It contained four villages: North Dana, Doubleday Village, Dana Center and Storrsville (from northwest to southeast). Post offices were located in Dana (1823-1938) and North Dana (1854-1938). When the Athol and Enfield Railroad was built through North Dana in 1873, that village became the most prosperous in the town. In the last years of North Dana's existence, state highway 21 passed through it.

The Middle and East branches of the Swift River passed through Dana and were fed by numerous brooks. The larger ponds within the town were Pottapaug, the largest, nearer the center; Sunk Pond, in the southwest corner; and the Neeseponset-Town Pond complex near north Dana. Rattlesnake and Soapstone Hills to the north, Skinner and Whitney Hills near the center, and Pottapaug Hill to the south were all landmarks.

Five faiths had churches within the town at one time or another. They were the Methodist, Universalist, Baptist, Congregationist and Roman Catholic. A Grange hall, a Lodge of Good Templars, and a Red Men's Hall were also located in Dana. Many summer camps were located on the lakes of the town, most notably Camp Dana. The Mount L Hotel, the Eagle House and the North Dana Hotel were the noted inns. Four schools were located within the town at the turn of the century.

Among the many small industries that flourished within Dana were grist mills, sawmills and factories making hats and table legs. Two of the foremost factories were the Crawford and Tyler Mills, and the Swift River Box Company (1890-1935).

The last town meeting in Dana was held March 7, 1938, and the town legally ceased to exist on April 28, 1938. All of the territory of Dana was absorbed by Petersham. Much of the central and northern parts of the town are still dry land, owned by the Metropolitan District Commission (MDC). (From J.R. Greene's "Atlas of the Quabbin Valley") See also PETERSHAM, QUABBIN RECREATION, QUABBIN RESERVOIR.

Doane's Falls

Located in Royalston approximately one mile north of the Athol line, Doane's Falls is described on a granite stone at the site as "an area of great natural beauty where the waters of the Lawrence Brook drop 200 feet over exciting cascades to the valley of the Tully River."

Doane's Falls: A great swimming hole (but be careful and don't litter!)

Lawrence Brook's final cascade at Doane's Falls

The falls and surrounding 30 acres is owned by Trustees of Reservation, the Milton-based conservation group, having been given to them by Richard Bullock in 1975 in memory of Brigham Newton Bullock (1831-1906), his wife Flora Bullock Poore (1864-1947) and Benj. Andrew Poor (1863-1940).

Starting at the topmost falls, where a stone bridge supports the roadway going between Athol and Royalston Center, a trail meanders along the northern side of the cascading brook. Access to the bottommost waterfall, where the swimming and jumping is the safest, can also be obtained from the bottom of Doane's Hill Road.

The area is interesting in all seasons, with glistening ice sculptures in winter and typical colorful foliage in the autumn. The flow of water, of course, is most dramatic with the spring runoff and is slowest during summertime drought. The "busy season" is the summer, when youths from near and far frequent the swimming holes at the top and the bottom falls, jumping from rocks into pools below. Swimming is officially described as "dangerous," but the occasional injuries at the falls are due to carelessness. Swimming is not prohibited, but a "Friends of Doane's Falls" group has been formed to discourage abuse of the area; pollution and littering are matters of special concern. Alcoholic beverages are prohibited.

The water of Lawrence Brook comes from Laurel Lake in Fitzwilliam, N.H., and flows into Tully Lake at Tully Dam, eventually flowing via the east branch of the Tully River into the Millers River, a major tributary of the Connecticut River which flows southward and eventually empties into the Long Island Sound. The water of Lawrence Brook at Doane's Falls is relatively clean, though it has a dark orange-brown color due to tannin from dissolved plant matter in wetlands that drain into the brook the whole length of Royalston. White foamy accumulations below the cascades are not due to soapy pollution, as is frequently believed, but are also the result of organic compounds in the water.

Doane's Falls was named for Amos Doane, who owned land in the vicinity and who, in the early 1800s, built a mill nearby to manufacture doors, sashes and blinds. Earlier, water power from the falls was used for a grist mill, a saw mill and for scouring and fulling mills, and in the manufacture of tubs and pails.

The waterfalls' usefulness dates back to 1753, when it was reported in Boston that a location had been found "for the erection of mills on Lawrence Brook, one mile north of the northern line of Pequoig," the original name for Athol.

Old foundations and millstones can be found in the area, including a millstone on display that has been engraved as a tribute to Edward Franklin Bragg (1863-1923), noting that "his love for these falls and his appreciation of their power and beauty will always be remembered."

Education

The public school system in the nine area towns involves many different school districts, as each town has autonomy in determining its affiliation. Are these "good schools" or not? That is a matter of opinion and lies beyond the scope of this guidebook. Per-pupil expenditure tends to be low in most area towns, but that is mostly an indicator of taxpayer concerns and is not the only indicator of school quality. As with many schools, the quality of education tends to vary greatly depending on administrators, teachers and physical plant. Area schools, like the people, reflect a mixture of conservative and progressive values, with strong influence of state and federal standards, whether the local communities like it or not.

Athol and Royalston are regionalized for grades kindergarten through 12, with elementary schools located in Athol, Royalston and South Royalston. Students on the secondary level attend Athol Junior High School and Athol High School.

Orange has its own elementary schools and a superintendent just for those schools. On the secondary level, Orange students attend Ralph C. Mahar Regional School; participants with Orange in the regional agreement for Mahar are New Salem, Petersham and Wendell. Erving formerly participated in Mahar but now sends its secondary students to Turners

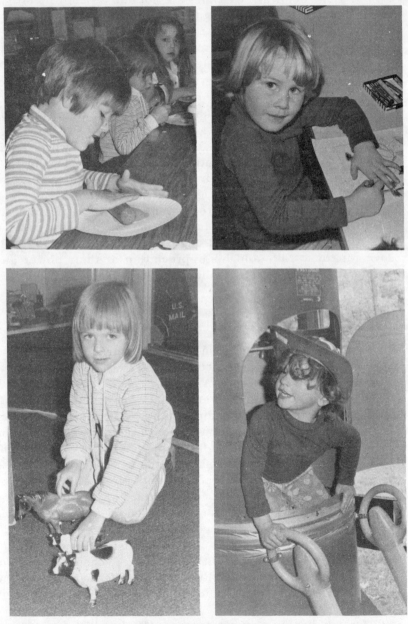

Children in unusual public pre-kindergarten classroom in Erving

At an Athol-Royalston Regional School Committee meeting

Falls. The superintendent for Mahar also serves as superintendent for the Petersham School Department, which operates the Petersham Center School.

The towns of Wendell and New Salem joined together recently to build the Swift River School right on the town line. There is a union superintendent of schools for the Swift River School, the Erving Elementary School and for schools in Leverett and Shutesbury. There are separate elected school committees for Athol-Royalston regional, Mahar regional, Orange (elementary), Petersham (elementary), Erving and Swift River schools. Phillipston and Warwick have their own elementary schools.

Secondary students from Warwick travel to Northfield to attend Pioneer Valley Regional School. Secondary students from Phillipston attend Narragansett Regional High School in Baldwinville (Templeton).

Under the jurisdiction of all public school systems, students from area towns attend various technical vocational schools and special needs schools.

Private schools in the area include:

Maple Valley School, Wendell Depot Road, Wendell, Tel. 544-6913; an alternative secondary school.

North New Salem Christian School, Elm Street, North New Salem, Tel. 544-6324; a Christian elementary day school.

Assumption Montessori School, North Main Street, Petersham, Tel. 724-6636 or 724-3468; a non-sectarian school for children ages 3-6.

New Salem Academy has plans to re-open in the near future as a private alternative secondary school. Catholic schools are available in Gardner and Fitchburg. Private preparatory schools of some renown within a short distance of the region include Northfield Mt. Hermon School, Northfield and Gill; Cushing Academy, Ashburnham; and Deerfield Academy.

Fisher Junior College Extension offers courses at Athol High School.

State-run colleges within reasonable distance of the region include Mt. Wachusett Community College, Gardner; Greenfield Community College; Fitchburg State College; Worcester State College; and Keene (N.H.) State College. The "five-college" area around Amherst and Northampton includes the University of Massachusetts, Amherst College, Hampshire College, Mt. Holyoke College and Smith College. North of the region are the School for International Training in Brattleboro, Vt.; Marlboro (Vt.) College; and Franklin Pierce College, Rindge, N.H.

Elderly Services

Programs for area elderly residents include special transportation routes, legal and health services, subsidized housing, meal centers (in Athol, Erving and Orange), and various advocacy programs. A booklet listing services is available free of charge from Franklin County Home Care Corp., Central Street, Turners Falls MA 01376, Tel. 413-774-2994.

Home Care also maintains SilverLine, a toll-free phone for information on these services: 1-800-322-0270.

The Athol Council on Aging is another agency focusing on helping elderly residents. It has an office in Memorial Building, 584 Main St., Athol, Tel. 249-8986.

Athol Public Library has a collection of large-print books, a large magnifier and small magnifying glasses, access to special services for the blind and physically handicapped and a portion of its book and periodical collection of special interest to elderly library users. See also HUMAN SERVICES.

Elliott Laurel Reservation

The Elliott Laurel Reservation is located in Phillipston off Route 101 just west of Queen Lake, somewhat north of the exact geographical center of the state. The 33-acre Elliott Laurel Reservation, owned by Trustees of Reservations, features large quantities of mountain laurel, known also by its Latin name, Kalmia latifolia.

The laurel blooms in late June, with purple, pink or nearly white cup-shaped flowers. Laurel, a shade-loving plant, thrives in sandy, peaty or loamy soil. The land here is uneven with bold outcroppings of granite ledge and boulders covered with lichens, moss and ferns. Hemlock, pine, oak and birch grow on the hillside, and from the top of the height, the visitor can enjoy a view of the surrounding country to the south.

Enfield

What became the town of Enfield – one of the four towns covered by the waters of the Quabbin – was originally parts of Greenwich and Belchertown. The area was probably first settled in the 1730s. It became the South Parish of Greenwich in 1787, and separated from Greenwich altogether to incorporate as the Town of Enfield on Feb. 15, 1816. The town was named for Robert Field, a prominent early citizen.

Enfield was about six miles long and five miles wide. There were two major villages within it – the center and the Upper Village, which was often called Smith's Village in homage to a prominent family. Part of the Pelham village of Packardville was within the northwest corner of Enfield. The west and east branches of the Swift River flowed through the town and joined below the center. Beaver Brook drained three small ponds in the eastern part of town. Three hills of note overlooked the town: Mount Ram, north of the center; Little Quabbin Hill, east of the center; and Great Quabbin Hill, south of the center.

The main churches in the town were the Methodist-Episcopal and the Congregational. A Grange Hall was located near the Congregational Church. Enfield's major inn was the Swift River Hotel, which thrived from 1832 until the final condemnation of the town. Visiting dignitaries stayed there when visiting the reservoir construction project. At one time there were six schools in Enfield, but a modern building replaced most of these in 1899. Many large fires, especially those of 1876, 1896 and 1900, ravaged the center, but each time the town rebuilt itself.

Enfield Center had a post office from 1823-1939, and the Upper Village had one from 1892-1936. The Athol and Enfield Railroad was built through both villages in 1873, and connected them with Athol and Springfield until 1935. State routes 21

Enfield town hall still stands during clearing (1939 photograph)

and 109 passed through Enfield in the last years of its existence.

Agriculture was always an important part of Enfield's economy, because of the good soil in the town. Industry was always foremost, however, because of the rivers and the railroad. The first mill was built in 1770, and manufacturing steadily increased until it peaked in the 1870s. Nails were made by hand after cutting the metal from iron plates by machine, and in 1804 a carding machine, the first of its kind in this part of the country, was built. The town's population remained around 1,000 between 1830 and 1900, then gradually declined to 495 when the reservoir was built in the 1930s.

The two major factories were the Swift River Company (1821-1925) in the Upper Village, which made cotton, satinets and other items, and the Minot Manufacturing Co., which operated at about the same time, making flannels, cassimeres and satinets. Other Enfield products were whetstones and potash.

Enfield was the most southerly and most populous of the four towns obliterated by Quabbin. The town officially ceased to exist on Apr. 28, 1938, and its territory was absorbed by New Salem, Pelham, Belchertown and Ware. (From J.R. Greene's "Atlas of the Quabbin Valley")

Engine Show and Fly-in

The noisiest array of antiques one might imagine can be found displayed in late June at the Orange Municipal Airport. At the same time, old flying machines and futuristic experimental aircraft are on hand. The occasion is a dual event with totally different sponsorship, held on the last Saturday and Sunday in June each year: the Yankee Engine-uity In Action show sponsored by the Central Massachusetts Steam, Gas and Machinery Association, Inc.; and the Fly-In sponsored by the Experimental Aircraft Association Chapter 726.

This event attracts thousands of people from local towns and around New England; it has become one of the area's major events. In addition to the displays of machinery and aircraft, there are booths selling food and crafts, flea market tables and other attractions. The show was begun in the early 1970s by three area men who enjoyed tinkering with old machines, Bruce Dexter, Doug Johnson and Ed Bergquist. From a small gathering initially, the show has burgeoned to one of the area's major family gatherings.

In recent years, these incredible hulking machines on display have included an 1892 Chase Shingle cutting mill made by the Chase Turbine Manufacturing Co. of Orange, powered by a 1922 Frick improved portable boiler and engine; various old power saws including a 1927 Ottawa drag saw, and a machine used to bore hollow logs (formerly used to provide gravity feed water to homes).

Information about the Yankee Engine-uity in Action show is available from the non-profit Central Massachusetts Steam, Gas and Machinery Association, Inc., Box 32, Orange MA 01364, or by telephone from Bruce Dexter, president, Tel. 544-2037. Information about the Fly-in is available from Paul Dexter, 15 Sunset Dr., Orange MA 01364, Tel. 544-6412

Erving

Travelers along Route 2, the main east-west road through northern Massachusetts, cannot fail to appreciate the power and beauty of the swift-flowing water of the Millers River as it parallels the highway for miles on the southern edge of Erving. The river water, a plentiful and powerful natural resource, has been essential to the economic well-being of Erving from the town's earliest days.

While water is of decreased significance as a power source, its use in the preparation of paper is vital in the manufacturing facilities of the Erving Papers Mills, an industry leader. This is Erving's biggest factory and is located in in the town center. The Millers Falls Paper Co., the town's second major industry, is in the Ervingside section of Millers Falls. These two companies are among the largest industries in Franklin County.

Most of Erving's 1,326 residents make their homes in three distinct sections of town, all along the Millers River. They are, from east to west, Erving Center, Farley and the Ervingside section of Millers Falls (a village located partly in Montague and once known as Grout's Corner).

An important part of the town's present economy is the Northfield Mountain pumped storage electric-generating plant. The "front door" of this facility is located in Northfield, off Route 63 north of Millers Falls, but most of the power station, including the Northfield Mountain hilltop reservoir, is within the Erving town limits. The owner of this multi-million dollar industry, Northeast Utilities, pays a significant portion of the town's real estate taxes. Erving's modern elementary school, located on Route 63, was constructed soon after the Northeast Utilities plant went on line in the early 1970s.

Relatively low real estate taxes remain one of the big pluses of life in this town, but Erving also offers most of the amenities of smalltown New England living. While the economy is based in manufacturing, this is a country town with lots of woods. The terrain is rugged enough to have prevented farming from ever being important to its economy. Erving has had a modest increase in housing units, up 23 percent from 461 to 567 between 1970 and 1980. The population grew from 1,260 in 1970 to the 1980 level of 1,326 – an increase of only 5 percent. In the previous decade the town experienced a sharp decrease but the population has remained steady in the 1,100-1,300 range through the entire century.

Erving is the smallest of the nine area towns, with 14.24 square miles, ranking it 263rd in size in the state. The population density is 93 persons per square mile, ranking it 276th in the state – about the same as Wellfleet, Buckland, Stockbridge and Gill and half as densely populated as neighboring Orange. Much of Erving's territory is occupied by Erving State Forest, which includes the Laurel Lake Recreation Area. (The lake was formerly called Long Pond.)

Erving is bordered by Northfield on the north, Warwick and Orange on the east, Wendell and Montague on the south

Scarecrow in Farley reflects its real-life family

and west, and Gill on the northwest. The Connecticut River forms part of the town's western boundary; the Millers River forms its southern boundary. The geography of the town is unusual in that it is one of the longest in the state and at the same time one of the narrowest – about 10 miles from east to west but only about two and a half miles from north to south. Erving's highest elevation is a 1,221-ft. peak in Erving State Forest off Great Swamp Road in the northeast corner of the town. (This hill, which appears on the Northfield quadrant geodetic map, has no name.) Close behind is the top of Hermit Mountain, also in the State Forest, 1,206 feet above sea level. The lowest point, where the Millers River empties into the Connecticut, is 199 feet above sea level. The elevation of the Northfield Mountain reservoir is 1,004 feet. It is 450 feet above sea level at Erving Center.

The possible relocation of Route 2 to eliminate this main commercial artery through Erving Center remains an issue here and throughout the region. The existing Route 2 winds its way through the town center, where truck docking at the Erving Paper Mills creates a hazardous situation. Community leaders maintain that the area's economic health is linked to a new east-west Route 2 alignment to bypass this curvy, narrow section. A plan by insensitive highway engineers to build a long bridge over the village was dropped several years ago after townspeople objected. Alternative routes proposed are a northern loop through Erving (which also faces local opposition) and an alignment along the southern bank of the Millers River in Wendell – which has met with considerable opposition from residents and officials of that town, many of whom believe environmental protection ought to outweigh the need for a new road.

The history of Erving begins in 1750 when John Erving received a grant of a tract of land. He bought more over a period of several years – possibly with real estate speculation in mind. Erving was a Boston fish and fruit merchant of considerable stature whose portrait, done by John Singleton Copley, hangs in the Smith College Art Museum, Northampton. Erving was no rustic or frontiersman, however, and the first settler of the town was Asaph White of Heath, who built a log house on the north side of Millers River and established a toll gate in 1802, later building various mills and roads. The town was incorporated on April 17, 1838, after the state legislature became concerned about what should be done with the various plantations and unincorporated territory of Massachusetts.

From Erving's earliest days, its inhabitants developed and worked in industries. J.E. Stone and Son did a big business in the manufacture of piano and billiard table legs, and cases veneered with oak, ash, walnut or rosewood. The Washburn and Heywood Chair Co., later affiliated with the Heywood-Wakefield Co. of Gardner, was a major employer for many years. A fire destroyed the factory in 1917, but heeding the pleas of the Erving employees, the company decided to rebuild. Some years later, the new plant was vacated and was taken over by the Fred T. Mears Heel Co., a successful business until Massachusetts' shoe industry was overwhelmed by foreign competition. Noah Rankin owned a chairmaking company, and Charles A. Eddy made sash and doors. Paper of all kinds have been manufactured here. The village of Farley is named for the Farley family which owned a large cardboard and paper product business. The Millers Falls Tool Co., begun in 1868 in the Millers Falls section of Erving, later moved to Greenfield and now occupies a large new plant in South Deerfield. A knitting mill was once prosperous at Farley. Other products made in the past in Erving include awnings, rubber goods and lock-corner boxes.

"Our forests have gone down in history," reads a centennial history of the town, "for in them hemlock was cut to build the textile mills which made cloth for soldiers' uniforms during the Civil War. The same forests furnished masts for many a sailing vessel in the early days and the oak timbers used in the famous steamship, 'The Great Eastern,' were sawed in a small mill that stood over one hundred years ago upon the site of the Heywood-Wakefield plant." (The Great Eastern was the ship that laid the first Atlantic communications cable.)

In Erving Center today, there are a few places of business, the Congregational Church and St. Blanche's Church (Roman Catholic), a new town hall and fire station and a post office, though village life is quiet and not as active as in days gone by. The present site of the post office, country store and The Cottage bar and grill was for many years the Formhals Store and prior to that was the Erving House, where innkeeper Frank Loveland "kept an excellent house and was famed for the good table his wife set," including cake known as the "Pride of Erving." Augustus J. Formhals, who owned the place for many years and was postmaster, was known for introducing automobiles for hire in Erving, "having four cars at one time to meet the traveling wants of the public." (The town has no taxi service at present, however!) Other places of business can be found in the Millers Falls area, including a bowling alley, restaurant and a motel with cabins .

One of the most curious bits of lore concerning Erving is that of the hermit of Erving Castle. This unusual man was John Smith, an actor born in Perthshire, Scotland, who came to the U.S. in 1866 and traveled to this area, finding a spot on Hermit Mountain which he described in a subsequent published memoir as "the rock that Moses smote in the wilderness. If ever there was a place for a hermitage, here it is." The centennial history continues the story:

"His presence on the mountain was not discovered until 1870 when three men came upon him as they were looking over timber. After that his habitat was a rendezvous for visitors and the jovial manners of the recluse made him popular. He lived in the cave which he called Erving Castle for two or three years and then collected driftwood and boards from Millers River with which he built himself a shack near the cave. Here he resided for nearly 30 years, buying what little he needed with money earned picking berries, cutting wood and weaving rugs from waste cord and rope he obtained from the factories in Erving. A striking figure with a long flowing beard that gradually became white, he welcomed company, though he always ate alone, claiming that this was the mark of a hermit. He was passionately fond of flowers and the stone walks he built are still to be seen. Well liked by everyone, he lived with his many cats

71

The hermit of Erving Castle in photograph taken around 1890

– stray and unwanted felines which seemed to sense in him a friend. His favorite cat was named Toby, and when it died, he had a stone with its name engraved on it, placed on the grave. Finally he became so old and feeble that the town fathers feared to have him alone and he was removed to the Montague town farm, where he died March 30, 1900, at the age of 82. His grave can be seen in Erving cemetery where a simple stone was erected by his friends." (The Erving Historical Society can be prevailed upon to arrange for group visits to Erving Castle.) See also CONNECTICUT RIVER, ERVING HISTORICAL SOCIETY, ERVING PAPER MILLS, ERVING STATE FOREST, FRENCH KING BRIDGE, LAUREL LAKE, NORTHFIELD MOUNTAIN, POWERHOUSE.

Erving Historical Society

The former Erving fire station on Route 2 now serves as the Erving Historical Society headquarters and museum. On the main floor, exhibits show old toys, including a "magic lantern" – predecessor of slide projectors, using kerosene light. Mrs. Pearl Care showed a recent visitor the lantern and commented, "This one's from about 1900, and there are some silly cartoons with it."

Mrs. Stacia Burnett, another society member, is an accomplished seamstress whose tiny hand-made clothing on a pair of beautifully dressed dolls is remarkable, including sleeves edged in lace and tiny tucks on the shirt of a frock coat worn by a male doll. She also sewed tiny gloves and put polished buckles on the shoes. The elegantly dressed lady doll is wearing pantaloons and full petticoats under a green hoop skirt.

Other items include old signs, tools, ballot boxes and a pair of piano legs from the old factory where parts for pianos and other musical instruments were made. (The piano company warehouse became the first building for Erving Paper Mills.)

The second floor of the old firehouse contains a 19th century apartment carefully laid out and arranged with Erving items. A hand-cranked ice cream freezer, a waffle iron on the wood stove and ironstone dishes add authenticity to the kitchen. In the washing corner are a tub, washboard and even a bottle of blueing and a box of starch.

The bedroom includes a washstand with cloth splasher behind it to protect the wallpaper. The parlor contains an old horsehair sofa from the 1890s and the dining room includes outline embroidery in red, fashionable in the 1890s. Candle holders in the apartment were made from pieces of railing from the old town hall.

The museum is open regularly in the summer or by appointment. Information can be obtained from Mrs. Douglas Burnett, High Street, Erving MA 01344, Tels. 544-3705 or 544-3872, or Mrs. John Care, 2 Prospect St., Erving MA 01344, Tel. 544-6339.

Erving Paper Mills

Bales of used paper – from old computer cards to glossy skin magazines – are stored outside the Erving Paper Mills

Waste paper is recycled into pulp at Erving Paper Mills

and are a familiar sight to travelers along the winding section of Route 2 through Erving center along the Millers River.

Erving Paper Mills, begun in 1905, was purchased by the Housen family in the 1930s. The current president of the firm is Charles Housen. Joel Rose, a company executive, said that Erving was one of the pioneers in the use of recycled paper, developing an effective process for de-inking used paper. Rose characterized the company as "one of the largest privately-owned paper companies" manufacturing napkins and towels. He said its leading competitor is the Fort Howard Paper Co. of Wisconsin.

The custom printing of dinner and beverage napkins has recently become a major growth item at the company, which has its own graphics design and color separation facilities.

In the Erving mill, where there are four pulpers, the fibers from waste paper are reclaimed by creating a soupy mixture of water, chemicals and used paper in a vat with blades much like a giant kitchen blender. The pulpy mixture is then transformed into paper as it is spread along a thin mesh wire and squeezed and sucked dry on the rollers of a "Yankee dryer," a cylinder about five yards in diameter. As the pulp dries, its water content is reduced from 99 percent to an average of 6 percent. A somewhat caustic chemical odor is noticeable during the drying process.

A computerized system, Measurex, monitors the paper in the manufacture phase, testing the product as it is produced. The paper ends up on a huge roll containing more than a ton and a half of paper. The rolls are cut to size before the printing or packaging phases.

Two million gallons of water are taken daily from the Millers River for the Erving mill's operation. Following the paper-making process, the water is transported to the treatment plant where 98-99 percent of the solids are removed, according to the company. There are 55,000 pounds of solids each day removed in the cleanup; these are transported to a landfill located between Route 2 and the Millers River west of Farley.

In addition to the paper mill in Erving, the company owns similar mills in Baldwinville and in Hinsdale, N.H. A large "converting operation – where paper is transformed into finished napkins and towels – is located in Brattleboro, Vt. The Vermont plant, with 325 employees working in 300,000 square feet, is the second-largest facility among Erving's holdings. It was acquired several years ago and includes packing and shipping facilities. Paper from the area mills is transported to Brattleboro for processing into finished products.

The company has been expanding its operations in recent years. In addition to the New England paper-making facilities, Erving owns the following subsidiaries: Sorg Products, Ligonier, Ind., a printing operation with its own graphic center; Pentex Corp., New Brunswick, N.J., which converts reusable non-woven materials into disposal products for use in health care services (such as disposable operating-room smocks); Flamingo Products, Hialeah, Fla., a small printing operation; Fox Paper Co., Lockland, Ohio, near Cincinnati, a paper-producing plant also using old paper to make towels and napkins; and LaGrange Paper, LaGrange, Ga., a converting plant that makes towels and napkins and pegged to be a duplicate of the Brattleboro operation. Unlike all the other subsidiaries, which were acquired through purchase, LaGrange was built by Erving Paper.

The company employs 1,300 people nationwide. Of these, 200 work in the Erving mill and 200 work in the corporate headquarters, including sales, marketing and accounting staffs.The headquarters is located in the modernized interior of an old industrial building on Arch Street, Erving.

The paper mill is approximately one mile east along the Millers River. Pollution in the river from the Erving and Baldwinville plants led the U.S. Environmental Protection Agency to intervene several years ago, and subsequent construction of wastewater facilities on both sites has improved the situation, although pollution problems persist.

Rose said the wastewater plants have been "operating extremely efficiently." Sludge, mostly clay and fiber, from the paper-making plants, is being deposited in landfills. Rose said a "proper use" has not yet been found, though experiments are taking place.

Operator of press that prints advertising designs on napkins

Company executives are proud of its recent energy-oriented reforms. The company has won awards for its van pooling program from the Associated Industries of Massachusetts, the American Lung Association and the Western Massachusetts Safety Council. There are four vans in use, two serving office workers, two serving the mill, with stops in Athol, Orange, Gill, Turners Falls and Greenfield. The van program is headed by Richard C. Spofford of Orange, the company's chief of security. Leo J. Roiko of Temple, N.H., director of industrial relations, said Erving received "inquiries from all over the country" about the van pooling.

The leasing of trucks from the independent Erving Transportation Co. allows the company "total flexibility" in transportation, Rose said. The trucks carry finished products all the way to the west coast and they often return filled with waste paper for recycling.

Another of the energy-conservation programs mentioned by the executives is "getting off oil." They said pelletized wood is a new fuel they expect to utilize.

Erving State Forest

Erving State Forest, comprising approximately 3,200 acres, is located north of Route 2 and 2A about five miles west of Orange and twelve miles east of Greenfield. The forest headquarters building, constructed in 1959, is on Route 2A in Erving. Supervisor is Michael Pelletier. Most of the forest lies in Erving with portions extending into Orange, Warwick, and Northfield. The principal entrance to the forest is by way of Warwick Road north from Route 2A in Wendell Depot. The forest may also be entered by way of North Street from Erving Center to Laurel Lake Road.

From a recreational point of view, the most popular attraction of the forest is the Laurel Lake Recreation Area, which lies partly in Erving and partly in Warwick.

The forest's current activities include camping, picnicking, swimming, boating, hiking, hunting, trapping, fishing, snowmobiling, snowshoeing, horseback riding and sightseeing.

Mountain laurel is prolific in many areas. The forest is managed for forest products, thereby providing the state's wood-using industries with a portion of their supply of raw materials. Oak is the predominant forest type in the Erving State Forest, covering approximately 50 percent of the area, mostly with northern red oak and some red maple intermingled. Other trees in the forest include white pine, red maple, black birch, white birch and eastern hemlock.

The soil type in the forest is characterized technically as belonging to the Shapleigh-Essex-Gloucester Association, which is described as shallow and deep well-drained soils in sandy glacial till.

Most of the forest is readily accessible by means of a network of roads and trails that traverse its acreage. The topography of the forest is generally quite hilly, but due to the heavy tree growth there are no scenic overlooks from the highest elevations (approximately 1,200 feet above sea level). A smaller hill near the Laurel Lake parking lot affords a nice view; its summit (1,047 feet) is reached by means of the only hiking trail as such, built by the Civilian Conservation Corps (CCC).

Three large brooks – Moss Brook, Darling Brook and Keyup Brook – as well as several smaller brooks drain the forest into Millers River south of the forest boundary. Laurel Lake is now the only body of water associated with the forest, although there is a long-range plan to reconstruct the former Harris Dam on Darling Brook to create a new Darling Brook Pond. A new camping area is projected for this area in the vicinity of Darling and Moss brooks, with the existing Laurel Lake campsites to be reserved for overflow.

Average annual precipation is 47.0 inches which includes the average annual snowfall of 63.2 inches.

Remains of old mills can be found on Moss and Darling brooks, and it is assumed that some of the dwelling foundations seen in the forest once belonged to some of the workers in these mills. There were three mills on Moss Brook, one of which was a sawmill located at the foot of what is now called Harris Swamp, which was a mill pond at that time. This sawmill supplied lumber for many years for construction in area towns. There was another mill part way down the brook towards Wendell Depot and another at Wendell Depot which at one time produced pianos. Laurel Lake was once known as Long Pond and at one time a canal, which still remains, diverted water from Long Pond Brook to a bucket shop at the foot of the hill near Harris Pond.

The initial purchase of property for a state forest was in 1918, consisting of approximately 1,200 acres. A plaque at the forest indicates it was officially established in 1921 by the state's Department of Conservation (now known as the Department of Environmental Management). In 1922 a forest nursery was started which was maintained until 1947 at the site of the present headquarters building. In 1931, there was a fire that destroyed 300 acres of the forest. Cleanup and reforestation occurred in 1933

Site of former Harris Dam on Darling Brook in Erving State Forest

with the assistance of the CCC. The CCC maintained a camp in the forest from 1933 to 1942, and carried out reforestation (including some 300 acres planted mostly with red pine and white pine with some Norway spruce and white spruce), road construction, waterhole construction, gypsy moth control, fire suppression and timber stand improvement.

Located near Quarry Road is an old stone quarry which ceased operation in 1928. This quarry was resurrected in the 1930s to obtain stone to rip-rap the river banks after the floods. In the northwest portion of the forest is an old town road, Great Swamp Road, now abandoned, which was a major road between Erving and Northfield and served several farms along the way.

Horseback riding is permitted on all of the forest roads except in the recreation area at Laurel Lake and on foot trails. Snowmobiling and cross-country skiing are allowed on all forest roads that are not plowed.

Long-range plans for the forest, in addition to the Harris Dam project, includes road resurfacing, construction of riding trails between existing secondary roads, improving the trail system and connecting them to the trails on Northfield Mountain developed by Northeast Utilities.

There are many species of wildlife to be found in Erving State Forest including both game and non-game species. The forest is open to hunting and fishing for the game species with the exception of the safety zones that must be observed near buildings and campsites.

The principal species of game animals that inhabit the forest are deer, snowshoe hare, ruffed grouse, fox and a few wildcat. Laurel Lake and the various streams include native trout and stocked varieties. Numerous species of small birds and animals can be found in the forest for those interested in observing them. There has been no wildlife management as such conducted in the forest, but such steps have been suggested as clearing around and pruning old apple trees and making wildlife plantings and adapting harvest cuttings to benefit wildlife. See also LAUREL LAKE.

Fall Foliage

The fall foliage spectacle that annually attracts tourists to New England is a natural phenomenon of chemical change in vegetation. For residents of area towns the colorful show is available in virtually everyone's back yard.

The foliage season is a fine time to take a day off and visit one of the many recreation and conservation areas in the region, especially scenic spots like hilly vistas and waterfalls and lakes. It's also a good time to explore back roads, especially those lined with lots of maple trees, because their leaves are the ones that turn the brightest red. Wheeler Avenue between Orange and North Orange is a good bet.

The favorite road for tourists in Massachusetts is Route 2 (the Mohawk Trail), but unless you're travelling on a weekday, it is advisable to avoid Route 2 at all costs; it can get very crowded with tourists, sometimes unflatteringly called "leafers" or "leaf-peepers."

By the way, in case you're curious about the whys and wherefores of those colored leaves, the process begins when falling temperatures (not necessarily sub-freezing temperatures or frost) produce an abscission or separation in the corky substance where the leaf joins the twig, stopping the flow of water through the stem. Deprived of water, the green color that comes from chlorophyll then breaks down and disappears. Yellow and orange pigments called carotenes that have been hidden by the chlorophyll become visible. Reds and purples also emerge in certain leaves, with the process accentuated by colder temperatures. The foliage is usually at its most brilliant in the first two weeks in October.

Farm Products

Many traditional New England farm products are readily available in the nine-town area, through relatively few people take advantage of this opportunity for the purchase of fresh food.

Most of the area's few farms and orchards run on a commercial basis welcome retail trade from local residents. In addition there are many small farms, part-time operations providing fresh-grown nutritious goods. The following is a partial listing resulting from responses to newspaper advertisements placed in conjunction with the preparation of this guidebook. Farmers are encouraged to submit a listing for future editions to Millers River Publishing Co., Box 159, Athol MA.

Kenneth Brackley, 1380 South Main St., Athol, Tel. 249-3671; poultry slaughtering service; suckling pigs for sale.

Checkerberry Hollow, Dorothy and A. Parker Cleveland, Moosehorn Road, Wendell, mail to RFD 1, Orange MA 01364, Tel. 544-2668; culinary herbs, capons, honey, maple syrup, self-contained winter herb gardens (potted plants), rhubarb.

Chimney Hill Farm, Ann and Stan Forrester, proprietors, Athol Road, Tully, Tel. 249-6903; tomatoes (greenhouse-grown, available July-December), raspberries, strawberries, honey ("when the bees oblige"), sweet corn.

Harry Currier, Warwick Road, Tully, Tel. 249-6690; vegetables.

Diemand Egg Farm, Mormon Hollow Road, Wendell, Tel. 544-3806.

Tom and Paula Duston, Tully Road, Orange, Tel. 249-6242; pick-your-own organically-grown strawberries.

Heart Acres, Skip Ciccarelli and Joan Katz, proprietors, intersection of Routes 68 and 32, West Royalston, mail to RFD 2, Athol MA 01331, Tel. 249-2605; maple syrup and other farm produce in season.

King's Farm, Dan and Gayle King, proprietors, 1743 White Pond Rd., Athol, Tel. 249-7441; since 1976; approximately ten acres under cultivation, including 35 different varieties of vegetables; wholesales to area restaurants and supermarkets; maintains vegetable stand at farm; quantity purchases available for home freezing and canning; raspberries, strawberries and blueberries under cultivation.

Maple Valley Farm, Dianne Salcedo and Bob Michaud, proprietors, North Orange Road, North Orange, Tel. 249-4328; since 1978; approximately 10 acres under cultivation, all vegetables; wholesale to stores and restaurants, sell at house on weekends, greenhouse-produced seedlings of vegetables and flowers; maple syrup.

George Northrop and Kathleen Collins, Ward Road, Royalston, Tel. 249-4407; home-made butter and other small-farm products.

Pequoig Farm, Ben Feldman, proprietor, 3346 Chestnut Hill Avenue, Tel. 249-3096; goat's milk.

Steven Richer, 75 East River St., Orange, Tel. 544-6580; white New Zealand rabbits bred and raised for meat (available live and dressed); lop-eared rabbits mostly for pets; breeder of Fancy and Teddy Bear (longhair) hamsters.

Stony Acre Farm, Art and Jeanne White, prop., Schoolhouse Road, Phillipston 01331, Tel 249-2582; Nubian goats, stud service; Bantam chickens.

Additional information on purchase of farm products and pick-your-own fruits and vegetables is available free of charge from the Franklin County Extension Service in Greenfield and the Worcester County Extension Service in Worcester. See also APPLES, HONEY AND HONEYBEES, HORSES, SHEEP AND WOOL.

Federation State Forest

Federated Women's Club State Forest is located mostly in Petersham (with a tiny piece in New Salem) near the northeast portion of the Quabbin reservoir. The entrance is off Route 122, New Salem, within a few feet of the Petersham town line. A sign indicates the entrance roadway. The 984-acre forest is also reached from the center of Petersham, via West Street.

A 140-acre portion of the forest was a donation of the Massachusetts State Federation of Women's Clubs and that portion only is set aside as a wildlife sanctuary (hunting and fishing prohibited). Part of the forest was presented to the Commonwealth in 1933 by the Diamond Match Co. The forest abuts Quabbin watershed lands.

There is a picnic area (24 fireplaces, 28 tables) with a small grassy area nearby. Unmarked trails lead from the picnic area to four "wildnerness" campsites and to the peak of nearby Soapstone Hill (890 feet above sea level), which offers a spectacular view of the Quabbin Reservoir from a rocky outcropping on the hill's south end. A boulder-strewn ravine called "The Gorge" is located just south of the picnic area.

Fever Brook running through the forest is stocked with

brook trout. Deer and other small game are hunted here. There are trails and roads for skiing, snowshoeing and snowmobiling.

The forest is shown on two topographical maps, the Quabbin Reservoir Quadrant and the Petersham Quadrant.

Fishing

Fishing is one of the popular pastimes of residents and visitors – from the teen-age youths carrying a simple fishing pole as they bicycle to a favorite spot to the most serious devotees of angling. While acid rain is a serious threat to fisheries in the entire Northeast, there are still many good catches to be had in area lakes and streams, as detailed in the following report prepared especially for this guide by Myron Becker of Wendell:

"Opportunities for angling devotees are here for the looking. Streams, rivers, ponds and lakes offer a broad range of game from the northern pike to the diminutive native 'brookies.' For convenience we can divide the fishing into two categories: warm water and cold water fisheries. The warm water species include largemouth and smallmouth bass, pickerel, northern pike, bullhead, and all varieties of panfish.

"The section of the Millers River between Athol and Orange is an overlooked, attractive, and productive warm water fishery. This slow and flat stretch can surprise the unwary with a toothsome northern pike on the end of six pound test line! If you don't connect with a monster pike, there are enough scrappy bass and pickerel as well as some outsized panfish to occupy your time. A canoe or light cartop boat is the best vehicle to work this water – there are no rapids or fast water. Access is easy at the bridge on Daniel Shays Highway in Athol, with takeout on the south side of the river near Orange Center (Hart's Landing), or you can paddle back upstream. Other waters worthy of effort from the warm water enthusiast are Tully Lake in Royalston, Lake Mattawa in Orange, and the chain formed by Lake Rohunta, White Pond, Eagleville Pond, and North and South Spectacle Ponds – easily accessible from Route 2 and Route 122. Pottapaug Pond in Petersham, a part of the Quabbin subject to different regulations from the main reservoir, is also a good bet.

"Cold water species are the salmonoids. In this area that means brook, brown and rainbow trout. Our only other salmonoid is the landlocked salmon found in limited quantities only in Quabbin. For convenience, we can subdivide into still water and flowing water trout fisheries. In this section of the state, the Millers River and its watershed deserve the closest scrutiny. Both branches of the upper Millers in Winchendon and South Royalston and its major tributaries (Priest Brook, Tully Brook and Lawrence Brook, all in the Royalston area) can provide about any type of flowing water a trout angler may seek. The stretch of river from South Royalston to Athol is largely inaccessible except by foot or canoe. For a committed trout angler with some initiative and sense of adventure, this piece of stream comes highly recommended. For the fly fisherman, good hatches and wild fish make this section worthy of effort. Other good streams are, from east to west, Beaver Brook and Tully River in Royalston, West Brook in Athol, Orcutt Brook in West Orange, Moss Brook in Warwick and Whetstone Brook and Osgood Brook in Wendell.

"Our nine-town area includes to our knowledge the largest concentration of trout ponds and lakes in the Commonwealth outside of Cape Cod. They vary in size from the Quabbin, with 39 square miles of water, to the tiny beaver bog which could be anywhere (requiring some good connections or a lot of luck, stamina, and skillful topographical map-reading to find!). Our pick of notable trout ponds, from east to west are: Long Pond in Royalston, Sheomet Pond in Warwick, Lake Mattawa in Orange, Moores Pond in Warwick and Laurel Lake in Warwick and Erving. On a quiet June evening the surface of any of these ponds will be boiling with rising trout; you should be there.

"Just remember: have a current state fishing license, don't violate landowner rights, and don't take any fish you're not going to eat."

Stocking by the state's Division of Fisheries and Wildlife is an important factor in area fishing. According to the division's official list, streams and ponds in the area stocked with trout include the following:

Athol – Ellinwood Brook, Riceville Brook and Tully River.

Erving – Keyup Brook and Laurel Lake.

New Salem – Swift River (middle branch) in New Salem.

Orange – Tully Brook (west branch), West Brook, Moss Brook, Orcutt Brook and Lake Mattawa

Petersham – Swift River (east branch), Fever Brook (east and west branches), Connors Pond, Nelson Brook, Moccasin Brook and Quabbin Reservoir.

Phillipston – Phillipston Brook and Beaver Brook.

Royalston – Lawrence Brook, Tully River (east branch), Little Pond, Boyce Brook, Priest Brook and Scott Brook.

Carefree angler on Lake Mattawa

Warwick – Tully Brook (west branch), Moss Brook, Moores Pond, Laurel Lake Mill Brook, Sheomet Pond and Orcutt Brook.

Wendell – Whetstone Brook, Lyons Brook, Mormon Hollow Brook and Osgood Brook.

Area ponds listed as "best bets" in a statewide Boston Globe fishing survey are:

Quabbin Reservoir – largemouth bass, smallmouth bass, chain pickerel, white perch, yellow perch, brown bullheads (hornpout).

Lake Mattawa (Orange) – largemouth bass, smallmouth bass, chain pickerel, yellow perch and brown bullheads.

Wickett Pond (Wendell) – largemouth bass, chain pickerel, yellow perch and brown bullheads.

Riceville Pond (Petersham) – largemouth bass, chain pickerel, yellow perch and brown bullheads.

See also QUABBIN FISHING.

Flowers and Plants

Wildflowers in woods and fields plus cultivated flowers and shrubs around area homes help give the region much of its beauty.

Several area greenhouses grow their own flowers for sale to home gardeners. Most popular varieties include petunias, marigolds, pansies, ageratum, alyssum, snapdragon, zinnia and geranium. House plants and flower arrangements (dried, silk and fresh cut) for all occasions from holidays to funerals are also available.

Places of business dealing in plants and flowers include:

Flowerland, Herb Wheeler, proprietor, **501 Main St.,** Athol, Tel. 249-3057.

Lanpher's Florist & Greenhouses, Christine Lavigne, proprietor, 51 Briggs St., Orange, Tel. 544-6029.

Ledge Greenhouses, Steve and Sue Baribeau, proprietors,

Engraver Ger Brender a Brandis found this lady's-slipper in Royalston

501 South Main St., Athol, 249-9191.

MacMannis Florist & Greenhouses, Vernon Brooks, proprietor, 2108 Main St., Athol, Tel. 249-3595.

Spectacular gardens of perennial flowers are maintained at the residence of Mr. and Mrs. Allan Sundberg, **634 New** Sherborn Rd., Athol, Tel. 249-3128; many of these plants can be purchased for transplanting.

There are also several nurseries and tree farms:

Landscape Nursery, North Main Street, Petersham, Tel. 724-3421.

Lawton's Tree Farm, Peter Gerry, proprietor, Townsend Road, Athol, Tel. 249-3340; popular spot for cut-your-own Christmas trees; the oldest registered tree farm in New England and the second-oldest in the nation.

Nye's Nursery, Harold Nye, proprietor, 1386 Pleasant St., Athol, Tel. 249-6118.

Noel's Nursery, Charles and Arline Noel, proprietors, 77 Tully Rd., Orange, Tel. 249-6957; specializing in fruit trees and evergreen shrubs, including live Christmas trees.

Among the more noticeable wildflowers are the ubiquitous goldenrod of late summer, black-eyed Susans frequently seen along roadways and the dandelions in people's lawns (whether they want them there or not!). In early spring, delicate pink lady slippers can be seen in partially-shaded areas – this flower is in the orchid family and is considered an endangered species so it should not be picked. Lilac bushes in late May perfume the air and decorate many yards. See also FARM PRODUCTS.

Fountains

They may not compare with the grandiose fountains of Europe's ancient cities, but there are three turn-of-the-century public drinking fountains in area communities which have their own charm and history.

The Ginery Twichell Fountain at the south end of the up-

J.F. Gilman painting of Uptown Common with Twichell Fountain

town common was given to the town in memory of one of Athol's most successful men: stagecoach driver, railroad magnate and U.S. Congressman. The donors were Miss T.H. Twichell and Richard W. Hale. The granite fountain, manufactured in Boston, was designed by a Petersham man who planned for dogs and horses as well as people to quench their thirst. The fountain is ten feet high and is decorated with the figures of four gargoyles. It was installed in 1898 near the site of an old tavern where Twichell drove up many times holding the reins of a team of horses pulling a stagecoach.

Although the fountain has been ignored and was damaged on occasion by vehicular traffic, residents of the uptown area have a proprietal feeling about it, as evidenced by murmurings that resulted when the president of the Athol Savings Bank suggested it be moved – for its better protection and preservation – to the new park adjacent to the bank. The suggestion to move the fountain was withdrawn.

In Orange, a fountain purchased by the Woman's Christian Temperance Union (WCTU) was installed in 1904 on the southwest corner of Central Square. The green and white Troy marble fountain cost $700; it included drinking cups and a small basin below for dogs. The water was shut off in 1910 when a new law was passed abolishing public drinking cups.

The WCTU was an organization that gained national prominence as it campaigned against the use of alcoholic beverages. Related to other popular reform movements, the WCTU blamed alcohol consumption for many of the nation's social ills, especially for domestic violence and the neglectful attitude of many husands and fathers. Its presentation of pure drinking water to the citizens of Orange in the town's main square was both a public service and a political message.

Fresh water from a spring on the side of Mt. Grace travels approximately one-half mile to a large fountain just north of the Warwick town hall. In the summer months, water flows from four fish heads; year-round a "jug filler" spout flows at the side of the fountain, serving residents and passersby. This handsome fountain was designed to serve animals and humans, and many Warwick residents can remember when cows and horses in the neighborhood regularly drank there. Even today, a horse can be seen now and then ambling up to refresh itself.

The Warwick fountain, made of steel and painted green, was refurbished in the late 1970s by the Volunteer Firemen's Association under the leadership of Chief Arlan Day Jr. The fountain was donated by Mrs. Edward C. Thayer of Keene,

N.H., on honor of Capt. David Ball. It was manufactured by Henry F. Jenks of Pawtucket, R.I.

French-Canadians

French-Canadians form the most apparent ethnic grouping in the Athol-Orange area.

The first French Canadians to live in the area came from the province of Quebec around 1885-95. A second migration came in the early 1900s, mostly from the northeastern tip of New York State. They became known locally as the Chateauguayans because they came from an area in New York State adjacent to Chateauguay County, Quebec, south of Montreal.

A 1962 memoir by Anselme Brouillet recalls the Chateau-guayans: "I remember some of the newcomers used to come down here in a railroad freight car loaded with home-grown potatoes. They used to bring them down, 600 or 800 bushels in a freight-car, and sell them to Frenchmen already living here who used to await their arrival at the freight yard. Most of the potatoes were sold right in the freight yard. The people here used to buy about 30 bushels each all at once, because they were much cheaper than those sold locally."

The third and by far largest migration of French-Canadians came from the maritime province of New Brunswick, beginning in 1905, primarily from the town or general area of Shippegan and Shippegan Island, in Gloucester County, which juts far out into the ocean.

"There's another bunch coming tonight," people used to say in response to the steady waves of immigrants, most of whom arrived by train. Like so many immigrants, they came to the U.S. seeking economic opportunity and, for the most part left behind their previous work as fishermen and farmers.

Le Club Franco-American or the Franco-American Naturalization Club was founded in March 1919 with 50 members and remains active to this day, although its purposes have changed over the years. The club sought to give the growing colony of French-Canadians quarters for social and patriotic activity while encouraging the continuing of old-country traditions, cultures, friendships and entertainment. A major aim has been "to aid French-speaking residents of this district, Canadian by birth, to become citizens and to achieve better citizenship; to urge the taking out of naturalization papers by those eligible, and transact other business of interest in town affairs and political rights," as stated in early records.

French-Canadians have played a major role in the Church of Our Lady Immaculate in Athol and other Roman Catholic churches in the region.

With immigration slowed to a near standstill in recent times, the naturalization function is virtually ended, but the Club, located at 593 South St., Athol, still serves a useful social function. Despite the assimilation of the younger generation, the Club's older members readily recall their experience as immigrants, and the sound of the French-Canadian language can still be heard occasionally on Athol's streets, and it remains the primary tongue in a few Athol homes. (Research courtesy Richard Chaisson).

French King Bridge

The region's longest and most spectacular bridge is the French King Bridge, carrying Route 2 high above the Connecticut River between Erving and Gill.

The bridge was built at a cost of $384,592 and was dedicated in 1932. It is 787 feet long, with an arch of 460 feet. The roadway is 137 feet above the water.

The bridge is decorated with high bronze poles with eagles atop stone pylons. According to a plaque on the bridge, it was cited by the American Institute of Steel Construction as the "most beautiful structure of its class" for the year.

The French monarch referred to in the name of the bridge is King Louis XV. The name for the bridge was suggested by

French King Bridge just prior to completion in 1932

the name of a fabled boulder, the French King Rock, located in the river upstream from the bridge crossing. A traditional tale was that during the French and Indian war of the mid-1700s, a party of French and Indian soldiers reached a conspicuous rock in the river as night approached, and the rock was named by the French soldier leading the party to honor his sovereign.

Underneath the bridge, the Millers River can be observed flowing into the Connecticut. There is an ample parking area on the Gill side of the bridge with a large information map showing various points of interest in western and central Massachusetts. A pedestrian walkway on the bridge affords spectacular views of the Connecticut River and the river valley north and south. The area is known as the French King Gorge. The bridge itself is best observed from the river (boat rides through the gorge are available from the Northfield Mountain Recreation Area) or from River Road, Erving, where it runs along the river under the bridge. See also CONNECTICUT RIVER, NORTHFIELD MOUNTAIN.

Greenwich

Some of Greenwich's most notable hills – Mount Pomeroy, Mount Liz and Mount Zion – are important landmarks above the deep waters of the Quabbin Reservoir, where they are perceived as islands.

Ice cut from the ponds of Greenwich (upwards of 100,000 tons a year) was shipped to Springfield, New Haven and New York City in the bygone era of the iceman and the icebox.

One of the four defunct Quabbin towns, Greenwich was formed as Narragansett Township Number Four in 1735. The land was a reward to troops who served in the Indian wars. The town was originally called Quabbin for a leader of the Nipmuc Indians who had lived in the area. The first church was built in the town in 1749.

Greenwich was incorporated on April 20, 1754, being named after the Duke of Greenwich, who was fondly rembered by many of the settlers of Scottish origin. (Local people pronounced the town's name "green-witch," not "gren-itch.")

The original town of Greenwich was quite large, about a dozen miles from one end to the other, but the fast-growing community had a number of villages within it, and movements for separation resulted. The southern part of the town formed its own parish in 1787, and formally separated to become Enfield in 1816. The northeastern section of Greenwich became part of Dana when that

THE TIP OF THIS MOUNTAIN
WILL BE AN ISLAND

View of Greenwich as published in a New York newspaper in the 1930s

town was incorporated in 1801.

What remained of Greenwich was about eight miles long and only three miles wide at its widest point. Greenwich Center and Greenwich Village (to the north) were the two villages, each with its own post office. Churches in town included Congregationalists, Spiritualists, Unitarians, Methodists and Independent Liberal. As many as six schools were located within the town. The Riverside Hotel and the Quabbin Inn were the most noted hostelries and there was a Farmer's Hall and a golf course.

The middle and east branches of the Swift River drained the hill-dotted plain that made up most of Greenwich. Several ponds were located here, the largest being East Pond or Quabbin Lake. Mount Zion was a prominent ridge on the border with Dana.

There was quite a bit of farming in Greenwich, including a profitable cranberry business. A grist mill was built in 1745 and there were many industries. Most depended on water power and were located in Greenwich Village. Among the many items produced were scythes, hats, matches, pewter, boxes (especially for apples), boots and wool – in addition to the vital ice industry. The weaving of palm-leaf hats was significant in the economy for part of the 19th century. This was done mostly by women and children working at home. The coming of the Athol and En-

92

field Railroad in 1873 aided some of the businesses and served as a route to the outside world. State route 21 served the two villages. In the latter years of the town, its biggest business during the summer months came from the hundreds of cottages and camps which dotted the lakes, ponds and rivers.

Many residents of Greenwich served in the Revolutionary War and approximately 50 participated in the Shays' Rebellion of 1786, when farmers attempted to combat the debtors courts that were ruining them.

The population of the town peaked at 1,460 in 1800 (before its loss of territory). The population was 699 in 1860 and had fallen to 450 by 1925.

Except for its hilltops, Greenwich was submerged. The land that remained was annexed by New Salem, Petersham, Hardwick and Ware. (From J.R. Greene's "Atlas of the Quabbin Valley" and from MDC publications)

Harvard Forest

Harvard Forest, a division of Harvard University, has approximately 3,000 acres of wooded land, including wetlands and ponds, in Petersham (with a small portion in Phillipston). The administrative buildings, museum, laboratories and residential facilities are located in Petersham on Route 32 north of the center of Petersham. Tracts of land owned by Harvard Forest are located elsewhere, including a small tract of virgin forest in Winchester, N.H., and a 3,500 acre section in the Lower Hudson Valley near West Point, N.Y.

The Fisher Museum of Forestry has dioramas describing the history of the countryside and forestry practices. The dioramas were made with great care and provide simple graphic instruction on land evolution in this region. The museum is open weekdays, 10 a.m. to 5 p.m. The museum is named for the founder and former director of Harvard Forest, Prof. Richard Thornton Fisher.

The newer laboratory building, financed by the Cabot Fountation, contains growth chambers and greenhouse facilities. Scientists from Harvard University in Cambridge and elsewhere work at the forest, including five to ten resident researchers, usually scientists in mid-career working on special projects. Harvard Forest is part of the university's biology department and the research covers such diverse topics as forest management, studies of soils, soil root relations and soil-affecting organisms, tropical botany, and purely silvicultural work (rather less active in recent years).

Undergraduate students also visit the forest for seminars and courses.

Of interest to the casual visitor is the Black Gum Trail, a hike of one and one half miles beginning at the Fisher Museum of Forestry. The trail criss-crosses the 75-acre farm once owned by Jonathan and Molly Sanderson. An explanatory leaflet available at the museum explains various features, including evidence of farm life 100 years ago, forest and other plant growth and results of chestnut blight and fire damage. The trail takes its name from the black gum in a swampy section, where spruce and sphagnum moss are also found. A touching plaque in the Fisher museum indicates that the Harvard Forest nature trails are dedicated to the memory of Richard Kerr McHenry (1940-77). The plaque explains, "As a U.S. Marine Corps captain, student and forester, his life was devoted to the conservation and preservation of the forest and water resources of the land that he loved."

Harvard Forest was founded in 1907. Prof. Martin H. Zimmerman, director, explains in a published article this was "the time when a number of forestry schools were established at North American universities in response to the public's concern that the country would run short of wood unless forests were managed carefully....

"Harvard Forest came to the university as a gift from interested friends and alumni....The basic idea was that the university would use it as a laboratory to train professional foresters, that it would operate it as a demonstration forest on a sustained yield basis so that the profit from timber sales would provide financial backing of the school, and conduct research as needed."

This scenario did not quite develop as planned, in part because training of foresters was seen as antithetical to a "purely scientific" approach. In the meantime, however, the forest acquired friends who gave it moral and financial support and supplied considerable endowments, so the land is now a conservation area more than a silviculture laboratory. Zimmerman wrote, "The concept of a demonstration forest, where proper silviculture is carried out and timber is harvested at a profit, has been almost completely dropped. It is no secret that raising timber in southern New England is not a profitable business. At the present time, forestry in this area will produce timber only as a by-product of managing land for urban purposes. Meanwhile, we try to learn how trees grow, and give students of biology, landscape architecture, etc., an opportunity to do field studies and discover how woodland can best serve the needs of urban and rural peole in this region."

Harvard Forest's land holdings are divided into tracts, the largest of which are the Prospect Hill Tract behind the headquarters buildings, the Tom Swamp Tract near the Athol line to the northwest of the Petersham Common, and the Slab City Tract just southeast of the common.

Because of its location in Petersham, Harvard Forest has undertaken detailed research into the history of land use in the town, much of which is applicable to all of the towns of this region. Much of this is recorded in Harvard Forest Bulletin No. 20, "The History of Land Use in the Harvard Forest," by Hugh M. Raup and Reynold E. Carlson (1941). The booklet includes maps and accompanying explanatory materials about the various forest tracts in town. See also SPIRIT FALLS.

Hatchet Hunt

On every Washington's Birthday since 1922, hundreds of youngsters have converged on the Bearsden Woods in Athol to search for a prized hatchet and other gifts hidden in the snow by the staff of the Athol YMCA. The event was begun and promoted for years by the late Alexander P. Johnstone of the YMCA, whose work with area youth earned him a legendary place in local history.

In recent years, the search area has been located in a hilly region off Green Street. The youngster who finds the hatchet has his or her name recorded in the YMCA Hatchet Hunt Hall of Fame.

Health Care Services

The primary health care institution in the region is Athol Memorial Hospital, 2033 Main St., Athol, Tel. 249-3511.

Founded in 1950, the hospital has 82 beds including medical, surgical, pediatric and alcoholism treatment units, with 24-hour emergency room coverage. There are coronary care and maximum care areas, a modern laboratory, blood bank, radiology, day surgery and operating room facilities. Programs include physical and respiratory therapy, a medical social service department, patient education and staff education, and patient consultations with pharmacists and dieticians.

There are outpatient clinics in orthopedics, neurology,

urology and alcoholism. The hospital has a governing board of area residents, an ongoing physician recruitment program, and an active auxiliary which operates a sales cart and gift shop and sponsors various fund-raising projects including an annual spring plant sale. A major fund-raising program to acquire an endowment to be used for purchase of modern equipment was launched in 1982.

The history of the hospital goes back to 1908 when Mrs. Sarah Kendall started a small hospital in her home. This functioned successfully as a voluntary institution until 1918, when it became a Massachusetts corporation. Five years later, heavily indebted, it was forced to close.

A crusade for a new hospital began in 1927 but the Depression and World War II sidetracked plans. Toward the end of the war, Lester Sawyer, an inventor from Leominster, offered to donate the 12-acre site of the Sawyer mansion on Main Street for a hospital. In 1947 the corporation was reorganized, the mansion was razed in 1948 and contracts totaling $738,000 were awarded. Construction began in 1949 and the new Athol Memorial Hospital was formally opened Sept. 10, 1950.

Substantial additions to the hospital were built as demand increased – first in 1958 and then in 1967-68. Ironically, the 1958 addition contained a new maternity ward but in 1975, yielding to pressure from the state Department of Public Health, Athol Memorial Hospital reluctantly closed its maternity ward. State health officials maintained there were not enough births to justify the expense of maintaining the maternity ward. Expectant mothers in the region now plan to give birth in more distant hospitals, including the Henry Heywood Memorial Hospital, Gardner, and Franklin County Public Hospital, Greenfield. (These hospitals are favored by some area residents for other hospital services as well.)

Other new construction at the Athol hospital has been two medical arts buildings to house doctors' offices – one on hospital grounds and one on East River Street in Orange.

An experimental federally-funded "health maintenance organization," the North Quabbin Health Plan, functioned here for several years but was phased out due to financial problems.

The hospital has its own Comprehensive Alcoholism Program with a 10-bed inpatient treatment center and specialized staff.

Community Health Service, a division of the hospital, has offices at 423 Main St., Athol, Tel. 249-5366. Its home health services are given by nurses in conjunction with home health

96

aides, physical therapists, medical social workers, dieticians and inhalation therapists. A brochure states, "Since recovery seems to occur faster at home than in a strange environment and since the overall cost of home health services is considerably less than hospitalization or other institutional care, many people find that Community Health Service provides a sound solution to their health care problems."

Those eligible for its services include residents of Athol, Orange, Erving, Petersham, New Salem, Warwick and Wendell, and patients eligible for third party coverage from Phillipston and Royalston. Specific information on eligibility requirements is available from the agency.

The boards of health in Phillipston and Royalston (along with other towns) belong to the North Worcester County Health Association (Norworco), which provides home nurse visits and educational and prevention programs in the public schools. The Norworco office is located in the Templeton town office building, Baldwinville, Tel. 939-2106.

There are approximately 15 doctors and seven dentists who serve patients at Athol Memorial Hospital. Most of these professionals maintain offices in Athol or Orange. In addition, about ten specialists are available for consultations; most of them maintain their regular offices in more distant communities. A list of these doctors is available from the hospital.

Excellent and low-priced dental care is available from various dentists in the community.

Other health care specialists residing and working in the area include chiropractors, podiatrists and psychologists.

The following nursing homes are located in Athol:

Fleetwood Nursing Home, Inc., Daniel Shays Highway,. Athol, Tel 249-3717.

Tully Brook Rest Home, 232 North Orange Rd., Athol, Tel. 249-4482.

Few alternative or holistic health care practitioners work in the nine-town region, but there is an abundance of them within easy reach in Connecticut Valley communities. "Many Hands," an excellent directory to holistic and alternative health care services (including acupuncture, vitamin therapy, therapeutic massage and a panoply of other "New Age" techniques) is available postpaid for $1 from the publisher, Beyond Words Bookshop, 150 Main St., Northampton MA 01060. See also ELDERLY SERVICES, HUMAN SERVICES.

History Trail

Twenty-four roadside signs in Athol commemorate places in the town's early history. The Athol Bicentennial Commission, formed to celebrate the 200th anniversary of the American Republic, undertook the Athol History Trail project in 1975-76 in the belief that "the more one knows a town, the more he or she is likely to appreciate it and do things for it."

As the booklet prepared for the trail by historian Richard J. Chaisson puts it, "Every town holds its fascinations for all who look close enough. Each has its own story of how it came to be and where it is heading. These signs tell some of the episodes in the story of Athol, Mass. Our hometown glimpses make up the bigger picture of America."

There is no simple way of viewing all 24 sites; however, the trail guide's proposed route covers 16 miles in an hour. Most of the sites are on private property and visitors are requested to respect landowners' rights and not trespass. The following is taken from the trail booklet, illustrated by Mary Pat Spaulding. Funds for this project were provided by various individual donors as well as clubs and the town meeting assembly.

1. EAST FORT (1736-1780), 786 Pleasant St. - Site of the first and strongest of three log forts defending Pequoig against Indian raids. It was 100 ft. square, made of upright logs, with a blockhouse, huts within for 20 families and a well still seen. The settlers of Pequoig, living in constant danger from Indian attack, built forts "in which, at the close of day, or at the alarm of danger, all the families in the vicinity gathered for mutual safety and protection."

2. FIRST HOME, 813 Pleasant St. - Here in 1735, Richard Morton built a log cabin, first one among the five settlers. It was the birthplace of our community's first boy and girl, Abraham Morton (1735) and Margery Morton (1737). The first pioneers of our town came here from Hatfield on Sept. 17, 1735, tracing their way through the wilderness by marked trees. They were the families of Richard Morton, Samuel Morton, Ephraim Smith, John Smeed and Joseph Lord. From these first five families our community was born.

3. SECOND MEETINGHOUSE (1741-1772), 831 Pleasant St. - Pioneers worshipped and governed in a crude cabin here. Fearing Indians, they kept muskets at their sides. In the yard were a whipping post and stocks to punish wicked men and naughty boys. This meetinghouse was built 12 rods (198 feet)

south of East Fort, after the first pioneer church on Hapgood Street burned. There was only one pew, it being reserved for the preacher. The 20 families did their praying and singing on planks set up on wooden blocks. From this beginning, Pleasant Street was to remain the "center" of town for 100 years.

4. OLD TOLL GATE, 1665 Main St. – From 1800 to 1830, travelers on this 5th Massachusetts Turnpike paid a fare to get past a toll gate here. It swung across the roadway from a toll house. Passage money paid for man and beast. The 5th Massachusetts Turnpike coming out of Boston in the early 1800s was the first major highway built across the state. To pay for its upkeep toll houses were set up every few miles. Travelers paid a few cents to get to the next toll gate.

5. HIDING PLACE FOR SLAVES, 1169 Chestnut St. – In this house before the Civil War ended slavery, Dr. George Hoyt hid and helped runaway slaves who fled the south. This "underground railroad" station was a haven on their freedom trail to Canada.

6. INDIAN TRAIL, Chestnut Street at Sanders Street playground – Many Indian tribes walked along this "great trail." It was 18 inches wide and hundreds of miles long, from Connecticut to Canada. The path followed Pleasant and Chestnut streets to Millers River off South Athol Road. For the Indians of New England this path formed the main "High Road" (mostly hill country) running from south to north. It began on the ocean shore in Connecticut and blazed through this inland forest to their great hunting and trade regions of the far north. The Pequiog Indians welcomed these travelers.

7. INDIAN CROSSING, South Athol Road at Riverview Avenue – On March 3, 1676, more than 2,000 Indians retreated to this riverside with their captive, Mary Rowlandson of Lancaster. Chased by 400 frontier soldiers, they escaped on rafts. After their bloody attack on Lancaster, the Indians marched 45 weary miles to this place with all of their women, children, aged and captive. The large boulder in the Millers River here is called "Rowlandson Rock." It marks the place of crossing.

8. FIRST MEETINGHOUSE SITE (1741), Hapgood Street near Cheney Street – Pioneers erected a log cabin for a house of worship halfway between the east and west settlements. Soon it burned, some said by Indians but others blamed a brush fire. One of the first public acts of the settlers of Pequoig was to build a house of worship and they chose this hillside near Mill Brook. Their first burial ground was nearby. This small and rough cabin was used only for a short time and

was not yet finished when flames destroyed it.

9. OLD BURIAL GROUND (1741-1777), 415 Hapgood St. – Here sleep the early settlers of Pequoig (Athol) in their first burial ground. Indians watched from behind trees as mourners armed with muskets came in sad procession. How many pioneers were buried here is not certain. At one time 40 graves could be clearly traced. A few of the names are known. Residents still debate whether Indians also were buried here, but there is no firm tradition or proof. In its center is seen the First Settlers' Monument, raised on July 4, 1859 by schoolchildren pulling on a rope.

10. UPTOWN COMMON and THIRD MEETING HOUSE (1773-1827), Main Street at Common Street – Seth Kendall deeded this land to the town "for public assembly and enjoyment" on Feb. 10, 1772. The meetinghouse, built on it a year later where the bandstand now rests, became the rallying hall for the local patriots of the Revolution. On July 18, 1776, a messenger arrived with a copy of the new Declaration of Independence. It was read to all from the steps of the meetinghouse. During the War of 1812, ammunition was stored inside. From this green in 1861, Athol soldiers marched to Civil War battlefields. A "Liberty Pole" rose high above for many years.

11. STAGECOACH STOP, 1505 Main St. – During the years 1790 to 1853 this corner was a busy stopping place for stagecoaches from distant points. John Brooks' Tavern stood here at the popular hub of five stage roads. Excited children watched the daily hustle of rattling coaches, foaming steeds, the transferring of passengers and mail, changing horses, and dust clouds heading 'round the bend.

12. TOWN HOUSE (1827-1847), 1476 Main St. – Athol's town hall for 20 years, it stood west of the Common until moved here in 1850. It also served as "Athol Academy" in 1828, then as a Congregational church in 1830-33. The town voted in 1927 to erect its first town house, two stories high, for use both as a public hall and church. Town meetings were held on the lower floor. Upstairs, John Crosby conducted an informal high school called "Athol Academy." Congregationalists worshipped on the second floor until they built their own edifice three years later.

13. FOURTH MEETINGHOUSE (1827-28) and OLD TOWN HALL, 1307 Main St. – Built on an acre of land donated by Samuel Sweetzer "for the public worship of God forever," this meeting house was used in its early days for religious services only. The town declared a holiday for its

100

dedication Dec. 3, 1828. Remodeled in 1847, it was Athol's seat of government until 1921. It was occupied by a woman's club 1921-57 and became the property of the Athol Historical Society in 1957.

14. TOWN POUND, 1251 Main St. - In the early 1800s there was a square enclosure of stone walls here, built by the town to hold stray cattle and other animals. Their owners had to pay a claim fee to the poundkeeper.

15. PIONEER HOMESITE (1737-1815), 416 Main St. - The downtown area began in 1737 when Jesse Kendall built a small home in the present middle of Main Street. Indians menaced this valley but the house stood firm for 78 years. The pioneer Kendalls, Samuel and son Jesse, owned nearly all of the downtown area when it was hostile wilderness. When Main Street was laid out in 1815, the house was moved to 47 Freedom St. and stood until 1875. Jesse Kendall had sold these 80 prime acres in 1795 to Simeon Fish for 700 British pounds.

16. FORT HOUSE (1745-1755), Exchange Street and Sally Fish Circle - On a small hill here that was removed in 1919, Samuel Kendall built for all "a garrison house, planked to the first story." It protected the few lowlands settlers from Indian attack. More pioneer homes began sprouting up in this lowland midway between the East Hill and West Hill settlements. A means of protection against Indian raids was needed for these isolated families. The garrison house was built atop a knoll that gave a wide view of this valley.

17. CAPTURED BY INDIANS, 151 Pequoig Ave. - Young pioneer Jason Babcock built his log cabin here in 1745. In the spring of 1747 he was captured by Indians in this open rear meadow, taken prisoner to Canada, then freed. Babcock came here at age 18 and bought most of this meadow and hillside. One day his cows strayed into the westside woods and he went to look for them. Suddenly shots rang out from Indians in hiding and Babcock was slightly wounded. The war whoops were heard by men at the mill near the present YMCA. They ran to his rescue but he was already carried off.

18. INDIAN MEADOW, 488 South Main St. - Pequoig Indians of the Nipmuck tribe built wigwams and planted cornfields all along this riverside meadow. Indian relics were found in a field close by until a generation ago. An unidentified historian wrote, "Konkeput was their chief. They built their council fires on these plains, gathered the wild grain on these meadows, hunted the deer of these hills. Here they gave their sons and daughters in marriage, and here they buried the

bones of their fathers. Relics of these noble men yet remain. But that once happy tribe is gone, faded away."

19. MOUNT PLEASANT CEMETERY, North Orange Road and Mt. Pleasant Street – Land donated by Samuel Morton before 1745. A memorial to many town founders. It has a marker to Ezekiel Wallingford, killed by Indians during a moonlit raid. The East Hill and West Hill pioneers were separated by two miles of wildnerness and a river crossed by foot at a fording place off North Orange Road. It became clear another burial place was needed for the settlers living north of the river.

20. OLDEST HOUSE IN ATHOL, 35 Moore Hill Rd. – Built in 1736 by Aaron Smith as a log cabin. Later enlarged. Menaced by Indians in 1746 and raided of food by Daniel Shays' army in 1787. Later served as a tavern and stagecoach stop. Its beginning was a two-room log cabin. The timbers were dove-tailed together so that wooden pegs or nails were not needed. His descendants added a second floor, and a major restoration in 1969 gives the house its modern look, but much of the original interior structure remains.

21. WEST FORT (1741-1780), Moore Hill Road – A strong defense against Indians, it stood in this lower field. Inside this log stockade were a solid blockhouse, huts for families and troops, and a well. Its remains were removed in 1869. "Our ancestors relate how, as night spread its mantle of darkness over the forest and around their infant settlement, all would gather together in the garrison and sit silently without lights, listening with cautious ear to every external sound, querying if each uncommon noise might not be the signal of danger from the hostile Indians."

22. SENTINEL ELM, Moore Hill Road – On the crest of this hill stood a majestic elm 93 feet tall. From its top branches Indians signalled across the valley, and later pioneer lookouts warned of hostile red men. It fell in 1931. The Sentinel Elm for more than 200 years created a dramatic silhouette on this hilltop. Used in early days as a "spy tree" by Indians and pioneers alike, in later years it became a favorite picnic spot. The tree is preserved in story, poetry, photography, art and song. The elm was visible for 20 miles and it was said that on a clear day Boston Harbor could be seen from its top branches. A bronze plaque marks where it stood.

23. SCALPED BY INDIANS, Moore Hill Road – On Aug. 17, 1746, Ezekiel Wallingford, thinking he heard bears trampling his cornfield here, left the fort to investigate. He was soon surrounded by Indians who shot and scalped him

dead. Indians lay in ambush here in Wallingford's cornfield and made noises like vandal bears to draw him out. A hundred yards from the fort, the Indians jumped from hiding and surrounded him. He turned and ran but in passing a fence was shot in the thigh and fell. Tomahawk and scalping knife ended his life.

24. COLONIAL HOME (1777), 1777 Chestnut Hill Ave. – John Haven Jr., a private in Gen. George Washington's army, built this home during the revolution. He had fought in the siege of Boston and the victories at Ticonderoga and Sarasota. Haven was one of Ethan Allen's "Green Mountain Boys" who captured Ft. Ticonderoga on May 10, 1775. Two years later his military service was completed, the war moved into the south, and he came home and built this house. It stands as a model of colonial sturdiness and design.

Honey and Honeybees

Bees are an essential factor in area agriculture, as they pollinate flowers making possible fruit and vegetable production. Two county associations meet regularly and individuals interested in locating locally-produced honey or in learning more about keeping bees can obtain information from the associations: Franklin County Beekeeping Association, Roger Augustine, president, North Cross Road, Gill MA 01376; and Worcester County Beekeepers Association, Frank LaGrant, president, Osborne Road, Ware MA 01082.

Honey produced by Kathy and Roger Augustine of nearby Gill is sold at Kathy's Kurling Korner, Mohawk Plaza, Athol. Locally-produced honey may occasionally be available from other area beekeepers.

Horses

Words like farrier, whiffletree, teamster and scoot, once a part of the working vocabulary around these parts, are rarely heard nowadays. All of these words relate to horsemanship, but it is uncommon to see horses at work as in the past – pulling carts and sleighs loaded with people and cargo, hauling logs out of woods, plowing fields. Some area residents nonetheless own these magnificent animals; corrals can be seen alongside homes and horses can be seen grazing in fields. Nowadays, horses are owned primarily for the pleasure they give rather than for the labor they save.

Lagrand, four-year-old chestnut stallion, at "The Farm" in Athol

Although there is no stable in the area offering trail rides, there are many forest roads ideal for horseback riding. Farm supply outlets in the area sell necessary equipment and the following businesses serve the horse-lover:

ABC School of Horsemanship, Anne Coombs, proprietor, Route 101, Phillipston, mail to RFD 1, Templeton MA 01468, Tel. 939-2023; lessons in all aspects of horse ownership, including riding, horse care, barn management, stable management including breeding; proper tack and attire use; leasing and boarding of horses; assistance to buyers and sellers; licensed personnel.

The Farm, Kathleen Woehl, proprietor, Vaughn Road, Athol, Tel. 249-3601; Arabian horses for sale, full training and equitation service for horse and rider; stallions standing at stud.

Human Services

Various human services, secular and religious, have been established in the area. Among the newest facilities are the Human Resource Center for Rural Communities installed in the town-owned former Main Street School and the Family and Children Services of Catholic Charities in a brand-new building near Our Lady Immaculate Church.

The Human Resource Center for Rural Communities, 100 Main St., Athol, Tel. 249-9926, defines itself as a center for mental health services for the people of Athol, New Salem, Orange, Petersham, Phillipston, Royalston and Warwick. The center "recognizes the dignity of every client in their desire to cope more successfully with a complex society." It cooperates with other agencies in building a network of rehabilitation services and assists clients with mental problems through individual diagnosis and treatment, counseling and workshops.

Trained psychologists on the center's staff assist individuals "with the stresses of everyday life," and their professional fees are covered by health care insurance, or, for those without insurance, sliding scale fee arrangements will be made.

Services include therapy, testing and evaluation, medication clinic, emergency assistance, alcohol and drug counseling, advocacy for mentally retarded adults and children, consultation to community groups and organizations, referrals, and workshops on stress, weight loss or smoking. Care is provided to all regardless of race, color, age, sex, handicaps, religious beliefs or ability to pay. A 24-hour on-call service (number above) is available seven days a week. The building is accessible to handicapped people; visits to home-bound individuals may be arranged.

People's Bridge Action, Inc., 485 Main St., Athol, Tel. 249-2248, was incorporated in 1975 and is "a community action agency." It was originally an outgrowth of grass-roots efforts to combine social and political awareness with the special skills of the helping professions. PBA's purpose "is to provide specialized services to persons and families in need of assistance in coping with the difficulties of life in a complex society." Offerings include direct guidance, advocacy, educational workshops, therapy and emergency shelter. These programs serve "individuals with special needs such as intellectual, emotional and/or physical handicaps, temporary family disturbances and drug abuse problems." The agency has several residential programs and specialized services for retarded adults, former mental patients and individuals with various mental health problems or those in crisis situations.

The advocacy program of PBA serves Worcester County citizens by providing housing information, including helping deal with tenant-landlord problems, as well as food stamps and welfare information. The fuel assistance program serves the four towns of Athol, Petersham, Phillipston and Royalston by providing energy assistance in the form of grants to help meet the cost of fuel as well as providing weatherization and self-help weatherization materials to those who meet income guidelines.

The family service outreach team of PBA provides family and individual counseling. An emergency shelter provides short-term emergency housing to children and adolescents up to age 22, with special 24-hour crisis telephone, 249-4249.

Franklin Community Action Corp., 26 North Main St., Orange, Tel. 544-6202, provides many of the same services as well as referrals. In some areas, such as fuel assistance and welfare rights advocacy, the Franklin County agency serves the Franklin County towns not covered by PBA. This agency is headquartered in Turners Falls and maintains an outreach office in Orange. Its non-profit Social Service Help program has helped area residents with such programs as locating inexpensive clothing for needy families, assisting in landlord-tenant disputes, mental health counseling, child care services, public assistance information, budget counseling, handicapped and chore services, non-payment of utility bills and other problems.

Family Planning Council of Western Massachusetts, Inc., 312 Main St. (rear), Athol, Tel. 249-2013, is a non-profit organization which offers comprehensive family planning health care. Medical and counseling services include all birth planning methods (contraceptive devices, pills and rhythm), pap smear and breast exam for cancer screening, VD screening, pregnancy testing and counseling, routine laboratory work and pelvic exam. There are educational programs and referral services available, including information about a shelter for battered women maintained in Greenfield by the New England Learning Center for Women in Transition. The council serves everyone, regardless of income, through a sliding fee scale, with free care available to limited income individuals.

Legal assistance for individuals who meet income guidelines is available from Central Massachusetts Legal Services (for Worcester County towns), 455 Main St., Fitchburg, Tel. 345-1946, and Western Massachusetts Legal Services (for Franklin County towns), 278 Main St., Greenfield, Tel. 413-774-3747.

American Red Cross, 584 Main St., Athol, Tel. 249-6257, arranges bloodmobiles, provides instruction in first aid and lifesaving techniques, helps families communicate with military personnel and offers emergency services.

Family and Children Services of Catholic Charities, 12 Riverbend St., Athol, Tels. 249-4563 and 249-6774, "provides outreach services to all people – regardless of age, color, creed, or ability to pay." Their counseling "seeks to maintain family relationships and help individuals in problem solving." They also offer homemaker/home health aides "to help maintain, strengthen and safeguard the care of children, and the functioning of the aged, physically or emotionally ill, or handicapped adults in their homes," and a "friendly visitor" program designed to provide friendship and advocacy to older people. There are also unwed mother services, adoption and infant foster care services and "lifeline" for women faced with a "troublesome pregnancy."

Salvation Army Corps and Community Center, 107 Ridge Ave., Athol, Tel. 249-8111, provides various services for the needy, including Thanksgiving and Christmas dinners, providing shelter for transients, and otherwise aiding those in crisis.

Most area churches provide assistance to needy community residents.

Various organizations, service agencies and advocacy groups serving particular groups such as Vietnam era veterans, handicapped persons, racial and ethnic minorities, gay men and lesbians, are located in larger nearby communities, especially in the Connecticut valley towns of Amherst and Northampton. These are listed in the Valley Advocate, a free weekly distributed in several Athol and Orange places of business. See also ELDERLY SERVICES, HEALTH CARE SERVICES.

Industry

Manufacturing is the major economic activity in the nine-town region, with most of the factories located in Athol and Orange, a legacy of the age of water power. These two towns have two and a half times as much of their economy engaged in manufacturing as either the state of Massachusetts or the United States.

More than half of the approximately 3,000 manufacturing jobs in the area are in the metal working machinery and special industry machinery categories. This includes the L.S. Starrett Co. and Union Butterfield Division of Litton Industries in Athol and the Rodney Hunt Co. and Leavitt Machine Co. in Orange.

The next most influential manufacturing type is paper products, with the two major employers in Erving – the Erving Paper Mills and Millers Falls Paper Co.

Utilizing native forest products, there are several

Lathe operator at Athol Table Manufacturing Co.

household furniture and toy manufacturers, including the N.D. Cass Co., Athol Table Manufacturing Co. and Eastern Furniture Manufacturers Inc., all of Athol.

Because of the nature of area industry, many highly-skilled workers in the metal and wood industries live in the area. See also ERVING PAPER MILLS, RODNEY HUNT CO., STARRETT'S, UNION TWIST DRILL.

Jacob Hill

Jacob Hill is a steep forested ridge located one mile west of Royalston Common, south of Warwick Road (Route 68). The steep roadway that ascends the hill between Falls Road and the center of town is sometimes called "Jacob's Ladder." A small unmarked automobile turnout off the road provides access for sightseers, via a short footpath, to a magnificent view to the west, including Long Pond (barely seen through the trees) and the east branch of the Tully River meandering sinuously through wetlands and flowing into Long Pond. Also flowing into the pond, down the westerly face of the ridge, is Spirit Falls.

The Trustees of Reservations owns 135 acres, including a major parcel purchased from Dr. Leonard B. Thompson of Gardner. The purchase price for the Trustees' part of the ridge was contributed "very generously by an anonymous donor." See also SPIRIT FALLS.

Keystone Bridge in New Salem

Keystone Bridge

One of the most beautiful structures in the region is the Keystone Bridge in New Salem, made of carefully laid stones. The middle branch of the Swift River flows beneath the round arch of this bridge, built in the late 1800s by Adolphus Porter, a Civil War veteran who lived in North New Salem and who is buried in the Orange Central Cemetery.

The bridge is located on Quabbin watershed land owned by the Metropolitan District Commission. The roadway atop the bridge, no longer in use, is reached from Gate 30 across from the intersection of Route 122 and Orange Road, New Salem. It's only a two-minute walk from the gate to the bridge.

Lakes and Ponds

Area towns are graced by numerous lakes and ponds, man-made and natural.

The biggest "lake" of all is the Quabbin Reservoir, although the word "lake" is rarely used to describe this body of water, 39 square miles in size. The Quabbin is stocked with fish and, while strictly regulated and policed, it is open to the public.

State-owned lakes stocked with fish and open to the public

include Ruggles and Wickett ponds in Wendell State Forest, Sheomet Lake in Warwick State Forest, Riceville Lake in Petersham State Forest and Laurel Lake in Erving State Forest.

Brooks Pond in Petersham is open to fishing by special permit obtained from Harvest Forest, which owns the pond.

Public swimming beaches on town-owned lakes are at

Long Pond on east branch of Tully River in Royalston

Lake Ellis and Silver Lake in Athol and Lake Mattawa in Orange. Swimming areas at state-owned lakes include Laurel Lake in Erving State Forest and Ruggles Pond in Wendell State Forest.

Several lakes have some or most of their shorelines covered with camps and year-round private residences. The largest of these are Queen Lake in Phillipston, Lake Mattawa in Orange and Sportsman's Pond in Athol (owned by a private association). Other lakes and ponds with private residences are Laurel Lake, Moores Pond in Warwick, Secret Lake in Phillipston, White Pond in Athol, and Packard Pond and Tully Pond in the Tully section of Orange.

Tully Lake in Royalston, not to be confused with Tully Pond, is formed by the Tully Dam and is under the jurisdiction of the U.S. Army Corps of Engineers. Upstream from Tully Lake along the "Dead River" section of the east branch of the Tully River is Long Pond, accessible by canoe and footpath.

Residents of Athol depend in part for their water on the Newton Reservoir (on the dammed Buckman Brook) and the Phillipston Reservoir.

Lake Rohunta, which lies in Athol, Orange and New Salem, is owned by the Rodney Hunt Co. of Orange. The private Pine Beach for Rodney Hunt employees is located on Rohunta's north end. Route 2 crosses over Lake Rohunta.

Other bodies of water include Little Pond and Beaver Pond in Royalston, North and South Spectacle Ponds in New Salem, Hastings Pond and Wheeler Pond in Warwick, Pottapaug Pond (connected to the Quabbin) and Carter Pond in Petersham and Fiske Pond and Bowens Pond in Wendell. See also LAUREL LAKE, PETERSHAM STATE FOREST, QUABBIN RESERVOIR, TULLY DAM AND LAKE, WENDELL STATE FOREST.

Laurel Lake

Located inside Erving State Forest, Laurel Lake offers one of the region's most popular public beaches and recreation areas. The lake is located partly in Erving and partly in Warwick. It is accessible from Route 2A in Wendell Depot via Warwick Road, or from Warwick Center by means of Wendell Road, as well as from Erving Center via North Street. There is a day use or seasonal fee charged for parking and for use of other facilities, including campsites.

Laurel Lake supports a population of several species of fish including pickerel and the brown and brook trout stocked by the state's fisheries and game division.

This was the first organized recreation area in Erving State Forest, being developed by the Civilian Conservation Corps in the 1930s as a picnic area consisting of twelve tables and six fireplaces. The CCC also constructed a spring house, bathhouse, toilets, parking area and 10 tent platforms (since removed), all of which were located in the vicinity of the present picnic area.

The recreation area currently consists of a bathing beach with lifeguard on duty during the season, 202 picnic tables, 160 fireplaces, a concession stand, bathhouse, toilets, contact station, parking lot and 32 campsites on the hillside above the picnic area. A trail up an unnamed hill near the campsites leads to a vista (elevation 1,047 feet above sea level). A state-maintained boat ramp can be found at the western end of the lake, but there are no boat rentals. Motorboats up to 10 h.p. are permitted, as well as canoes and rowboats.

There is some private property on the lake shore. See also CAMPING, ERVING STATE FOREST.

Leonard Monument

In his 1963 history book, Warwick resident Charles Morse tells the story of the James Leonard monument:

"For over 140 years people traveling along the Wendell road have seen what appeared to be a gravestone by the side of the road, just a few rods below the southern edge of Moores Pond. A closer examination reveals that this is a monument erected to commemorate a tragedy which took place in 1824. The inscription tells that James, the three-year-old son of Francis Leonard, was killed here when he fell from a cart and the wheel passed over him.

'Here I passed from Earth to Glory.
In a moment quick as thought;
Passing strangers read the story
On this consecrated spot.'"

Libraries

"Books are the treasured wealth of the world and the fit inheritance of generations and nations." So wrote Henry David Thoreau in his book "Walden" – one of those treasures that can be found in just about every public library in the United States.

The largest public library in the area is the Athol Public Library, which celebrated its 100th birthday in 1982. This well-run library serves not only residents of Athol but many readers from surrounding communities. Its book collection consists of 25,000 hardbacks, 18,000 for adults and 7,000 for children. The library suscribes to 10 daily newspapers (including The New York Times) and more than 100 periodicals. There is an audio-visual collection of records, cassettes, and paintings, plus projecters – all available for circulation. A coin-operated copy machine and a microfilm reader-printer are available in the library.

Library activities include lunch-hour book reviews and art and photographic expositions, some of these sponsored by a Friends of the Library organization. There is a children's librarian and special programs in a separate children's room.

Every area town has its own public library, though only the Wheeler Memorial Library in Orange comes close to offering the collection size and range of services offered in Athol. Inter-library loans and other services are offered by regional systems to which all area libraries are affiliated – the Franklin County communities belonging to the Western Massachusetts Regional Library System and the Worcester County towns belonging to the Central Massachusetts Regional Library System.

Five area communities – Athol, New Salem, Orange, Phillipston and Royalston – were the focus of "The Athol Area Library and Community Analysis," undertaken under a grant in 1980-81. The published report recommended more inter-library cooperation and praised each library as having "great potential as a cultural, educational, recreational and social force."

Area libraries depend on state and local tax funds for their operation. Most of the libraries were originally built on donated land with funds from philanthropists. The Athol library was built with a donation by America's most famous giver of libraries, Andrew Carnegie, on land given by Laroy S. Starrett. Orange's library was built with money given in memory of John Wheeler by his widow, the former Almira Johnson. At least three area libraries, the Athol Public Library, the Wheeler Memorial Library in Orange and the Phinehas S. Newton Library in Royalston, have handsome grandfather clocks donated when the libraries were originally opened in the early part of this century.

Lithuanians

Lithuanians form one of the visible ethnic communities in Athol. Leaving their Eastern European homeland to escape persecution at the hands of the Russians, they came to America in search of freedom and quickly sought suitable farmland to continue their previous lifestyle. The first Lithuanians in Athol arrived shortly before 1900, but the number increased just after the turn of the century, and an association was formed in Athol in 1904.

As with other ethnic groups, these benevolent societies were formed to help newcomers adjust and to prepare immigrants for U.S. citizenship. Some of the Lithuanian efforts were in cooperation with the smaller Polish population. Athol's Lithuanians established their own parish, St. Francis of Assisi, in 1913. The brick St. Francis Church that serves the parish today was built in 1919.

The American-Lithuanian Naturalization Club has its headquarters at 365 South St. See also WAYSIDE CROSS.

Lodging

In days gone by, Athol and Orange had several handsome hotels, and still further back in area history there were inns serving stagecoach stops in local communities. These are now mere memories. Athol's four-story brick Pequoig Hotel, once popular with travelers, remained empty for several years; placed on the National Register of Historic Places and with the help of state and federal programs, the building has been saved from demolition and will be converted into a housing project for the elderly.

Unfortunately, none of the nine towns currently offers travelers the charm and comfort of lodging and dining at a traditional New England country inn. This kind of accommodation is available in some nearby communities, including the Fitzwillian Inn in Fitzwilliam, N.H. (Tel. 603-585-9000).

There are five motels serving the nine towns of the region:

Bald Eagle Motel, 110 Daniel Shays Hwy., Orange, Tel. 544-2101.

French King Motor Inn, Route 2, Millers Falls, Erving, Tel. 413-659-3328.

King Philip Motel, Athol Road, Phillipston, Tel. 249-6300.

Quabbin Gateway Motel, Daniel Shays Hwy., Orange, Tel. 544-2986.

Weatherhead's Motel & Cabins, Route 2, Millers Falls, Erving, Tel. 413-659-3831.

More rustic facilities are available at the Warwick Inn, Route 78, Warwick, Tel. 544-8549; and for men only at the YMCA, 545 Main St., Athol, Tel. 249-3305.

Arrangements for lodging in the case of emergencies can be made through the Salvation Army, 107, Ridge Ave., Athol, Tel. 249-8111.

Maple Syrup

Maple syrup is traditionally associated with Vermont more than with any other state, but Massachusetts has its share of maple sugar production. Pure maple syrup is made simply by boiling down the sap of the sugar maple tree, with approximately 40 gallons of sap yielding one gallon of syrup. The syrup is not cheap – current prices running in the range of $20-$25 per gallon – but authentic 100 percent pure maple syrup is a special natural treat. Most "pancake syrup" sold in supermarkets consists of corn and cane sugar syrup with artifical maple flavoring and, in some cases, a tiny percentage of the real thing.

In the nine-town region, the largest commercial sugaring operation is at the Philip Johnson farm on Wheeler Avenue in Orange. Each spring, when the weather conditions are right, causing the sap to run, the maples along Wheeler Avenue can be seen with sap buckets hanging from them, and the sugar house across from the Johnson residence and barn has steam rising from its roof. Visitors are welcome at the sugar house, and syrup and sugar are sold at the farm until the supply runs out, usually several months later.

Maple syrup is also available at the Apple Barn in New Salem, Maple Valley Farm in North Orange, and Putney's Mill in Royalston. Other residents of the region produce smaller quantities of maple syrup, sometimes selling it from their homes and advertising it only by means of a small sign. See also FARM PRODUCTS.

Maps

To help one become familiar with any place, a map is an essential tool. An excellent road map of the Athol-Orange-Barre area, covering all the towns of the region and then some, is available at Countryside Realty Gallery of Homes, 253 East Main St., Orange, which publishes it for advertising purposes and as a community service. This map includes an index and shows all streets.

A map of Quabbin Reservoir indicating gate numbers and fishing areas is published by the North Worcester County Quabbin Anglers Association. A copy may be obtained by sending a self-addressed stamped envelope to the Association at Box 79, Athol MA 01331.

The best maps of all for hiking and any detailed exploration are the 7.5 minute series topographical maps published by the Geological Survey of the U.S. Department of the Interior. These maps cannot be recommended too highly to longtime residents and newcomers alike. Although some of the surveys are slightly out of date, the amount of information on them is phenomenal, including every structure and roadway as well as all topographical features. These maps come in various "quadrants," including ones for Athol, Orange, Royalston, Petersham, Quabbin, Mt. Grace and Millers Falls (covering Wendell). The "topo maps," as they are often called, are available locally from two dealers:

Virginia Frye, Town Clerk's Office, Prospect Hill Road, Royalston, Tel. 249-3005.

Charles Richardson, 90 Ward Rd., Orange, Tel. 544-2889.

Because these two dealers sell the maps from their homes, it is advisable to call first to make sure they are at home and have available the quadrants being sought. These maps are also available during regular business hours at retail outlets in nearby communities, including Barrett & Baker in Greenfield and A.J. Hastings and Eastern Mountain Sports in Amherst. A catalog with complete listing and prices for the 7.5 minute quadrant maps and other topographical maps covering larger areas is available from the U.S. Geological Survey, Branch of Distribution, Eastern Region, 1200 South Eads St., Arlington VA 22202; mail order requests are filled.

Another useful item is the Western Massachusetts Atlas published by the Arrow Map Co. This includes all indexed street maps of all towns in Franklin, Hampshire, Hampden and Berkshire counties. The atlas is sold in many stationery and variety stores in those counties.

A copy of the Official Transportation Map of Massachusetts is available free of charge by writing to Department of Commerce and Development, 100 Cambridge St., Boston MA 02202. This is probably the best available road map of the state; it also shows railroads.

Metacomet-Monadnock Trail

The Metacomet-Monadnock Trail, which passes through the region, is a marked interstate footpath linking the extensive Connecticut trail system with the New Hampshire trail system that converges on Mt. Monadnock. From Montague, the trail enters Wendell and continues through Erving, Northfield, Warwick and Royalston before crossing the state line into Richmond, N.H.

Beginning in the Hanging Hills of Meriden, Conn., the trail runs north along the traprock ridge bordering the Connecticut River Valley, crosses the river past Mt. Tom to follow the ridge of the Holyoke Range, then proceeds through the Amherst-Pelham-Montague area to enter Wendell at Ruggles Pond. Near the pond there is an Adirondack shelter for 8-10 people. The trail runs north from the Ruggles Pond parking area on a tote road alongside Lyons Brook, joins Jerusalem Road and follows it to Davis Road in Mormon Hollow and then skirts the western slope of Bear Mountain along Farley Road to cross the Millers River into Farley Village.

Crossing Route 2 at Farley, the trail continues northward steeply to heights overlooking the Millers River. The outcropping of ledge in this area is some of the most precipitous in the region, offering a dramatic view of the Farley flats.

Northwards, the trail continues to include Crag Mountain in Northfield, crosses the Bald Hills and enters Warwick on White Road to ascend Mt. Grace in Warwick via the old Snowshoe Trail, with descent on the Winchester Trail. The trail proceeds through backwoods sections of Warwick to Bliss Hill Road in West Royalston where a recent re-routing of the trail takes the hiker through forestland and across Route 32 to the old Newton Cemetery and from there to Royalston Falls before crossing the state line into New Hampshire.

The Metacomet-Monadnock trail is marked by white painted rectangular blazes about two by four inches in size. Two blazes, one above the other, are used to indicate abrupt changes in trail direction ahead. The trail includes public lands and public roads but also crosses much private property, and users are advised that respect for landowners' rights is essential so that the route will remain open to hikers.

This scenic trail uses pathways which have been traveled for decades by naturalists along the ridgetops, game trails, forest service roads and wood roads in territory often inaccessible directly by car or horse. As the trail guidebook published by the Berkshire Chapter of the Appalachian Mountain Club states, "It follows in the cool shade beside dancing sylvan streams, climbs on sunlit ridges high against the sky, and runs generally for miles through the serene forest solitude of central Massachusetts. The trail in Massachusetts and New Hampshire was created by and is now maintained as a public service of the Appalachian Mountain Club, the Green Mountain Club, the Metawampe and similar organizations. Its existence is a tribute to the cooperation of numerous state forest and park organizations, town watershed managements, wildlife sanctuaries and private landowners in making this fascinating countryside available to all who love and enjoy it."

This guidebook is available by mail for $2 postpaid from Walter Banfield, Pratt Corner Road, Amherst MA 01002. Users of the trail are advised to obtain the guidebook and topographical maps to avoid getting lost. In some ways this trail sounds better than it is. The woodland pathways are not always apparent – due to their infrequent use – and thus are difficult to follow in some sections. The use of the Metacomet-Monadnock Trail is recommended only to the adventuresome and woods-wise person.

Millers River

"The spirit of a wild river is a blend of water, earth, air and human memories, and if it dies it dies in quiet agony. When death comes swiftly suffering intensifies, for those who have loved the river see it as it is and as it was; there has been no buffer generation to immunize them to ugliness. Of our many dead and dying rivers few have been more swiftly and savagely desecrated than the Millers in north-central Massachusetts."

Those sad, angry words were written by Ted Williams in an article published in Massachusetts Wildlife in 1972. In a decade's time, so much progress has been made in cleaning up the Millers River – the sparkling artery of water that runs through most area towns – that the tragic prose of the magazine now seems melodramatic.

In fact, however, it was the tireless efforts of writers like Ted Williams and conservationists such as Robert Gray of Athol, that have given the Millers River a new lease on life. Slowly but surely, the river is being cleaned up, though the optimum level of cleanliness and a return to desired wildlife abundance have not yet been achieved.

Millers River and bridge in Farley section of Erving

The Millers River rises in the towns of Winchendon and Ashburnham through the confluences of several streams draining bog swamp areas and the warm waters of Lake Monomonac, Naukeag Pond and Whitney Pond. From its immediate source, Whitney Pond in Winchendon, the river flows south and west through an area called the "Central Uplands," decreasing in elevation by 867 feet with an average drop of 19 feet per mile. It drains 391 square miles on its 35-mile course to the Connecticut River at Montague, and is the smallest of Massachusetts' four main tributaries of the Connecticut River.

The Millers River called attention to itself nationwide in late September 1938 when, during a hurricane, it overflowed its banks and inflicted considerable damage on the riverside towns, so much so that federal disaster aid officials were called in and military surveillance of the area was ordered – and a few years later, the U.S. Army Corps of Engineers began work on two flood control projects in Royalston, Tully and Birch Hill dams.

During the historic flood, most streets, highways and railroads in the area were rendered impassable by falling trees and other debris, or were simply washed away, while in the low lands, "waters poured into the windows of many dwellings, reaching nearly to the ceiling of not a few homes and business places," as reported by William G. Lord in his history of Athol. For many years, a sign posted on the edge of Route 2 where it skirts near the edge of the river in Erving noted that the 1938

119

floodwater level was more than five feet above the highway surface, but inconsiderate souvenir-hungry thieves repeatedly removed the historic sign, and as of this writing the state has stopped replacing it.

Atlantic salmon once made their way upstream from the Long Island Sound to spawn in the Millers, and as recently as the 1950s, although polluted in parts, it was still one of the state's best trout streams. But in the early 1970s, the pollution problem was grave, and as Williams put it, the river was "a smudgy, sudsy mess, barren of trout, except for a few unfortunates occasionally swept down from feeder streams by high water."

The river's woes began in the 1890s when towns along the watershed began piping sewage directly into the river. By the early 1970s, it was clear that any cleanup of the river would have to involve new high-technology sewage treatment plants in area towns and industrial waste processing at various industries, most notably paper mills in Erving and Templeton. A principal Millers tributary, the Otter River, polluted by waste from the Baldwinville Paper Products, a division of Erving Paper Mills, was considered for a time as one of the filthiest waterways in the state.

Throughout the 1970s, due to a mixture of local efforts and national environmental consciousness, millions of dollars were spent on this cleanup, and the river has been slowly recovering, although some town sewage treatment plants still need upgrading while the paper mills, recalcitrant through much of the cleanup effort, have been successful in obtaining approval from the U.S. Environmental Protection Agency to continue placing impurities in the water.

Swimming and fishing are currently not common practices in the Millers, except in Ashburnham and Winchendon (upstream from the confluence with the Otter River). The section of the river between Athol and Orange is ideal for flatwater canoeing. Below Orange through Erving, white-water canoeists can be seen during springtime freshets, although this section of the river is often the scene of incidents of boats being capsized. The section of the river through the Birch Hill Wildlife Management Area in Winchendon is characterized by long, slow riffles and ponded pools. The bottom is largely mud and silt; banks are well-shaded and swampy. This is also the area that is frequently inundated in the winter and spring due to the Birch Hill Dam. The entire area becomes a virtual pond and fishing is poor when the dam is closed.

Stocking of trout took place in South Royalston and Erving

Millers River above old dam near downtown Athol

in the spring of 1983 - an event that made headlines in Massachusetts newspapers. Prior to that, the stocking was limited to cleaner sections upstream. Salmon smelt were placed in the river below Orange in 1983, part of a tri-state salmon restoration project. Top credit for the river's revival must go to environmental laws and to the Millers River Watershed Council, Inc., formed in 1970 "to work for the restoration and maintenance of clean water, and the wise use and proper management of water and related natural resources" in the 20-town watershed.

The Council (Box 23, Athol MA 01331) has been active in opposing plans promoted at various times by the Metropolitan District Commission and the U.S. Army Corps of Engineers to divert water to the Quabbin Reservoir from the Millers itself or from smaller streams in the Millers watershed (including the Tully River and Priest Brook in Royalston). The Council's major focus, under the leadership of founder Robert Gray and others, has been to promote basic cleanup by urging local communities to deal with sewage and to urge industries to stop treating the river as if it were their private disposal system.

Another means of calling attention to the problems and potential of the river has been the annual River Rat Spectacular canoe race from Athol to Orange, which attracts hundreds of canoeists and thousands of spectators annually.

A more recent development involves a proposed "greenway" to protect the river and encourage its appreciation from a users' point of view by means of walkways, vantage points, boat launches, resting and picnicking areas - possibly by obtaining easements from property-owners. Under a state program, an advisory council has been meeting regularly to develop plans for the greenway, although some riverside landowners have expressed concern that the plan threatens their property rights. (More information is available from Jonathan Geer, Scenic Rivers Program, Department of Environmental Management, 100 Cambridge St., Boston MA 02202, Tel. 617-727-4704.)

Pollution is not the only Millers River problem. Dams built at various sites in South Royalston, Athol, Orange and Erving harnessed the Millers for hydropower for industry during and after the industrial revolution. Many of these dams have fallen into disuse, but there are new plans afoot to reconstruct several dams along the river for the generation of electricity – an approach welcomed by alternative energy enthusiasts but questioned by sportsmen who are concerned that dams will interfere with maximization of the river's potential for fishing and recreation. See also ATHOL, BIRCH HILL DAM, ERVING, ORANGE, RIVER RAT RACE.

Millers River Wildlife Area

The Millers River Wildlife Management Area consists of 1,850 acres of land in Royalston and Athol owned by the state's Department of Environmental Management. This land is managed by the Division of Fisheries and Wildlife.

Most of the acreage is located on the north side of the Millers River in a remote area known as The Gulf, just north of the Bearsden Woods. It includes miles of frontage along a particularly wild and fast-moving portion of the river. The terrain is rugged and forested primarily with hardwoods. Smaller streams running into the Millers here are Gulf Brook and West Gulf Brook. There is little open land and thus no stocking of pheasants. Typical upland wildlife species are found here and the land is open to hunting, trapping and fishing.

After some years of being rated too polluted to justify stocking, the Millers River in this area has been substantially cleaned up. Trout stocking took place in South Royalston below the Birch Hill Dam in 1983. State biologists hope to establish a wild turkey population here and have been releasing turkeys.

Access to the Millers River Wildlife Management Area is by means of Gulf Road from either Athol or South Royalston. See also BEARSDEN WOODS and MILLERS RIVER.

Mt. Grace State Forest

At 1,617 feet above sea level, Mt. Grace's peak is the second highest elevation in Massachusetts east of the Connecticut River. (The highest is Mt. Wachusett in Princeton, 2,006 above sea level.)

The mountain is contained in Mt. Grace State Forest, which covers 1,458 acres in Warwick.

A leisurely hike up the mountain takes no more than an hour and a half; the descent is quicker. A trail begins on the western side of the mountain near the administration building on Route 78 just north of Warwick center; it connects to a jeep road that ascends from the southern side. The jeep road is not open to public vehicular traffic.

A fire tower at the top offers a spectacular view of surrounding countryside, especially the Sunny Valley of Winchester, N.H., to the north. Also visible from the peak are Mt. Monadnock, Jaffrey, N.H.; the Vermont Yankee nuclear power plant in Vernon, Vt.; and some of the houses in the center of Warwick. The view to the south is mostly obstructed, however. In addition, public access to the tower is made difficult, though not impossible, by a chain-link fence.

A telephone microwave tower is located near the fire tower.

The old fire tower is no longer used in connection with fire prevention but the cabin at the top contains various radio

Mt. Grace framed by maple trees on Hastings Heights Road in Warwick

equipment and is not accessible to the public. The view is from the staircase – without climbing the staircase the visitor will not see over the treetops.

The fire tower is one of the oldest in the state. The original tower was erected in 1911. It was 40 feet high, made of galvanized iron with a six foot square box on top and about one and one half miles of telephone line connecting it to the New England Telephone Co. line in Warwick.

The state did not hold title to this land but was given permission to use the land by its owner, Charles A. Williams.

In 1920, a new 68-ft. tower was erected and the state purchased a half-acre of land from Williams. The next year the state erected a small open bungalow to accompany the fire watch, but this structure is gone. Acreage was added over the years.

The tower was blown down in the hurricane of Sept. 21, 1938, and was replaced after that with a temporary wooden one. In the summer of 1939, the present tower, 68 feet tall and made of galvanized steel, with a 10 ft. square room atop it, was installed.

In subsequent years, a pole line was constructed and radios were installed.

Aside from hiking and sightseeing, recreational activities in Mt. Grace State Forest include snowmobiling (six miles of trails), hunting, and picnicking. The picnic area, in a pine grove off Route 78, includes 50 tables and 25 grills. Manning Field is a five-acre cleared area available to groups for a day use fee. Warwick residents gather there frequently for Sunday volleyball games and the field is used for weddings and other gatherings. The area can be reserved. A day use or seasonal fee is charged for the field and picnic facilities.

At one time, a downhill skiing area was maintained on Mt. Grace by the state. According to a 1940 edition of "Conservation Bulletin," there were four trails, Gulf Link, Snowshoe, Tripod and Mt. Grace. The principal trail was the Mt. Grace Trail, more than a mile long and "designed to meet U.S. Eastern Amateur Ski Association requirements." According to the listing, Mt. Grace had "complete ski facilities including three large parking areas, two Adirondack shelters with council fireplaces."

A spokesman for the state's department of environment management was unable to provide information on the circumstances that led to the eventual closing of the ski area. Warwick historian Charles Morse recalls that the area was closed in the early 1960s. He said by that time many New

England ski areas had modern facilities. Mt. Grace had problems with inadequate parking, and skiiers were increasingly dissatisfied with the fact that the only means to the top was a rope tow. Now, from Route 78, motorists can view considerable growth of trees and brush in the remains of the main trail's corridor on the slope.

There is a popular legend that goes with the mountain. A state information sheet on the park, for example, says this: "Legend has it that Mount Grace was named after the infant Grace Rowlandson who died while a captive of Indians and was buried at the base of the mountain."

This tale is not accepted by historians, however. The legend is based on the facts stemming from the so-called Lancaster massacre in February 1675. The story goes that Mary Rowlandson and her infant daughter were being held captive by a band of Indians headed for Canada, but the baby died and was buried at the foot of the mountain. The legend is perpetuated in this way in Lord's history of Athol, "A kindly Indian assists her in digging a rude grave, and as she reluctantly leaves this spot, she gazes at yonder hilltop and humbly prays to God that it may hereafter bear the name Mount Grace, in memory of the beautiful child who now sleeps at its feet."

The truth came out years later when a diary kept by Mary Rowlandson was analyzed more carefully by historians. It was determined that the child's name was Sarah, not Grace, and the burial took place in New Braintree. In other words, Mt. Grace has nothing at all to do with the Rowlandson legend, except for the possibility she passed through the area. Morse reports that the mountain was named Mt. Grace even before the original Warwick land grant of 1735. He said it is a "mystery" how the legend evolved and endured.

Museums

Few museums as such are located in the region, but the area is rich in history, and local historical societies preserve artifacts, housewares, photographs, furniture, manuscripts, genealogical records and other remembrances of things past.

The L.S. Starrett Co. in Athol has its own museum to record the tool manufacturing firm's history.

The Cabot Museum, stressing natural history, is located at Harvard Forest in Petersham.

Various historical and fine arts museums can be found within a short drive of the region, including Springfield Fine

Arts Museum (and other museums on "The Quadrangle"), Clark Institute in Williamstown, Gardner Museum, Farmers Museum in Hadley, Fitchburg Museum, Worcester Fine Arts Museum, Old Sturbridge Village and Historic Deerfield, as well as substantial collections in various institutions in Boston and Hartford. See also ATHOL HISTORICAL SOCIETY, ERVING HISTORICAL SOCIETY, HARVARD FOREST, ORANGE HISTORICAL SOCIETY, OLD ROYALSTON SCHOOLHOUSE, PETERSHAM HISTORICAL SOCIETY, STARRETT'S, WHITAKER-CLARY HOUSE.

Music

Musical tastes in the region range broadly, as in most places in the United States, but music to satisfy virtually all preferences can be heard in area towns.

Children who want to learn a musical instrument can find experienced and dedicated teachers offering lessons through the musical programs in the public school system, starting as early as fourth grade. School bands provide entertainment at parades, athletic events and seasonal concerts. Lessons by private teachers are also available.

The Orange Community band is composed of interested musicians from the area. Members rehearse Sundays from February until April for their annual pops concert usually held the last Saturday in April or the first Saturday in May. Summer rehearsals are Wednesday evenings at the armory for the summertime concerts at the beautiful timber-frame octagonal bandstand in the town park off East River Street played Friday evenings late June and all through July. More information is available from conductor Tony Bosco (Tel. 544-3701) and band president John Tandy (Tel. 544-7348).

The Petersham Community Band performs six concerts on summertime Sundays. More information is available from the director, Earl Olson, Hardwick Road, Petersham, Tel. 724-3362.

Area night spots frequently offer live musical entertainment. Among the places best-known for live music are the Depot Lounge in Athol, featuring rock bands, and Silver Spur in Route 2A in Orange, with its country and western motif.

Local performing groups include rockers Outerspace Band, Hot Pursuit and the Dave Rivers Band, Colt 45 for a country sound, the new wave E Sharps and Loose Caboose for

Members of Outerspace band at Old Home Day in Wendell

reggae/rock. Some of these groups travel outside of the area for bookings.

Solo performers include Al Williams, pop vocalist; Steve Schoenberg, composer and improvisational pianist; and Scott Smith, folk singer – to name a few.

John "Klondike" Koehler of Wendell is a professional sound man who has brought several top-notch acts to the Orange Town Hall – including Maine folk recording artist Dave Mallett – in the "Homefront Concert" series.

The annual minstrel show sponsored by the Athol Area Y.M.C.A. annually brings together a large cast which enthusiastically carries on the tradition of American vaudeville. Information about the minstrel is available from the Y.

In the classical vein, the Elizabeth Carpenter Concerts are given twice yearly in Petersham. This program is entirely supported by private donations. The concerts, usually held in Petersham churches, offer a particularly beautiful and serene surrounding for the enjoyment of classical music. The Elizabeth Carpenter series has also included jazz and dance performances. Potential donors and individuals who wish to be notified about these concerts by mail may obtain further information from Olive Marsh, West Road, Petersham, Tel. 724-3247.

The Merri-Tones is a women's singing group performing popular songs in harmony. Information is available from its president and director, Clarice Cone, 181 Park St., Athol, Tel. 249-4438.

The Singing Men is an all-male vocal ensemble. Information is available from its president and director, Lawrence Cone, 181 Park St., Athol, Tel. 249-4438.

Organ music can be heard regularly in area churches. Jim and Judy Willis of Royalston and the Rev. and Mrs. Ted Boren of New Salem are veteran gospel performers who often perform locally. Visiting gospel groups and "singspirations" are frequently heard in area churches.

Within a short drive of the region, musical performances by top performers in their fields are available most weekends. Rock groups perform regularly at the Wallace Civic Center in Fitchburg, the Centrum in Worcester and the Springfield Civic Center. Folk and jazz performers appear regularly at the Iron Horse Coffee House in Northampton and other locales in Amherst; Brattleboro, Vt., and Peterborough, N.H. Musical productions are offered by the Arena Civic Theater in Greenfield, Stage West in Springfield, and at area colleges. Summertime folk and rock festivals have been held at Mt. Watatic, Ashby. Classical music in country churches and town halls is offered each summer by Monadnock Music in the Monadnock region of New Hampshire and the Mohawk Trails Concerts, Charlemont.

New Salem

For many years, the town of New Salem was best known for New Salem Academy, which provided outstanding secondary education to boys and girls not only from this town and nearby communities, but from more distant places. The school was established in 1795 through public subscription and a grant of public land from the state legislature.

New Salem Academy was a focal point of the area's cultural and educational life for many years. For much of its history, the school functioned not only as preparatory school (with some boarding students from faraway places) but also as the town's public high school. Many of its students from area towns, attending on a contract basis, came from families of workers, farmers and owners of small businesses. They received a college preparatory education generally not available to youths of their social class. Many of the Academy's graduates went on to the finest colleges and universities and joined the ranks of the various professions.

The school was first set up on the ground floor of the town house, but this was destroyed by fire in 1837. Another struc-

New Salem scene during town's bicentennial in 1953

ture, later used for a time as the town library, was erected. The prominent stone building with its unique domed tower was built in 1908, and other school buildings were added in the 1930s and 1940s.

With the development of regional schools, New Salem Academy went into decline, however, and its last class was graduated in 1968. Attempts to revive the Academy failed and eventually the trustees even considered demolishing some of its buildings. In 1982, under the leadership of New Salem resident Nathaniel Needle, a new burst of enthusiasm and energy was provided, fund-raising began and after several months the school's reopening was scheduled. Needle, who will be headmaster, plans a program incorporating high academic standards and contact with "the real world," including business, industry and the out-of-doors.

The Academy is a major feature of the New Salem common, a peaceful, quiet enclave only a few hundred feet from the heavily-traveled highway, Route 202, that skirts the western side of the Quabbin Reservoir. The town hall, beautiful homes, the Unitarian Church (1794), the Congregational Church (1854), the library (between the two churches in the former town hall built in 1839), the post office and a small green with a few monuments share the center of this picturesque New England village. Through the efforts of the New Salem Historical Commission, 37 buildings and sites and five monuments in the center of town have been listed in the Federal Register as an historic district.

129

This town, more than any other area town, has felt the impact of the massive Quabbin Reservoir, however. Three of the streets leading from the Common dead end at Quabbin gates. The Quabbin waters are but a mile to the east, and a good portion of the town – the Prescott peninsula south of the town center – is an off-limits wilderness privately controlled by the Metropolitan District Commission (MDC). The New Salem village of Millington, formerly located southeast of the center, was razed when the reservoir was constructed in the 1930s.

The town's current population of 688 is unlikely to increase a great deal as so much of the land is MDC-owned watershed and cannot be built upon. There has been some recent population influx, however, with an increase of 45 percent in the decade from the 1970 population of 474. Housing in New Salem rose from 180 units in 1970 to 278 in 1980 – an increase of 54 percent. Some of this is due to the influence of the University of Massachusetts in Amherst, 15 miles to the southeast, which grew in the 1960s from a small agriculture college to a great state university. Because of this proximity, New Salem has developed strong ties to the five-college area in the Connecticut Valley. Approximately ten percent of the townspeople are students in higher education, and 16 percent are listed as having professional occupations.

The town's small amount of commerce emphasizes quality. The New Salem Restaurant and Store is located on Route 202 near the historic town center, offering residents and travelers a taste of good New England home-cooking and occasional farm products. Studio 45 offers the latest in solar energy devices. Hamilton's Orchard and the Apple Barn on West Street is a popular place for visitors, with its "nature trail," a maple-sugaring operation, pick-your-own apples and home-cooked refreshments. The Whitaker-Clary House on Elm Street, headquarters of the Swift River Valley Historical Society, is one of Massachusetts' outstanding small museums – it has limited summertime hours. While home gardening is popular, New Salem can no longer be characterized as the farming community it once was, but here and there homegrown produce is available.

Elementary school students from New Salem attend the Swift River School on the New Salem-Wendell town line; the modern schoolhouse is administered by a progressive administration under the guidance of an active school committee. Secondary students attend Mahar Regional School in Orange and the Franklin County Technical School in Turners Falls – with the possibility in the near future of New Salem

Academy, too. New Salem and Wendell co-sponsor a rural arts program.

The town's history is usually dated from Dec. 31, 1734, when the grant of a township six miles square by the General Court (state legislature) was made to 60 residents of Salem, the historic seaside community in Essex County. "Wanted, a stout heart to start settlers to New Salem." Those words were circulated by the proprietors of the wildnerness. It took some years, however, until Jeremiah Meacham, identified as the first settler, paid ten pounds and led the way; that was in 1737. Subsistence farming was augmented by such trades as millwrighting and blacksmithing. In 1740, James Cook set up the first grist mill on a site now in the Quabbin area. Ten years later, Jeremiah Ballard and Jeremiah Meacham set up a sawmill on the middle branch of the Swift River in the section that became known later as New Buffalo.

For some years, the town was governed in Old Salem. Eventually the frontier and agrarian settlement was incorporated as the district of New Salem on June 15, 1753. Only a few small industries were developed, among them tanneries. As in other area towns, the braiding of palm leaf hats by women was an important cottage industry – records show 79,000 hats were made in New Salem in 1837. New Salem was once part of Hampshire County, but when Franklin County was established in 1820, New Salem was its largest community with a population of 2,145. In 1900, the population was down to 809, partly because much of the territory was lost to neighboring towns, including Orange, Athol and Prescott. Some of the Prescott territory was later returned to New Salem when the Quabbin Reservoir was created in the 1930s.

The community of Houlton, Maine, has its roots in New Salem. During the early days of the New Salem Academy, the town appealed to the state legislature for help in maintaining the school, and a grant was made to the Academy of a township of land in the district of Maine (then controlled by Massachusetts). When the Academy could not sell the land in Maine, James Houlton and others from New Salem and nearby communities paid the Academy a total of $5,000 for it, sold their farms and moved to Maine to settle. Their town was named Houlton, now the seat of Aroostock County, heart of Maine potato country.

Ferns and butter are two products important in New Salem's history. On Aug. 16, 1903, the Springfield Republican reported that "the Crowl fern company of New Salem is supposed now to control the eastern market in ferns and laurel. The florists in this city (Springfield) depend to a large extent on this company for their supplies. Down at the isolated little New Salem station nearly every train that comes along finds shipments ready on the lonely platform for some big city or other. The ferns go to Boston, to New York, even to Chicago, Canada and the far-off 'Frisco – replanting, temporarily at last, New Salem hills in a thousand places." As many as 300-400 pickers were engaged in gathering ferns from the slopes of New Salem and surrounding towns. The Crowl company stored a crop of thousands of ferns in special cold storage cellars. The ferns and laurels were used as decorations, especially at weddings.

Around the same time, dairy farming in town was so well developed that local creameries were producing 250 pounds daily. Under the management of L.E. Beebe, the creamery in Millington was awarded the sweepstakes prize, consisting of a $50 watch, at the Massachusetts' butter-makers exhibition held at Northampton in December 1899. "A careful observer says on this point that the farming outlook in New Salem is encouraging," according to the Springfield Republican article, but this "careful observer" was not taking seriously enough the plans, already afoot, to build a reservoir in the Swift River valley.

New Salem's face was changed considerably by the building of the reservoir. Although it gained territory, most of this was the newly-acquired property of the Metropolitan District Commission. Today, New Salem has an area of 59 square miles – approximately 45 square miles of land and 14 square miles of Quabbin water. In total area, the town ranks sixth in the state – behind Plymouth, Middleborough, Petersham, Barnstable and Dartmouth. The population density is 14 people per square mile, ranking the town 341st in the state. New Salem is the least densely populated Massachusetts town east of the Connecticut River.

New Salem's highest elevation is Packard Mountain near North Prescott, 1,281 feet above sea level. The elevation at the town center is 1,048. The surface of the Quabbin, 524 feet above sea level, is the town's lowest.

On June 1, 1935, as the reservoir was being built, the last regular train of the Athol-Springfield branch of the Boston and Albany Railroad traversed its route. Known as the Rabbit Run, this railroad was opened in 1873. It took three hours to make the trip fom Athol to Springfield. The New Salem station was dismantled and rebuilt at the center as a firehouse.

The relocated federal highway 202, which traverses the

entire length of New Salem, was completed in 1935. It was named for Capt. Daniel Shays, leader of the Shays Rebellion, whose men passed through this town in 1787.

Another group of soldiers equally significant historically passed through New Salem only ten years before. These were a thousand Hessians, German mercenaries, who had surrendered to the American colonists in the Revolutionary War and were being marched through here en route from Saratoga, N.Y., to the Boston area for probable deportation. A road called Hessian Lane and a stone marker are permanent indicators of this bit of history. The marker, inscribed in the early 1900s by Eugene Lehrman of Wendell, says simply: "Oct. 25th, 1777 – 1000 Hessians Who Surrendered At Saratoga Passed Here." The marker is at the corner of Elm Street and Hessian Lane near the Whitaker-Clary House.

Dick Chaisson, writing in the Jan. 6, 1960, edition of the Athol Daily News, quoted North New Salem resident Eugene Bullard as stating (back in 1903) that while in New Salem en route from Greenfield to Petersham the Hessians were given apples by Thomas Andrews "from his orchard. These were of the very poorest quality, but they were very acceptable to the prisoners. Several of these men remained in this town and Petersham; all of whom took unto themselves American wives, and today several of their descendants are numbered among the residents of this town...."

New Salem today retains much of the traditional community awareness of a small New England town, a spirit celebrated annually at Old Home Day. In 1982, two residents of the New Salem common, Steve Schoenberg and Dorothy Johnson, combined talents to create a popular hometown musical called "'Smalltown Life." This was by no means the town's introduction to top-notch entertainment, however. In the 1890s, this town was the summer headquarters of the McGibney family, a famous theatrical group consisting of eight McGibney sons, four daughters and two daughters-in-law. The family, which toured the country in a palatial railroad car, prepared their shows during their summer residence here. Nearby, at the corner of Millington Road and South Main Street, a large house was the property of Thomas Reddy, who established the summer programs of the Dorothea Dix Hall Association, later called the Boston Children's Theater Company. A 1922 news item reports a show for locals to benefit the Grange to be performed under Reddy's direction by eight children – "all professionals, and they are sure to give a performance equal to that seen in any of the vaudeville theaters of the cities."

One of New Salem's natural features is the scenic, historic Bear's Den on Neilson Road, owned by Trustees of Reservations. Several Quabbin gates are located in New Salem, but some are in the off-limits Prescott Peninsula. Gate 35 at the end of South Athol Road is one of the most popular entryways for Quabbin hikers as it quickly leads to open space along the water. Gate 31 off Route 122 in the South Athol section of New Salem provides access to Fishing and Boat Mooring Area No. 2. See also BEAR'S DEN, KEYSTONE BRIDGE, PRESCOTT, QUABBIN FISHING, QUABBIN RECREATION, QUABBIN RESERVOIR, QUABBIN WILDLIFE, STACY MONUMENT, WHITAKER-CLARY HOUSE.

Newspapers

The major news source for the Mt. Grace Region is the Athol Daily News, published every day but Sunday, serving the nine towns of Athol, Orange, Erving, New Salem, Petersham, Phillipston, Royalston, Warwick and Wendell, with offices at 225 Exchange St., Athol. The paper, founded in 1934, is locally-owned.

A weekly newspaper in Orange, the Enterprise and Journal, went out of business several years ago following a fire. The Pioneer Junior Woman's Club in Orange recently began publication of a community monthly, the Orange Oracle (Box 193, Orange MA 01364). Another community monthly, the Wendell Post, is published in that town (Box 113, Wendell MA 01379). Residents in Warwick publish the Warwick Community Newsletter every month (c/o Nancy Kemerer, Old Winchester Road, Star Route, Warwick MA 01364).

The Greenfield Recorder, a daily, regularly covers the Franklin County communities of Orange, Erving, New Salem, Warwick and Wendell. The Worcester Telegram, a morning paper, and the Worcester Gazette, an evening paper, with similar contents, cover the Worcester County towns of Athol, Petersham, Phillipston and Royalston, with occasional coverage of Orange. The Springfield Union (daily) and Sunday Republican have sporadic coverage of area communities.

The Valley Advocate, an "alternative" weekly published in Hatfield, is circulated free of charge at several area businesses, with the new edition arriving late Tuesday; its listings of Western Massachusetts cultural events is especially useful. A similar weekly, Leisure, is published in Keene, N.H., but is not distributed locally. The Boston Globe and Herald-American can be purchased daily in area outlets. The Wall Street Journal and New York Times Sunday editions can be purchased at area newsdealers if pre-ordered.

North Common Meadow

The North Common Meadow is a 24-acre property of Trustees of Reservations located on East Street just east of Petersham Common. Cattle once grazed here, and the Trustees hope to manage the meadow as a wildflower display area and to preserve the open space character of the community. There is a small pond.

The land was formerly owned by Duane Sargisson of Worcester and was acquired by the Trustees in 1975 by funds contributed anonymously. A portion of the meadow borders the Brooks Woodland Preserve's Roaring Brook tract.

Northfield Mountain

A recreation and environmental center at the Northfield Mountain Pumped Storage Power Station offers numerous programs and events open to the public free of charge or for a nominal fee. These include films, nature walks, trails for hiking, horseback riding and cross-country skiing, lectures, campfires, orienteering, canoeing and camping. The programs take place at the center in Northfield, just over the Erving line, and at the Barton Cove area in Gill.

Perhaps the most exciting and interesting of the programs is the Connecticut River boat ride, including the French King gorge under the French King Bridge, aboard the Quinnetukut II, which operates from the spring through the fall foliage season. The Northfield Mountain Newsletter listing events is published four times a year. A free subscription can be obtained by sending a request (with your zip code) to Northfield Mountain, RR 1, Box 377, Northfield MA 01360. Information about programs is available by telephone: 413-659-3713. See also POWERHOUSE.

Old Royalston Schoolhouse

"The object of this Society shall be 'to preserve Old Royalston Schoolhouse for historic and civic purposes, to

Royalston Historical Society building and U.S. Post Office

foster and encourage the improvement of the Town of Royalston and to foster the educational value of the history of our town for both present and future generations.'"

Thus was given the statement of purpose of the Royalston Historic and Village Improvement Society, Inc., owner of the Old Royalston Schoolhouse on the south end of Royalston Common.

The society maintains a museum with various articles and furnishings on the second floor of the building. The post office is located on the ground floor (with a community bulletin board in the corridor). This schoolhouse was originally built in 1835, although it was not the town's first school. Indeed, it was in 1777 that the town voted to create nine school districts, each with a schoolhouse.

The Royalston Historic and Village Improvement Society arranges for afternoon open houses at the building during the summer months, and by appointment. In recent years, the society has held a summertime flea market and pancake breakfast on the common to raise funds to maintain its building. It has arranged special tours of Royalston houses for groups concerned with architecture and historic preservation. Information about the society's activities and visits to the building is available from Peter Kraniak, Winchendon Road, Royalston, Tel. 249-7625.

Orange

The people of Orange are clustered in several distinct communities in various parts of the hilly and mostly forested town, but the overwhelming majority live in or near the town center on the Millers River, which has been the lifeblood of the town for most of its history.

The town's 1980 population of 6,844 is the largest in its history, up 12 percent from 1970. The population throughout the 20th century has been in the 5,000-6,000 range, increasing gradually before that from 1,622 in the 1860 census.

Orange has 35.81 square miles, ranking it 55th in the state in area. The population density is 184 people per square mile, ranking it 230th in the state. Of the 26 towns in Franklin County – the most rural county in the state – Orange is the third most populous, after Greenfield (the shire town or county seat) and Montague.

In the southern part of town, residents live on or near the shores of Lake Mattawa, a town-owned body of water stocked with trout and popular for fishing, swimming and sailing. The town maintains a public beach on the lake.

In the eastern part of Orange, lakeside properties at Tully Pond and Packard Pond provide population clusters, including

Aerial view of Central Square, Orange

Tully Mountain as seen from Walter Shaw's millyard

summer camps or part-time residences. The village of Tully, labeled Tulleyville on some maps, has its own identity – a fire station, the private Tully City Council Club, an historic cemetery and a mixture of old and new homes – ranging from traditional frame houses and several mobile homes on Tully Road and Royalston Road to a cluster of experimental solar homes on Canon Lane.

The west branch of the Tully River, often called Tully Brook, passes through Tully where an old industrial building, still used as woodworking shop, stands as a reminder of the harnessing of water power in days gone by.

Tully Mountain, one of Orange's most unusual geological features, rises sharply from the adjacent flatlands. Tully Mountain is not public land but hikers frequently climb to the top to enjoy the spectacular view from atop the cliffs at its southern end. This hump-shaped hill, with its peak at 1,163 feet above sea level, is not the town's highest elevation as is sometimes claimed. That honor belongs to Pitt Hill in a northern corner of the town near the Warwick line, 1,252 feet above sea level, according to the geodetic map. A close second is Chestnut Hill in the southwest corner at 1,247 feet. Another prominent hill is Temple Hill in North Orange at 1,125 feet. Elevation at the town center is approximately 500 feet along the Millers River.

Another focal point of population is North Orange, a lovely village with old houses, the Community Church of North Orange and Tully (built in 1781 and originally serving as both church and town hall), a school building (now vacant), a library and little Goddard Park, the town's oldest. This was the town's original center, though not its oldest settlement. The oldest settlement was established on West Pequoiag Hill in 1734; this "West Pequoiag" part of Orange, about two square miles, was ceded to the town by Athol.

Orange is named after William, Prince of Orange, although the reasons for this are rather obscure. The original Prince of Orange, William the Silent, lived in the Netherlands from 1553-1584. It is more likely the town was named for William VI, Prince of Orange, who was alive when Orange was in its formative years. He moved from Holland to England in 1795 after the French invasion and sided with Prussia against Napoleon, all of this possibly bringing him some renown across the Atlantic. It has also been speculated that the naming of the town in his honor was the idea of Orange's first minister, the Rev. Emerson Foster, a graduate of Dartmouth College, which received philanthropic contributions from the prince.

Orange was established as a "district" in 1783 from parts of Athol, Royalston, Warwick and Ervingshire. The district (a status somewhat akin to "territory") was incorporated as the town of Orange on Feb. 21, 1810, in what is now the village of North Orange (though it was not called "North Orange" in those days.)

Settlement of the southern part of Orange coincided with the development of water power on the Millers River. The first dam across the river was constructed in 1790 by James Holmes, who built a sawmill and a grist mill the same year. In 1804 a carding mill was set in operation. With the mills came an increase in the number of residents in the riverside area, which came to be known as South Orange, In 1837, the town annexed portions of New Salem and Erving and as a consequence South Orange was closer to being the geographic center of town. Because it also continued to develop as the commercial center, in 1845 South Orange became known as Orange Center and the original village in the north was renamed North Orange.

In her 1976 history of Orange, Mrs. Beatrice Miner offers a review of the development of industry in the town – serving as a reminder that even for the region's pioneers agriculture did not stand alone:

"The first industries were always in the home: spinning wheel, loom, dye-pot for fabrics for household or clothing which the village seamstress, going from house to house, would convert into coats and pantaloons for men and dresses and capes for women. Spring brought soap-making; Summer, making cheese; Fall, taking up bees and honey; Winter, making sausage and applesauce, and drying out tallow. Spinning, weaving, knitting, sewing, braiding hats, weaving and binding Shaker bonnets, gathering herbs for flavoring and medicine; checkerberry leaves for distilling, and sorrel for dying, and setting color filled the year for our North Orange ancestors. The men of the family tanned hides, cut and sawed wood, tapped maple trees for sap made into sugar, raised rye, oats, barley,

Orange gardener with butternut squash crop on a sunny fall day

Industrial buildings and dam site on Millers River, Orange

buckwheat, built stone walls for which there were many backaches. In Tully, checkerberry leaves taken there by the neighborhood women were distilled into that old-fashioned lotion, wintergreen oil, and one resident, using a lage rake, would gather many bags of the leaves and send them away to be distilled."

Manufacturing and food-processing facilities in the various parts of Orange produced pails, bedsteads, shoddy cloth and woolens, boxes, tanned hides, bricks, earthenware, butter, cider, tools, baseball bats, cane and wood seat chairs, and fancy iron work such as door-knockers, candlestick holders and fireplace fixtures.

The building of the railroad through Orange in the 1840s led to growth and diversification of industry. A mill used to manufacture wooden pails was taken over by a sewing machine factory that created single-thread machines – these machines must have seemed magical to the thousands of men and women used to the drudgery of hand sewing. The machines were sold under such names as "Home Shuttle," "New England," "Gold Medal" and finally "New Home" (a name still in use though the machines are made in Japan!). John Wheeler, secretary and treasurer and later president of the New Home Co., became the town's most prominent industrialist prior to his death in 1910, and promoted the development of the settlement of "Wheeler" (later called Wheelerville) on the eastern part of town near the river and railroad tracks. (Wheeler's man-

141

sion is now the Eastern Star Home and his large "summer home" on Wheeler Avenue with its profusion of rhododendron bushes now belongs to a local doctor.) During World War I, the New Home Co. had contracts involving more than a million dollars to turn out shells and supplies for the army.

The name of Grout, an early automobile, is important in Orange lore. The model developed by Fred and Charlie Grout evolved from their bicycle business in 1899. It was steam-powered and won a prize in 1901 at the Philadelphia Automobile Show. Thomas Edison once came to town to take delivery of one. By 1907 a Grout was sold for $2,500 – it could travel 30 miles an hour and was tested on the steep grades of Walnut Hill and Mechanic Street. In the 1970s, civic-minded Orange citizens purchased one of the 12 Grouts known to exist and return it to its home town for complete restoration.

Minute Tapioca, a processed dessert food sold in grocery stores today, had its origins in Orange, being first produced in 1902. The Minute Tapioca Co. processed the cassava root (known as manioca in Brazil from where it was imported) in a factory building on West Main Street. The company was sold to General Foods and became one of the town's leading employers in the 1920s and 1930s, but the corporation moved its operation to Delaware in the 1960s. The building – with the monogram "MT" still visible on the tall chimney – was used for a time by the George Bent Co. for furniture manufacture but in 1983 it was unused and for sale.

Manufacturing remains crucial to Orange's well-being. Industries include the Rodney Hunt Co., manufacturing water control equipment and other machinery; the Adell Corp. making metal stampings; the So-Jo Corp. (formerly Union Tool) manufacturing small hand tools; Riveto Manufacturing producing "Slencil" pens; Leavitt Machine Co. producing valve reseating equipment, used in movement of steam, especially for nuclear power plants and the U.S. Navy; the Chase Manufacturing and Supply Co., producing sawmill machinery and belts; NRG Industries, formerly the Orange Foundry, making rough iron castings, cast iron tea kettles and wood-burning stoves and accessories.

The wood products industry has always played a role in the life of Orange. Richard Fairman, Fred Heyes, Kenneth Prue Jr. and Walter Shaw, with their own sawmills, are independent sawyers and purveyors of forest products. Hyde Park, Inc., manufactures wooden desk accessories. Ralph Henley is a master craftsman whose inlaid woodwork has attracted national attention.

#1 High Street: One of Orange's outstanding houses

In 1974 (the last year for which figures are published), there were 103 firms in Orange reporting to the state's Division of Employment Security, with 1,110 persons employed and an annual payroll of $8,521,797, primarily in manufacturing. The next most important aspect of Orange's economy is retail trade, and the town's shopping district includes numerous stores – a mixture of veteran merchants with decades of business experience and novices seeking to serve shoppers in imaginative ways.

A private sport-parachuting center is operated by Parachutes Inc. at the municipal airport.

Mt. Grace Sportsplex is a modern health and fitness center with Nautilus equipment and racquetball courts.

The town is not without a continuation of its agricultural tradition. There are several dairy farms, the largest being the Hunt Farm on South Main Street with its herd of registered Holsteins. The Johnson Farm on Wheeler Avenue includes the region's largest maple sugar operation. Haley's Orchard in North Orange is being revived by a new owner. The Wintergreen Cooperative Solar Greenhouse offers services to the region's many gardeners including educational programs in solar greenhouse applications for home and possible commercial use.

Orange's population is homogeneous, with many of its residents descending from European peoples, including Scots-English, French Canadian, Scandinavian and Irish. Less than one percent belongs to a racial minority and less than five percent are foreign-born or had foreign-born parents. Swedes formed a unique ethnic group at the turn of the century and some Old World traditions endure. Bethany Lutheran Church, organized in 1889 to provide Swedish language services, has one of the area's largest Protestant congregations. The Mission Covenant Church was originally known as the Swedish Evangelic Mission Church and was organized the same year.

The town's recent population increase, which has occurred despite economic stagnation, is apparently less a result of the back-to-the-land trends than in other area towns. Since 1970, three elderly housing complexes (Colonial Acres, Red Brook Village and King James Court) have been built on southeasterly side of Orange providing 240 dwelling units. The Putnam House in Central Square, an historic structure being refurbished, contains eight units of subsidized elderly housing. The influx of elderly, retired residents has contributed to the population jump of 12 percent since 1970. In addition, the same area of Orange on the southern side of the Millers River has a trailer park and a recently-built family housing complex (Pine Crest) with rents established according to income. Both of these residential sites attract younger couples with school-age chldren.

Orange is home for the Ralph C. Mahar Regional School, named for State Senator Ralph C. Mahar, a native of Orange. The town maintains its own elementary schools.

The town has many fine homes, including a number of attractive Greek Revival and Victorian buildings in the center. Some of the old structures, especially on North Main Street, have undergone renovation with the help of a federal rehabilitation project.

Orange boosters have traditionally kept their sights high. After World War II, when the United Nations interim committee announced its intention of searching for a site in the United States, the Orange Chamber of Commerce published an attractive brochure entitled, "Presenting Orange, Massachusetts, as a Permanent Seat for the United Nations Organization..." Townspeople continue the quest to improve the community's economy. A controversial proposed racetrack, favored by some residents, was defeated by voters. A new industrial airpark, promoted and defended by selectmen and other town leaders despite some wariness by others, has been outfitted with paved roads and underground utilities. It awaits the dawning of a new era for Orange and surrounding communities. The town has invested local and federal tax dollars in this facility in a spirit of optimism, fueled by the knowledge that the "Friendly

Town" – as Orange has been called for decades – is a nice place to live and work. See also AIRPARK, AIRPORT, ARCHITECTURE, BICENTENNIAL PARK, ORANGE HISTORICAL SOCIETY, ORANGE STATE FOREST, PARACHUTING, RADIO, RODNEY HUNT and SOLAR GREENHOUSE.

Orange Historical Society

The Orange Historical Society is housed in a handsome yellow building at 41 North Main St., the former homestead of the prominent Stephen French family.

Among the thousands of items on display are the town's first machine-made carpet, Parisian and American dolls, an old parlor pipe organ, antique china and furniture, memorabilia of town government, schools, industry, business and family life.

The imposing blocks of granite in the building's lawn wall and the grand steps came from the Warwick quarry owned by Samuel S. Dexter near Long Pond, now Laurel Lake. John Frawley, an Erving stonecutter, did the carving on the corner near the Universalist Church.

A noteworthy member and instigator of the historical society was Miss Phoebe Lee Hosmer, its first president, well-known in the community as a conscientious and erudite teacher. For the society's music room, Miss Hosmer willed her musical instruments and autographed photos of world-famous musicians.

Orange Historical Society building on North Main Street

The Orange Historical Society was formed in 1942 and took over the premises at 41 North Main St. in 1944. The property and much of the collection was previously owned by the Mt. Grace Chapter of the Daughters of the American Revolution. A precursor of the modern society was the Orange Historical and Antiquarian Society formed in 1895.

Because the building is not heated, regular visiting hours as well as visits by appointment are scheduled only in the summer months. Information is available from Wheeler Memorial Library, East Main Street, Orange, Tel. 544-2295.

Orange State Forest

Three tracts of land on the western edge of Orange, all of them adjacent to Wendell and Warwick state forests and administered with them, are designated as Orange State Forest by the state's Department of Environmental Management.

The northernmost of these, 188 acres, is in a northerly corner of Orange abutting Erving State Forest to the west and Warwick State Forest to the north. This tract is about midway between Laurel Lake and Millers River; it is traversed by Wendell Road north of Wendell Depot. The second tract, 128 acres, lies south of Wendell Depot, between Coolidge Swamp and Kempfield Road (in Wendell). The third tract is still further south encompassing part of Chestnut Hill (though not including the hill's highest peak). This tract abuts Wendell State Forest and contains 196 acres.

The Orange quadrant topographical map indicates the location of this forestland, which is open to the public for cross-country skiing, hiking, hunting and other "passive recreation purposes."

Parachuting

More than 21,000 parachutists have had their first jump at Orange Municipal Airport. Indeed, the sport parachute industry in Orange is probably the town's best-known business and its most current "claim to fame."

Parachuting in Orange is not a town-sponsored activity, but rather is the endeavor of a private enterprise, Parachutes Incorporated (PI), which was founded in U.S. in 1955. In 1959, the world's first, largest and safest sport parachuting center was opened at the Orange airport by PI.

Jacques-Andre Istel, the founder of PI, which also has installations elsewhere, led in the effort of several developments in sport parachuting, including reducing landing shock and patenting the lift effect for parachutes. PI wrote the basic safety regulations for parachuting, created Parachutist magazine, trained the U.S. Marine Corps in free-fall parachuting, and sponsored the World Champion Wings of Orange team.

In the early 1960s a world championship competition was held in Orange – giving the town considerable publicity. To this day, there are many people who associate Orange with parachuting. A picture of a parachute appears on the patch of the town police officers, and Orange's square dance club calls itself the "Jumptown Twirlers." There are many residents in Orange who remember the days of the championship, including at least one woman who was 14 years old in those days. (She recalls a starry-eyed though innocent romance she had with a dark, handsome Rumanian who, like many of the international visitors, lived in tents on the airport grounds.)

Despite recent disputes with the town over a lease arrangement, Parachutes Incorporated still maintains its sport parachute center, and it boasts an injury rate in Orange of approximately two-tenths of one percent.

Most of those jumping in Orange come from out of the area. However, Richard Kilhart observed in a recent issue of the Orange Oracle, "Try it sometime. It might be the greatest experience you will ever have." Kilhart wrote the following summary of how it's done:

"It takes approximately four hours to complete your instruction, training and jump. To make your first jump, the first step is to register in the office in the airport. One must be at least 18 years of age or 16 with parental permission.

"Once registered, you receive your boots, helmet and coveralls. You then receive classroom instruction, which includes procedures of exiting the plane, maneuvering the parachute, landing techniques and emergency procedures.

"Classroom instructions are followed by practical training, which includes exiting the plane with a good arch and spread, and practice landing falls. At this point you are chuted up with a main rig and reserve. Then you run the 'mock up,' which is actually exiting the plane with a good arch and spread with your full gear intact.

"You are loaded into the plane. At the altitude of 2,500 feet, you are signaled by your instructor when to exit the plane. Your parachute opens automatically by the static line as you leave the plane. There is a gentle tug at your shoulders that indicates the opening of your canopy. You then float gently to earth and steer your chute according to the advice your ground instructor gives you through radio communications. Then you land safely by doing a good practice landing fall and the efficient ground crew will greet you and assist you with your equipment.

"You then return to the classroom so the instructor can give you an individual evaluation of your jump and present you with the first jump certificate."

For current information on fees and hours, Parachutes Incorporated can be reached at 544-6911.

Peace Statue

An impressive "peace statue" graces a small park in the center of Orange. The 12-foot high bronze sculpture by Joseph Pollia of New York attracted national attention when it was unveiled as a memorial to veterans of World War I. Favorable comments on the statue were made by various newspaper editorial writers and by many luminaries such as Eleanor Roosevelt, wife of Franklin D. Roosevelt, who was president at the time of the unveiling.

The statue, weighing 1,120 pounds, was installed on two granite blocks, and its inscription "It Shall Not Be Again" has attracted peace activists to the park even in recent years.

In the spring of 1935, the Mt. Grace Chapter of the Daughters of the American Revolution presented its annual medal given to a high school pupil for excellence in civics to Robert Elliot Babbit, 14, a freshman in Orange High School. The essay on which the award was made follows. Written nearly a half-century ago, this essay tells the story of the statue and offers one boy's plea for peace that is as urgent today as it was then:

"On Thursday, May 13, 1934, a bronze statue was unveiled at the Memorial park. This statue was sculptured by Joseph Pollia of New York.

"It depicts a doughboy just returned from the war torn fields of France. He is seated on a stump with weariness emanating from every line of his body. His shirt is open at the neck and his khaki coat is thrown across his knees. On his head he wears an overseas cap.

"Beside him, dressed in the clothes which would be worn by the average American schoolboy, and carrying a book, stands a typical American schoolboy of perhaps 10 years, who is partially embraced by the soldier's left arm. He appears to be listening intently to the soldier's words with fist clenched.

"The doughboy may be telling him of how horrible and uncivilzed war is; how futile and destructive. Maybe he speaks of fond parents, wives, sweethearts and brothers who wait in suspense for the dread news that some loved one is killed. Perhaps he speaks of the hundreds of thousands of men who

'Never Again': Memorial to Orange men killed in World War I

149

were killed or horribly injured and mutilated by explosive bullets, gas, shells, and other death-dealing machines of war.

"On the base of the memorial, which is made of granite is a bronze plaque. In the foreground is an inscription which further brings out the idea of the statue – 'It Shall Not Be Again.'

"In the background a shrouded form of abject grief stands. The remaining part is studded with 11 stars. One for each man who gave his life from Orange.

"On the back of the base is another inscription reading thus: 'Dedicated in memory of those of Orange who served their country during the World War, 1917-1919.'

"The statue typifies the American ideal of peace. Nothing about it signfies war, death or destruction. The soldier carries no weapons. A steel trench helmet is not worn by him. Even the inscription signifies peace.

"This is one of the world's greatest problems. How can war be prevented and peace be sustained? The United States and the other great powers are working for it but what do they do? Nothing. They hem and haw and go on increasing their armaments. Peace cannot be attained in that way. There must be no armies of thousands of trained men ready to move immediately. There must be more cooperation and friendliness between the various countries.

"Now let us consider the monetary side of the story.

"Billions of dollars are spent annually. Money from the taxpayers' pockets going for bigger armies, navies, air forces, when they could all be done away with if it were not for the petty jealousy existing between nations. Bigger, better schools could be built. Other similar useful peace-time projects could be put into effect.

"Then too, what good is war? What is gained by it? Everyone loses in war. Therefore, let us all strive for peace and cooperation between nations in the world. Also bear in mind the significance of our statue and its noble words: 'It Shall Not Be Again.'"

Petersham

Petersham is one of those places that readily satisfies the popular image of a picturesque New England village – but beyond picture postcard prettiness, the town is home to a community of vibrant, creative people resolved to both preserving and enjoying the beauty that surrounds them.

This town combines the comforting closeness of village

life in the town's center with many square miles of unspoiled woods – much of it watershed and conservation land protected in perpetuity from development. Chances are just as good that the elegant town center will also remain unspoiled for such is the commitment of the townspeople.

In the center of Petersham is its common, the proverbial village green, including an octagonal bandstand that is not merely decorative but is used each summer for concerts. On either side of Main Street – along a ridge approximately 1,050 feet above sea level – are Petersham's public buildings and homes, including some typical New England architectural treasures. These varied buildings display the traditional simplicity of white-painted wood with dark green shutters, the majesty and strength of stonework, the elegance of brick, the classic stylishness of columns. In all, some 45 buildings are included in the historic district including the common and environs, listed in the National Register of Historic Places. A monument adjacent to the brick building of the Petersham Historical Society recalls the farmers' rebellion led by Daniel Shays, a crucial event in the history of the American Republic, which came to an end here on a winter's morning in 1787.

Among the structures included in the historic district is the Deer Farm on North Main Street, readily identified by the large cast-iron deer on its front lawn – placed there in the 1800s. This unusually large and handsome residence, used now as a private home, was built before the American Revolution. It was owned by John and Nathaniel Chandler whose

A look at Petersham's historic Deer Farm close up (with deer!)

151

family store in this building was well-known in the region. The Chandlers were active merchants involved in the exchange of goods between these woods and forests and the busy port of Boston.

The only businesses on the common are the White Pillars Restaurant and Gift Shop and the Petersham Country Store. Across the way is the Maria Assumpta Academy, a former Catholic school and nuns' residence that has been offered for sale. Among other buildings of note are the Unitarian Church, built in 1910 on the site of previous churches destroyed by fire, and the town hall, rebuilt in 1960 after a fire. On several side streets near the center, many of Petersham's 1,024 residents make their home. The remainder of the population is scattered throughout the town in an assortment of country dwellings – on West Road and Turnpike Road close to the waters of the Quabbin Reservoir, in Ledgeville at the towns' eastern end, on more than two dozen gravel and paved roads in all directions.

Some of these places are modern owner-built homes. Many are modest old farmhouses from the 18th and 19th centuries; others are nothing less than estates. Indeed, "elite" and "affluent" are words that are sometimes used in connection with Petersham, not without some validity, yet the town is populated by many earthy, friendly people. Edward C. Hutchinson, former owner of the country store who retired and moved to Maine in the early 1970s, once offered a few succinct comments about Petersham: "I agree with most folks, we've got to keep the town the way it is – quiet and spacious....Summer people, professional people, and we up-country 'regulars' – there's no class distinction at all. At meetings, one man's words are just as important as the next. We're quite independent people but we get along well together."

As for affluence, Petersham's neighbors may consider the town "rich," but a study by University of Massachusetts researchers using 1980 census data listed Petersham's median family income at $21,484, considerably below the figure for the state's ritziest towns – Weston with $51,339, Sherborn with $43,779 and Dover with $42,514. In the same study, the median family income in nearby Athol was listed at $18,432; and in Royalston, which like Petersham boasts fine houses on an historic common, the median income was $16,397.

The beauty of Petersham is found not only in its lovely buildings, community spirit and spacious woodlands, but in the panoramic vistas that can be appreciated from the plateau of this "Hilltop Town," as it is sometimes called. From Route 32 north of the common, there are good views of the distant curved top of Mt. Wachusett in Princeton, tallest mountain in Massachusetts east of the Connecticut River. From other spots, there are views of Mt. Monadnock to the north (snow-capped even after spring fills the air), the Winchendon hills, Mt. Grace in Warwick and the Berkshires to the west.

Petersham, along with nearby Greenwich, was for many years a popular summer resort for city residents who could afford a full summer of leisure. Many of these people built summer homes, others restored old farmhouses – and there were those who stayed at the wood-shingled Nichewaug Inn (now the Maria Assumpa Academy).

Some executives of Athol industries make their homes here but most of Petersham's residents are professional and working people, with an assortment of farmers, craftsmen and artists, too. The largest working farm is a dairy farm on Maple Lane owned by David Perkins, who took the place over upon the retirement of his father, Charlie Perkins. Most of the cornfields and hayfields seen in Petersham are cultivated for Perkins' livestock.

Self-sufficient farming by ambitious, courageous pioneers marked the beginning of Petersham in the mid-1700s. The formation of the town was the result of a petition by 67 soldiers who, under the leadership of Capt John Lovell of Dunstable and Capt. John White of Lancaster, fought in military expeditions against the French and Indians. Their petition was granted by the General Court in 1733 and the new township was temporarily named Volunteers Town. Shortly thereafter the name of a local Indian settlement, Nichewaug, was adopted and was used for this place until the town's incorporation on March 27, 1754, as Petersham. The plantation of Quabbin was incorporated at the same time as the town of Greenwich, with both towns being given the names of places in England. These names were apparently assigned by officials in Boston rather than being chosen by residents. (By the way, today's residents call the town "Peter's HAM," not "Peter SHAM.")

The evolution of Petersham's ecology is chronicled in a Harvard Forest bulletin, "The History of Land Use in the Harvard Forest," published in 1941, which states, "The early influx of population into Petersham was substantial and for a while the community gave promise of becoming one of the leading towns in Worcester County." The population peaked in 1840 at 1,775, a year when neighboring Athol had 1,591 people. The building of the railroad through the Millers River valley did more than any other factor to establish Athol as a commercial center and decrease the importance of Petersham. Fire damage to houses and industries in Petersham was another factor.

Subsistence farming initially involved crops such as Indian corn, rye and wheat, as well as harvesting of hay from natural meadows and tilled uplands seeded with timothy, red clover and other plants. By the mid-1800s, the hay crop was in the range of 2,500 tons. There was much grazing land, with nearly 1,000 sheep in town. Early industries included tanneries, potash processing plants and woolen mills.

Two major household industries were boots and shoes and the weaving of palm-leaf hats, both using a type of industrial organization called the "putting out" system. The Harvard Forest researchers described the process: "In the case of the palm-leaf hats, the agent would make his rounds in the fall to those households desiring employment and provide them with a quantity of straw. During the ensuing winter months members of the family – usually the women – would weave the straw into hats. A normal winter's work was 250 hats, for which they were paid at the rate of ten cents each. Then in the spring the agent would return, collect his hats and pay off his employees. This institution provided a small but steady supplementary income in cash to many farm families and continued into the first decade of the 20th century. In 1836, 130,525 palm-leaf hats were made in Petersham.

"The making of boots and shoes was the second major domestic industry managed on the 'putting-out' system. Agents delivered shoe material, uppers, soles, linings, etc., and the farmers assembled the shoes in their homes, returning the finished commodities to the agent on his return trip. In 1836, 11,000 pairs of boots and shoes were processed by this method and in a local factory employing 35 hands."

Abandonment of farms was a factor in Petersham as throughout New England. Census figures show the ratio of woodland to total area as gradually increasing from 14.5 percent in 1865 to 55 percent in 1905. Some industries in Petersham used timber, including factories making ladders, chairs and cabinets and casks – most of which employed a handful of employees each. Today, Petersham is mostly covered by forest. The evolution of farm and forest in Petersham is portrayed vividly in the dioramas at the Fisher Museum in Harvard Forest.

The making of the beautiful Petersham that remains today is in large measure due to the fact that many of the town's early inhabitants practiced a trade in addition, and often incidental to their farming. "There were brickmakers, clothiers, cordwainers [shoemakers], tanners, blacksmiths, house carpenters, joiners, millers, curriers and not a few Jeffersonian politicians," to quote the Harvard Forest study. Many of these people had a hand in creating the pillared white wood and brick homes and public buildings around the Common,

The town hall in the center of Petersham

built mostly between 1835 and 1850.

As Athol historian and journalist Richard Chaisson has observed, Petersham's story "is one more of small incidents than large:

"Daniel Webster stopped by one day and left behind his oversized hat for giggling youngsters to try on. It added to the large treasury of local folklore.

"During World War II, in a precaution against possible bomb damage or shelling, art masterpieces by Whistler, Gainsborough and Copley were taken from Harvard University in Cambridge and hidden in a vacant building of the University's School of Forestry here.

"A host of literary figures came here in generations past to rest their weary minds. The noted American historican and evolutionist John Fiske was one of them. He stayed, wrote his great books under a maple tree, and lectured in the parlors of the old Nichewaug Inn for the benefit of the library fund.

"Fiske once had as his house guest the eminent British biologist Professor Thomas H. Huxley. A happy summer resident years ago was Norman Hapgood, editor of Colliers and Harpers magazines. Calvin Coolidge came here for years to enjoy fishing in Carter Pond and a branch of Swift River.

"The work of some of Petersham's people is world recognized; Solomon Willard designed and built the Bunker Hill Monument, and William Austin Burt invented the world's first practical typewriter."

The town thrives not only on its beauty but on its cultural and festive activities and institutions, including the Petersham Craft Center, Harvard Forest, Elizabeth Carpenter Concerts, the annual levee of the Unitarian Church, antique shows and various programs of the Petersham Historical Society and other civic groups.

Public tours of the town's stately homes were once conducted by the Petersham Historical Society. Mrs. Delight Haines, a member of the historic district commission and one of the town's most active participants in community affairs, told a newspaper reporter what happened: "In a few years we were besieged with onlookers. More than 500 people took the tour in 1962. That's quite a few people to pass through one house at a time. We had to give it up. Nowadays, the tours are open only to members of the Historical Society. Even then, we must handle a group of 50 at each home."

Mrs. Haines points out that town meeting actions over many decades have reflected a concern for keeping the main thoroughfare unspoiled, whether it involves placement of new street lights or putting up a store sign. As far back as 1920, burial of many utility lines was required.

Petersham gained considerable territory in the 1930s with the addition of Dana and parts of Prescott and Greenwich – including dry land and much of the Quabbin lake. Much of Petersham lies within the watershed of the Swift River (east branch). The east and west branches of Fever Brook also feed the reservoir. As a result of the massive gains in watershed territory, Petersham ranks third in the state in size, with 68.18 square miles. Only Middleborough and Plymouth are larger. The town's population rose only one percent between 1970 and 1980 – from 1,014 to 1,024. There was a somewhat larger increase during the previous decade, from 1960-1970. The population density is 20 people per square mile, about the same as Royalston and Wendell – ranking Petersham 329th in the state in population density.

Petersham is bordered on the northeast by Phillipston and the northwest by Athol, on the southeast by Barre, on the south by Hardwick and Ware, and on the west by New Salem. This area includes not only much Quabbin water (including the Pottapaug Pond section)and watershed land but also thousands of acres of Harvard Forest, state forest land and conservation land owned by various private agencies. The lowest elevation is 524 above sea level, at the Quabbin; highest is Sherman Hill, 1,209 feet above sea level in the southeast portion of town, not much higher than the town center at 1,050 feet – thus the name "Hilltop Town." See also ARTS AND CRAFTS, BROOKS WOODLAND PRESERVE, CURLING, DANA, FEDERATED STATE FOREST, HARVARD FOREST, NORTH COMMON MEADOW, PETERSHAM HISTORICAL SOCIETY, PETERSHAM STATE FOREST, QUABBIN RECREATION, QUABBIN RESERVOIR, SHAYS REBELLION.

Petersham Historical Society

A small brick structure, patterned after a Harvard University chapel, houses the Petersham Historical Society. Located on the common, the two-story building contains a variety of local memorabilia including genealogical documents. The building was erected by John S. Eames.

Adjacent is a plaque recalling the defeat in Petersham in 1787 of the rebellious farmers led by Daniel Shays. The Shays plaque was dedicated by members of the New England Society of Brooklyn, N.Y., at the behest of a member who spent his summers in Petersham. The building is open to the public during the warmer months. Information about visiting hours is available from Delight Haines, West Street, Petersham, Tel. 724-3380. See also SHAYS REBELLION.

Petersham State Forest

The main feature of Petersham State Forest, which lies mostly in Petersham with two small sections in Athol, is Riceville Pond, 100 acres in size, regularly stocked, and characterized as having excellent fishing for warm water species.

In addition to fishing, activities here include hunting for all small game and deer, hiking, snowmobiling, snowshoeing and cross-country skiing.

The forest's area totals 539 acres, purchased in 1933. The Civilian Conservation Corps had a camp here in 1939-40. The dam creating Riceville Pond was rebuilt in 1960. The pond was used for storage of logs from hurricane damage in 1938. Most of the pond is in Petersham, but the northwestern corner lies in Athol.

Best access to the forest is via Pleasant Street and New Sherborn Road from Athol or Turnpike Road from Petersham, off Route 122. Nelson Road in Petersham cuts through the middle of the main tract.

Phillipston

"The town center is probably the quietest spot in Central Massachusetts as far as communities go. A few white buildings, including the graceful Congregational Church, form a circle. And that's all. Grass and trees predominate. Near the old town hall stands the ancient public pump. Those in the area make it a point to stop off, give the handle a few energetic pumps and drink from the old font..."

Thus Ivan Sandrof, Athol bureau chief for the Worcester Telegram, described Phillipston in a 1956 article. Twenty years later, in the same newspaper, Sandrof's successor, Richard Chaisson, wrote: "This pleasant country town is held together by a fine blend of serenity, neighborliness, public socials, special events and an endless necklace of pretty fieldstone walls."

The town center and the serenity remain as they were

Phillipston church bazaar during U.S. bicentennial year

then, despite some population increase as more and more people from the cities look to rural America for quiet clean places
they can call home. Population growth in Phillipston has been
moderate, increasing nine percent between 1970 and 1980,
from 872 to 953 people. The town is relatively small, with
24.29 square miles, ranking it 131st in the state. The population density is 41 people per square mile, ranking is 303rd in
the state – quite rural in character but double the population
density of neighboring Royalston and Petersham.

While Phillipston has some public land, notably a state-
owned wildlife management area that has been gradually expanding plus a portion of the Petersham-based Harvard
Forest, there is room here for a moderate increase in population without threatening the town's rural character. The
townspeople who love this "rolling town with steep hills and
plunging dips into valleys" (Sandrof's description) are wary of
too much growth, however. A building moratorium for major
projects was approved by town meeting voters in the mid-
1970s, a reasonable response to a situation documented in the
1980 census: housing units in Phillipston up from 246 in 1970
to 412 in 1980, an increase of 90 percent, one of the highest in
the state.

Phillipston's elevation is 1,166 at the town center. The highest point is Prospect Hill, at 1,383 feet above sea level, near the Petersham line. Second-highest is Baldwin Hill, 1,355 feet above sea level, close to the Athol line, giving its name to a road and to the unusual sourdough whole wheat bread baked in brick ovens in an old Phillipston farmhouse, one of the town's few "industries."

The Millers River forms less than a mile of the border between Athol and Phillipston, and the elevation there, 790 feet above sea level, is the town's lowest. Phillipston's land drains several watersheds. Beaver Brook and Thousand Acre Brook flow north to the Millers River. The east branch of the Swift River, which flows into the Quabbin, rises from the convergence of Bigelow Brook and Popple Camp Brook. Burnshirt River, forming part of the border between Templeton and Phillipston, flows into the Ware River.

The terrain is mostly rough and stony, although the southern portion of town – quite near the geographical center of Massachusetts – is more level with some swampy areas. Queen Lake, the town's largest body of water, covering 160 acres and averaging 13 feet in depth, is one of its best-known features. It is one and one quarter miles long and a half-mile wide and is located at the southern end of the town.

The first of many cottages was built on the lake, then called Phillipston Pond (earlier records show it was called Jackson's Pond), in 1891. That same year a fisherman from nearby Barre, George A. Simons, wrote a poem about the lake. "Oh, Queen of the Lakes among the hills, 'bove Goulding Village's ruined mills," he wrote, lines which captured the imagination of Athol real estate developer Sumner L. Morse who used the name "Queen Lake" in advertisements. As people bought lots and built cottages, the name stuck. Queen Lake became a popular summer resort. From the 1920s to the 1960s the Queen Lake Camp for Girls was active and popular. At present there is a mixture of year-round homes and summer camps on its shores.

Several years ago, Athol frogmen diving to the bottom of Queen Lake discovered what is believed to be a portion of an ancient dugout canoe. The relic is displayed at the Phillips Memorial Library.

Queen Lake is private, as is the more recent "Secret Lake" development off Ward Hill Road on the shores of a body of water identified as Reservoir No. 2 on the geodetic map.

One of Phillipston's prominent hills is Ward Hill in the western part of Phillipston (the part that once belonged to

Athol), which offers a scenic view of surrounding countryside. The north slope of the hill was used by the former "Snow Hill" ski area, which was closed in the 1970s and has been for sale. Land on this hill was once the home of a "famous son" of Phillipston. He was Ithamar Ward, son of Artemus Ward, who preceded George Washington as commander of the colonial army. Ithamar Ward came to Athol before the close of the Revolutionary War and settled on the road and hill that bears the family name today. He served the community in the state legislature and was town clerk for 30 years. Headstones in the cemetery in the center of town are reminders of the once prominent Ward family.

Phillipston is bordered on the east and southeast by Templeton, on the south by Hubbardson and Barre, on the southwest and west by Petersham and Athol, and on the north by Royalston. Route 2 passes through Phillipston, as does parallel Route 2A, Route 101 (passing Queen Lake between Templeton and Petersham), but none of these numbered highways goes through the town center. Except for a few hundred yards of the now defunct Boston and Albany line, passing through the southeastern corner of town, Phillipston has had no railroad. Indeed, when the principal east-west railroad bypassed these hills in the 1840s, Phillipston declined as a trading center for this part of Worcester County as neighboring Athol became more prominent and populous. Up to that point, Phillipston's town center included a well-stocked general store visited by customers from a wide area.

This town, like Warwick and others in the area, began as the spoils of war, in this case the war against the Narragansett Indians, waged furiously in 1675 under the command of General Josia Winslow, governor of Plymouth Colony. "If you play the man," he promised, "take the fort and drive the enemy out of the Narragansett country...you shall have a gratuity of land, beside your wages."

In 1733, the land bonus came through in the form of several large grants. One of them, Narragansett No. 6, became Templeton, given to 60 men. What became Templeton West Precinct included most of the territory that is now Phillipston. Gradually the area was settled and roads built – including one completed by 1751 from Templeton to Pequoig (Athol), passing directly through what is now Phillipston Common. On March 6, 1792, both Pequoig (Athol) and Templeton were incorporated.

Residents of the area were dissatisfied with their inconvenient church affiliations in Athol and Templeton (everyone went to church in those days and only church members were legal voters), so they moved to form a separate church and soon after that a separate town.

The original application of the settlers sought to name the town Gill (for Moses Gill of Princeton, a state senator). The name of Elbridge Gerry of Cambridge (one of the signers of the Declaration of Independence, a delegate to the Continental Congress and a member of the Congress under the Articles of Confederation) was also suggested, and Gerry promoted himself by offering to "glaze this meeting house."

Gerry it would be. The town of Gerry was officially established by the state on October 20, 1786. Gerry, who eventually became vice president of the United States under James Madison, had a long and stormy political career. He is probably best known for the redistricting controversy that gave us the word "gerrymander." He was embroiled in many areas of controversy on the state, national and even international level, and in 1814 a special town meeting was called and a petition was adopted asking that they be relieved of their obligation to "support the name of a man who from the beginning was opposed to the National Constitution, and to the politics of Washington; and who is reputedly hostile to the ministers and ordinances of religion." The petition included a request – speedily granted by the state – to change the name from Gerry to Phillipston, honoring the then lieutenant governor of the Commonwealth, William Phillips, well known in politics, education, philanthropy and religion.

The meeting house windows were probably never provided by Gerry in any case. That meeting house, raised in 1785, which is today's Congregational Church, is a masterpiece of church architecture. As late as the mid-1950s, the church was not wired for electricity, being lit by a dozen oil lamps from swinging wrought iron wall brackets. Inside the steeple is a wonder of Yankee ingenuity, an unusual church clock built in 1891 by "Cabbage" Clifford who carved the clock's 29 wheels out of cherrywood. Its pendulum is a 14-ft. wooden shaft with a 417-lb. boulder hanging from it. The clock lacks a face but its chimes announce the time.

As Phillipston developed, farm and forest products were the backbone of its economic life. Timber in the 1700s and early 1800s was hauled by oxen to water-powered sawmills where it was cut into lumber for furniture, boxes and pail staves. Factories in the 1800s produced cotton and woolen goods. Braiding of palm leaf hats was an important cottage industry, chiefly involving women, while men bottomed boots for factories in nearby Brooks Village and Athol.

Thomas White of this town experimented with sewing machines, and his efforts contributed to the eventual establishment of the New Home Sewing Machine Co. in Orange and the White Sewing Machine Co. of Cleveland, Ohio.

The population peaked at 932 in 1820 and dropped off to only 441 in 1900, down further to 357 in 1930. Not until the 1970s did Phillipston's population surpass that 1820 peak. Earlier in this century, the principal occupation of the community was agriculture, including the making of cheese and butter, market gardening, poultry raising and fruit growing.

The Red Apple Orchard on Highland Avenue remains one of the town's most important businesses. The orchard, operated by the Rose family for more than five decades, is a place of great beauty and visitors are welcome.

A few miles south on Ward Hill Road is the Fox Run Restaurant, well known throughout the region. This establishment was begun in 1954 by Mrs. Dorothy H. Harrington and her daughter, Tillie. The two women created the dining rooms and bar from an old ordinary barn and decorated them with an unusual decor including old horse collars which frame mirrors and a huge mounted moose trophy called Hector the Head. The tradition of country dining is carried on under the current owners, Mr. and Mrs. Derek Anson.

Other businesses include the Baldwin Hill Bakery, an automombile salvage yard, a motorcycle sales and repair business, and a few small retail stores. There is no sizeable industry or retail trade, however, and residents work and shop out of town, mostly in Gardner and Athol. Home gardening and backyard farm animals are common but farming as a full-time occupation is virtually unknown nowadays as Phillipston joins the long list of Massachusetts "bedroom communities."The 1981 "Library and Community Analysis" indicates Phillipston is a "working class town," most of its residents working in non-professional occupations.

Phillipston is served by the Athol telephone exchange and post office, as the town's own post office was closed in 1954. Phillipston belongs to the Narragansett Regional School District, which also includes Templeton, and Phillipston students on the secondary level attend Narragansett Regional School in Baldwinville (Templeton's largest village).The Memorial School in Phillipston, built in the late 1940s and expanded in the 1970s, accommodates pupils through grade 6. The Phillips Memorial Library serves these schoolchildren as well as adult residents. The Narragansett Historical Society in

Templeton houses Phillipston historical materials.

Among the events in town that attract a large number of residents and visitors are the annual Congregational Church bazaar, traditionally held on a June weekend, and the October weigh-in on the town common for the Phillipston Pumpkin Commission annual contest. See also APPLES, BREAD, PHILLIPSTON WILDLIFE AREA, PUMPKINS.

Phillipston Wildlife Area

The Phillipston Wildlife Management Area and the adjacent Popple Camp Wildlife Management Area cover 2,750 acres in Phillipston and Petersham. Some expansion of the Phillipston area is anticipated, and the owner of all of this land – the Massachusetts Department of Environmental Management, Division of Fisheries and Wildlife – is already the largest landowner in Phillipston.

A broad range of upland mammal and bird species are found here in mostly forested and swampy terrain, with the area open to hunting, trapping and fishing, as well as bird-watching and hiking. The Popple Camp area borders both sides of the east branch of the Swift River, which is stocked with trout.

There is very limited stocking of pheasants in the Phillipston area.

Access to both areas is off Route 101 and via Bakers and Narrow lanes. There are no buildings or resident staff here, but parking areas are provided.

Powerhouse

Northeast Utilities' Northfield Mountain pumped-storage hydroelectric plant is undoubtedly the Mt. Grace Region's most modern and technologically complex industry. When it went into commercial service in 1972, it was the largest facility of its kind in the world. The plant's "front door," so to speak, is located in Northfield, but the powerhouse itself is hidden 700 feet deep inside Northfield Mountain in the town of Erving. The utility is, as a result, Erving's main taxpayer.

Electricity cannot be stored in bulk; water, however can – and that is the principle on which this plant is based. At night, or at times of lower customer use of power (minimum demand), water is pumped from the lower reservoir (the Connecticut River) to the upper reservoir where it is stored as a potential energy source. The man-made upper reservoir is located atop Northfield Mountain, also in the town of Erving. When customer usage is high (peak demand), this stored water is released. As it flows back to the lower reservoir it passes through a turbine which is connected to a generator and electricity is produced.

Water from the Connecticut flows into the tailrace canal, continues down a mile-long tunnel to the powerhouse, where four motor-driven pumps send the water up the pressure shaft to the upper reservoir. Each pump has the capacity of pumping 20,000 gallons of water per second to the upper reservoir. The 300-acre upper reservoir is located approximately 900 feet above the powerhouse; it is capable of storing 5.9 billion gallons of water.

When electricity is needed, this process is reversed, and water is released from the upper reservoir. It flows back down the same pressure shaft to the same pumps; however they now operate in the reverse direction functioning as turbines, which drive the generators and produce the electricity. Each turbine-generator produces 250,000 kilowatts of electricity for a total station capacity of one million kilowatts. The water continues down the tailrace tunnel to the tailrace canal and into the river.

The Northfield Mountain Station is designed to go from complete shutdown to supplying a million kilowatts of capacity in less than three minutes. The electricity is fed into transformers, located within the underground powerhouse, which increases the voltage to 345,000 volts. The power is then transmitted 2,500 feet through two pipe-type cables, installed in a 26-ft. diameter underground access tunnel, to a switchyard. From this switching station the power is distributed not only to serve the needs of Northeast Utilities' customers (in Western Massachusetts and Connecticut) but also throughout New England via the New England Power Exchange. The electricity used to power the pumps that send the water to the upper reservoir comes from that same exchange, which utilizes nuclear, fossil fuel and hydroelectric power.

The powerhouse is reached by a half-mile-long tunnel from the entrance on the east slope of the mountain. The cavern it occupies is as high as a 10-story building, as wide as a four-lane highway and longer than a football field. The total generating capacity of the plant is enough electricity to serve cities the size of Springfield and Holyoke combined.

Engineering studies for the Northfield Mountain project began in 1964. Earth and rock core samples were drilled and analyzed to see if this would be a suitable site. Tests showed Northfield Mountain is a 560 million-year-old metamorphic rock formation called gneiss. Actual contruction began in 1967. It was completed in 1972 and began commercial operation the same year.

Building the facility cost $140 million, of which about $1 million was spent on landscaping the Northfield Mountain area. Some of the 250,000 tons of rock excavated from the cavern and access tunnel was used as fill. The rock removed from the inside of the mountain could fill 69,000 freight cars – making a train stretching from Boston to Cleveland, a distance of 550 miles. In the landscaping project, topsoil was added and grass and trees were planted to provide a natural-looking area that helps hide the plant's switchyard and other facilities outside the mountain. As part of arrangements with the state surrounding the construction of the plant, Northeast Utilities agreed to provide elaborate recreational facilities in the area and to maintain an ongoing program of environmental education, which the company does very successfully.

However, there are some environmental questions about the project. For one, there is a plan to use the Northfield Mountain reservoir and pumping system to divert water from the Connecticut River to Quabbin Reservoir – this plan is widely opposed in Western Massachusetts. In addition, there is considerable concern about erosion of soil along the riverbank due to the constant rising and falling of the river's level. This problem has been discussed by the Northfield conservation commission.

A film about the construction and operation of the plant can be seen at the visitors center. Regular tours to the upper reservoir and special tours to the interior of the mountain are offered to the public. Information about these tours is available by calling 413-659-3713. See also NORTHFIELD MOUNTAIN.

Prescott

The name of Prescott lives today in a unique piece of land known as Prescott Peninsula, within the town of New Salem, where a wilderness area is maintained under the jurisdiction of the Metropolitan District Commission (MDC). It is the home of important wildlife programs including attempts to naturalize wild turkeys and eagles. But the town of Prescott is no more.

The area that was later to become Prescott, one of the four

defunct Quabbin towns, was first settled in the 1740s, and the first school was erected there in 1754. In 1786, the East Parish of Pelham was formed, and this, added to a section of southern New Salem, became the town of Prescott on Jan. 28, 1822. This Hampshire County town was named for either Dr. Oliver Prescott (who helped suppress Shays' Rebellion) or Col. William Prescott.

The town consisted of about 12,700 acres, and was shaped like a sidewise L. At its widest point it was six miles wide, and up to four and a half miles long. Three villages were located within it – North Prescott, on the boundary with New Salem; Atkinson Hollow; and the center, on Prescott Hill. Most of the long section of the town was on a ridge, punctuated by Prescott, Pierce, and Rattlesnake Hills. In the eastern section, Mount Russ and Mount L looked over a plain. The west branch of the Swift River formed the boundary with Pelham to the west, and the middle branch of the Swift flowed through the eastern corner of the town. The Athol and Enfield Railroad passed through this same corner of town, with a flag station named Soapstone.

Because most of the town was located on a ridge, the main occupation was farming. A few mills were located on the west branch of the Swift River, producing such products as carriages, cloth, batting, cider and cheese. Soapstone was mined for the manufacture of sinks. Stores were located in each of the villages, and post offices functioned in Prescott and North Prescott.

There were five schoolhouses within the town at one time. Baptists, Methodists and Congregationalists were the main religious groups. The town hall was in Prescott Center and a Grange Hall was located in the Hollow.

Since the population of Prescott had decreased to only 230 people by the time the building of the Quabbin was authorized by the Swift River Act of 1927, and because many of those remaining had decided to sell their land to the MDC, the town was the first to be taken over by the state. The MDC appointed agents to run Prescott from 1928 until its final dissolution on April 28, 1938. Parts of the town were absorbed by New Salem and Petersham.

In fact, most of the area of Prescott's territory is still above water, and an astronomy observatory run by the University of Massachusetts was built at the site of the center in the early 1970s, somewhat undermining, unfortunately, the value of the peninsula as a wilderness area. (From J.R. Greene's "Atlas of the Quabbin Valley") See also PRESCOTT HISTORICAL SOCIETY.

Prescott Historical Society

While former residents of all four "lost" Quabbin towns – Dana, Enfield, Greenwich and Prescott – banded together to form the Swift River Valley Historical Society, headquartered in the Whitaker-Clary House in New Salem, some of the former residents of Prescott resolved to preserve their history by means of the separate Prescott Historical Society.

The former North Prescott Methodist Church, originally built in 1837, was moved to Orange in the 1940s to serve specifically as a home for the society and as a resting place for Prescott memorabilia. The building is located on South Main Street across from the Mahar Regional School driveway. The group has 65 members scattered hither and yon, with an annual meeting held on the first Saturday in August. This is the only day of the year that the building is open to public inspection.

The society is exploring the possibility of giving up its separate identity and turning its possessions over to the Swift River Valley Historic Society. The old church might then be moved or sold. See also PRESCOTT and WHITAKER-CLARY HOUSE.

Prison Camp

The Warwick Forestry Camp is located on Richmond Road in Warwick on the site of a former "transient camp" where the federal government in the mid-1930s housed unemployed men with no legal residence. The camp buildings were dismantled after World War II, and new facilities were built in the early 1960s for a prison camp.

MCI-Warwick (Massachusetts Correctional Institution-Warwick) is the westernmost facility within the state Department of Correction. The camp is "primarily minimum security," according to a department information sheet, and was designed to serve inmates near the completion of their sentences.

The camp's main building houses all residents, two of them to a cubicle. This building also contains administrative offices, television room, weight room, barber shop, kitchen, and dining room as well as a visiting room.

The department states: "Eligibility to Warwick is limited to those not currently serving a sentence for a sex offense. Additionally, lifers are not eligible, but a second degree lifer may be considered if he has served 12 years. Residents assigned to a forestry camp receive an additional two and one-half days credit per month."

The camp is rated for an occupancy of 50 males. In late 1982, its population consisted of 65 inmates with a staff of 22.

Various programs are offered here, with average attendance of 10-12 inmates "which allows for individuality and creativity." Among the programs are Alcoholics Anonymous, drug counseling, literacy and other educational programs, and Bible study (directed by a local clergyman and volunteers).

Recreational activities include team sports, weight-lifting, films and avocational activities such as wood carving, painting, leathercraft and music. Space is made available each summer to all residents who wish to maintain a garden.

Under work programs, inmates are involved in maintenance of the camp and such camp jobs as laundry and kitchen; a forestry crew working on state lands; the Fernald School program providing assistance in maintenance at the state school for retarded adults in nearby Templeton; "functional equipment program" assembling materials for schools serving children with physical handicaps; and "work release" offering jobs to certain inmates in furniture factories and foundries, primarily in the Gardner area.

Public Transportation

Englander Bus Co. of Greenfield offers east-west bus service along Route 2 between Boston (Greyhound Terminal) and Williamstown, with several buses daily plus weekend service to Albany, N.Y. Passengers in the Athol-Orange area are served by several buses daily stopping at Cullen's Sunoco, Daniel Shays Highway, Orange, at the intersection of Routes 2 and 202. Information about fares, schedules and package service is available from Cullen's, Tel. 544-8565. (The company name is "Englander," not "New Englander," and some of these buses are marked "Bonanza" even though operated by Englander.)

There are connections in Greenfield (at Charron's Pharmacy, Tel. 413-773-9410) with Greyhound and Vermont Transit to points north and south. (Trailways Bus Co. formerly offered service to the centers of Orange and Athol on its route between Haverhill and Springfield, with direct service to New York City, but that ended several years ago.)Vermont Transit Lines, with stops in Fitzwilliam, N.H., Winchendon and Gardner, on its lines between Boston and Vermont, New Hampshire and Quebec points, may be useful to some residents.

Amtrack service departs for points south and west from Springfield several times daily. There is also Amtrack service on "The Montrealer" with stops in Springfield and Northampton, as well as Brattleboro, Vt., but as of this writing the trains stop during inconvenient early-morning hours both northbound and southbound. Amtrack's toll-free telephone is 1-800-523-5720. The Massachusetts Bay Transportation Authority (MBTA, known as "The T") provides subsidized commuter train service between Boston and Gardner. The T's toll-free line is 1-800-392-6100.

The closest airfield offering scheduled air service (to New York and Boston, with connections to other points), is the Dillant-Hopkins Airport, Keene, N.H., on commuter-size aircraft of Precision Airlines. Bar Harbor Airlines offers service at the Worcester airport. More frequent service by major carriers is available at Logan International Airport, Boston; and Bradley International Field, Windsor Locks, Conn., serving the Hartford-Springfield area. Charter service is available at Turners Falls and Keene airports.

For most long distance travel, as well as locally, residents depend on the private automobile. It was not always this way. Local and regional bus and train service functioned as recently as the 1950s, and earlier in the century, street railways or trolleys running east-west connected many area towns; it was possible to take the trolley from Athol to Gardner, for example.

Various attempts have been made in recent years, some with the help of federally-funded programs, to provide local or regional transportation by bus and van, but these services have not caught on, except those provided for the elderly and handicapped. The most recent effort is scheduled bus service between Athol and Orange launched under the auspices of the Chamber of Commerce in the fall of 1982. Taxi service is available from Athol Taxi, 41 School St., Athol, Tel. 249-2727 and Friendly Town Cab, 22 Water St. (Depot Square), Orange, Tel. 544-3535, for local and long-distance travel. See also AIRPORT and ELDERLY SERVICES.

Pumpkins

Pumpkins, a kind of squash, are among the native New England plants that the Indians grew. The first settlers learned to grow them, and they remain popular not only for the traditions of pumpkin pie and Halloween jack-o'-lanterns but because the incredible size they reach even in a short growing season is a reminder of the wonderful nurturing forces of Nature. One favorite variety among seed-lovers is the Lady Godiva, so named because their seeds have no hard hull and are especially easy-to-eat. Other varieties are favored by pie-

Phillipston pumpkin-growers and potential prize-winning giant

lovers. For really big pumpkins, however, the place to go is the annual weigh-in of the Phillipston Pumpkin Commission, which claims to grow the largest pumpkins.

The participants in the contest each pay a $50 entry fee, and 98 per cent of the money goes to the winner. However, contest rules specify that the winner must take all of the losers out to dinner at a restaurant of their choice.

The Phillipston pumpkin-growing contest "started out as a drunken bit" between two friends in the late 1970s, according to one of the two, Craig Twohey of Ward Hill Road. The other founder is Don Schlicke of Highland Avenue, whose 1980 contest-winning pumpkin weighed 209 pounds. Twohey is a chef at the Fox Run Restaurant; Schlicke manages the orchard at the Red Apple Farm.

Most of the contestants "are good serious gardeners," Schlicke pointed out, noting that successful pumpkin-growing is a result of careful seed selection, soil care and watering. Precise details of Schlicke's own techniques for growing the squash family vine known in Latin as Cucurbita pepo are "nobody's damned business," he said.

Most of the contestants grow the Burgess giant from the Burgess Seed and Plant Co. or the Big Moon variety from the Gurney Seed Co. The original Burgess giant strain was propogated some decades ago through selective breeding by Howard Dill of Nova Scotia, Canada. Schlicke explained that since the Burgess giant is not a hybrid seed, growers must select the baby pumpkin they think is most likely to grow into a giant; if they nip the wrong baby pumpkin they won't grow a winner.

The contestants use a mixture of manure and bagged chemical fertilizer and depend on watering to maximize weight. Twohey said his giant pumpkin added 50-75 pounds a week during the height of the season, and watering the plants was essential during periods of summertime drought.

An autumn weigh-in is scheduled every year "rain or shine" with commissioners borrowing a large grain scale from Agway's of Athol. Lots of large pumpkins are on sale – some contest winners as well as the also-rans from contestants' gardens.

Area residents interested in entering can write to the Phillipston Pumpkin Commission, Phillipston. "Ralph knows where to bring the letters," Schlicke said, referring to local rural route carrier Ralph Duteau.

Quabbin Fishing

The Quabbin Reservoir is a good place to fish, although surprisingly few people know about it. Initially, only shore fishing was permitted. The water level in the reservoir stabilized in 1946, and by the early 1950s, the large pickerel and perch that were abundant became scarce due to changes in the underwater environment. Fishermen began to apply pressure for the extension of the shore fishing area and permission to use boats.

During 1951, the Metropolitan District Commission (MDC), Division of Fisheries and Wildlife and Department of Public Health conducted a survey on the recreational potential of the reservoir. A report was filed and in 1952 the reservoir was formally opened to boat fishing.

It may seem strange or ironical, given the concern for water purity, that motorboats using gasoline outboard engines are permitted on the lake while sailboats are excluded. In any case, state law specifies that the reservoir is not open to recreational boating as such but only to fishing; this is apparently a result of the political clout of organized sportsmen. The rules specify that there must be at least one individual with a fishing license in each and every boat launched on Quabbin's waters, whether or not the occupants of the boat engage in fishing. Shore fishing is permitted; ice fishing is not.

Although there are dozens of entranceways into the Quabbin, marked by numbered "gates," only three provide access to

Successful Quabbin angler with lake trout

boat mooring areas – boat mooring area number one at Gate 8 in Pelham off Route 202, area two at gate 31 in New Salem off Route 122, and area three at Gate 43 off Route 32A in Hardwick.

Rowboats and motorboats meeting current MDC specifications may be launched at any of three areas; they are also available for rent. Rental equipment cannot be reserved, and it is advisable to arrive early, especially during the early part of the fishing season. Canoes (also restricted to fishing) may be launched only at the Pottapaug Pond section at Gate 43; canoes are not available for rent.

Fishing in the Quabbin Reservoir generally falls into two broad categories, coldwater and warmwater, which characterizes roughly the requirements of different groups of fish. The salmonoids such as lake trout, rainbow and brown trout, and landlocked salmon as well as as their principal forage, smelt, are all examples of coldwater species. On the other hand, the basses, pickerel, white and yellow perch, and bullheads are considered warmwater fish.

The difference in groups relates not only to the best time of year to catch a particular species but also the type of habitat that fish prefer. A depth contour map of Quabbin readily shows that the majority of deep water in the open fishing zone occurs on Quabbin's west branch side available to fisherman in area one (Gate 8, Pelham). Shallower water occurs in the Quabbin's middle branch accessible from area two (Gate 31, New Salem) and the east branch accessible from area three (Gate 43, Hardwick).

The trout species (including salmon) are caught readily from any gate, prior to Memorial Day weekend. At first the fish are concentrated around the mouths of brooks and then, as surface waters warm, they work their way into deeper water. Rainbow trout are taken on occasion right at the surface through May and into the early part of June. Lake trout prefer cooler water temperatures and so tend to congregate near the bottom in water depth of 80 or 90 feet. During the summer and early fall, all trout are found in deep, cold waters. This requires a change in angling methods. Fisherman who change their style successfully land trout throughout the fishing season.

By the middle of May the fishing for bass, white perch and bullheads picks up especially on the middle and east branch side and fishing for these species as well as pickerel, yellow perch and largemouth bass continues through summer.

While serious trout fisherman continue to work the deep

water available out of Gate 8 through the summer, others revert to warmwater fishing, working the extensive shallows and islands on the east and middle branch areas, seeking largemouth bass, bullheads and pickerel. Others concentrate on somewhat deeper water (15-30 feet) looking for white perch, generally near bottom; yellow perch; and if rocks and logs are present, smallmouth bass.

With the arrival of cooler surface waters by late September, the coldwater species, especially rainbow trout, become more active and are available again in shallow waters. Their catch generally shows an upswing during this latter part of the season. Although few people fish for bass at this time of year, serious fishermen often do quite well especially when fishing for largemouth.

A fish management program by the Division of Fisheries and Wildlife of the Massachusetts Department of Environmental Management has been in effect since the early 1950s. This has included stocking of walleye pike and lake trout, followed by the introduction of smelt as food for the lakers. Problems with the clogging of intake systems and flow meters resulted, and a chemical smelt control program (using copper sulphate) was undertaken in 1959. Damage to other species, especially brown trout, also occurred. Screen intakes were installed solving the clogging problem, and in 1968 and 1969, more smelt were released. Stocking of rainbow trout, brown trout and landlocked salmon is an additional feature of the fish management program.

Approximately 400 fishermen belong to the North Worcester County Quabbin Anglers Association (P.O. Box 79, Athol MA 01331), which promotes the interests of fishermen and seeks to raise the consciousness of anglers and the general public about protecting the Quabbin so that the area remains open for recreational use – there are those in the MDC who would prefer to close it to the public altogether. A tagging program and fishing derby is one of the association's various activities. Anthony Brighenti of Athol is the association's president and spokesman.

Up-to-date information on fishing, including a useful map of Quabbin, is available from the association. An important resource is the Quabbin Area Sportsman's Guide, prepared by Ellie Horwitz, published by the Massachusetts Division of Fisheries and Wildlife and the MDC. This pamphlet, from which most of the information in this section has been taken, is available free of charge, in person or by mail, from the MDC Water Division, 485 Ware Rd., Belchertown MA 01007. The guide includes current information on gate opening and closing hours and boat rentals, not included here because it is subject to change. This information is also available by phone from the MDC Water Division, 413-323-6921, or the MDC Police, 413-323-7561.

Quabbin Recreation

The use of the massive Quabbin Reservoir and surrounding watershed lands by the public for recreational use is highly restricted or surprisingly open, depending on one's interpretation. The only activities officially sanctioned are hiking and fishing; in contrast, there are those who believe the protection of the water would be best served by closing the area altogether.

The potential seems enormous, even if one takes into account this concern for water purity. Certainly limited recreational boating, especially sailboating, is one activity that could be introduced without major impact to its cleanliness.

Unfortunately, even shockingly, however, some members of the public, including outdoorsy types, are stupid and thoughtless – even now the Quabbin area suffers from the results of littering and other violations of common-sense.

Common sense aside, there are 27 items in the rules and regulations for the use of the reservoir and watershed, and any

Hiker's reward: view from Soapstone Hill in Petersham inside Gate 37

violation is punishable by a fine up to $500 or by imprisonment not exceeding one year in the house of correction. The Metropolitan District Commission (MDC) has its own police force, with a station at Quabbin headquarters in Belchertown, and every now and then the district courts in Gardner and Orange handle cases brought to them by MDC police (though in

White birch catches sunlight inside Gate 35

Quabbin driftwood seen from roadway inside Gate 35

practice punishments meted out are usually not severe).

Questioned about bicycling in the Quabbin, Lt. James L. Sullivan of the MDC police provided this response: "This letter is to inform you that in the Quabbin area there are no areas set aside for the specific use of bicycles. The use of bicycles as a means of access to the fishing areas where shore fishing is permitted, has never been denied. These areas are the gates and access routes to the water between Gates 22 and 43. The above roads are not designated bicycle paths, but the use is allowed, provided the rules of the commission are obeyed."

One must read between the lines: a well-behaved bicyclist is welcome to enjoy the Quabbin lands, while a polluter, litterbug or rowdy may be caught by the long arm of the law. The same goes for picnicking, prohibited under rule number four, which also prohibits smoking! Motorized vehicles are strictly forbidden.

The activity of hiking, which is permitted, is not to be belittled in any case – and this includes bird-watching and the proverbial "communing with Nature." Hiking in the Quabbin is made all the more special, perhaps, when the hiker knows that no one is present on the land for any other purpose than to peacefully observe and enjoy this incredible little wilderness located only a short distance from the cities of the northeastern megalopolis.

Of the twenty access gates in the North Quabbin area, the most popular ones for hikers are Gate 35 off South Athol Road in New Salem, and Gate 40 off Route 32A in Petersham. Gate

178

40 provides access to roadways leading to the old center of Dana, including some paved roads especially good for bicycling.

A copy of the Quabbin rules and regulations may be obtained from the MDC Police, Quabbin Reservoir, Belchertown MA 01007. See also DANA, QUABBIN FISHING, QUABBIN RESERVOIR.

Quabbin Reservoir

Many Massachusetts residents have noticed the large blue lake that clearly dominates the center of the state on any current map. Few, however, know the story of that lake – the Quabbin Reservoir – and among the ignorant, sad to say, are many who depend on Quabbin's clear water for daily sustenance.

Aside from offering clean water to millions, this lake also provides ample opportunities for recreation – fishing and hiking in particular – although there are very strict regulations enforced on the lake and in the thousands of acres of surrounding watershed lands.

The history of this reservoir is worth appreciating as much as is its water and its recreational possibilities. Long before April 26, 1927, when the state legislature approved an act to

Aerial view of Quabbin Reservoir from the north

take the Swift River valley and create the Quabbin Reservoir, there were rumblings of massive changes to come in the valley. By 1895, rumors were rife in the area and by 1922 the first survey was made to provide information which would serve in construction of the reservoir.

The building of the reservoir was a direct outgrowth of Boston's quest for water. Ever since the Revolutionary War period, New England's largest city has had problems supplying itself with clean water. In the 1820s, the first comprehensive study of the problem was completed, and as a result Lake Cochituate, west of Boston, was turned into a reservoir by 1848.

This reservoir and others proved inadequate after 40 years, so another study was commissioned by the state board of health. From 1893-95, the study surveyed such possibilities as the Merrimac River, Lake Winnepesaukee, the Nashau River and the Ware and Swift rivers (as possible backup supplies). The construction of a reservoir on the Nashua River in Clinton was the recommended solution to the water problem. Land was soon purchased in Clinton, Boylston and West Boylston, and the Wachusett Reservoir was built by 1908. Aqueducts connected this reservoir with Lake Cochituate and the Sudbury River reservoir system. The Wachusett Reservoir proved to be adequate for little more than a decade.

A tremendous surge of population growth took place in the Boston metropolitan area around the turn of the century, and around this time the populace found itself surrounded by polluted rivers, filled with industrial wastes and with sewerage from riverside communities. To address this and related problems, the Metropolitan District Commission was created in 1919 and asked for a report on how to increase the supply of clean water available to Boston, Worcester and surrounding communities.

Reports in the 1920s recommended the construction of an aqueduct to connect the Ware River with the Wachusett Reservoir as well as the use of waters from the Swift River watershed, thus continuing the tendency of Boston to look westward for its water.

In 1926 the legislature passed the Ware River Act to provide for the construction of the aqueduct and impoundment of the Ware River. The villages of West Rutland, North Rutland, White Valley in Barre and Coldbrook Springs in Oakham were affected by the land-taking for this project.

On April 26, 1927, after much debate, the legislature passed the Swift River Act, which provided for the con-

Demolition of Swift River bridge, Enfield (1939 photograph)

struction of a reservoir in the Swift River valley and an aqueduct to connect this to the Ware River. A sum of $65,000,000 was appropriated to finance the project. Since the act meant destruction for the towns of Dana, Enfield, Greenwich and Prescott, and would affect towns around them, political and legal conflict resulted. The state of Connecticut went to court but in 1931 the U.S. Supreme Court ruled that Massachusetts was within its rights.

The exodus of the valley had already begun. In addition to ending the four towns, 36 miles of state highway were relocated and sixteen miles of railroad tracks were abandoned. About 2,500 persons living in 650 houses in the area were compelled to find new homes. A detailed survey of properties in the area, including photographs, was completed. (In 1982, a selection of the photographs was exhibited by the Massachusetts Historical Commission.)

A cemetery, called Quabbin Park Cemetery, was built in the town of Ware and 7,561 bodies previously buried in 34 cemeteries in the area taken for the reservoir were moved to the new cemetery, which is maintained by the MDC. At MDC headquarters in Belchertown, records of the old towns are maintained, and the Quabbin superintendent continues to serve as town clerk for the four eradicated towns.

Quabbin was created by erecting two large earth dams

with concrete cut-off walls: the Winsor Dam and Goodnough Dike (formerly Quabbin Dike), both named for engineers who worked on the project. The Winsor dam, named for Frank E. Winsor, is 2,640 feet long, rises 170 feet above the bed of the river and contains 4,000,000 cubic yards of earth fill. The Goodnough Dike, named for X.H. Goodnough and located approximately three miles east of Winsor Dam, is 2,140 feet long, rises 135 feet above the bed of old Beaver Brook and contains 2,500,000 cubic yards of fill.

The valley was empty by 1939 and the reservoir was filled by 1946. Twenty-eight people lost their lives during the course of construction. The Swift River Valley Historical Society, based in the Whitaker Clary House, New Salem, preserves the history of the Quabbin towns and their people.

Quabbin Reservoir impounds the run-off from 186 square miles of the Swift River watershed (including parts of Wendell, New Salem, Petersham, Orange and Athol) and from 98 square miles of the Ware River watershed. It has a capacity of 412 billion gallons. The reservoir is approximately 18 miles long with a water surface area of 38.6 square miles and a shore line of approximately 118 miles, not including the shore line of some 60 islands. The maximum depth of water in front of the dam is 150 feet and the average depth eight miles above the dam is approximately 90 feet. It is believed that this is one of the largest, if not the largest, reservoirs in the world constructed entirely for domestic water supply purposes.

Water from the Quabbin Reservoir and aqueduct system flows by gravity or is pumped through MDC's distribution system to the water mains of 34 municipalities which are members of the Metropolitan Water District. These members lie within a 15-mile radius of the state house. They are: Arlington, Belmont, Boston, Brookline, Cambridge, Canton, Chelsea, Everett, Lexington, Lynnfield Water District, Malden, Marblehead, Medford, Melrose, Milton, Nahant, Needham, Newton, Norwood, Peabody, Quincy, Revere, Saugus, Somerville, Stoneham, Swampscott, Wakefield, Waltham, Watertown, Wellesley, Weston, Winchester, Winthrop and Woburn. In addition, the MDC supplies all or a portion of the water supply to the following non-members: Chicopee, Clinton, Framingham, Leominster, Marlborough, Northborough, Southborough, South Hadley Fire District #1, Wilbraham and Worcester. (This long list is provided here with the hope that Quabbin users may become informed about the source of their water and will learn to appreciate and conserve that precious resource.)

Due to the high quality of the water impounded in the various reservoirs, and enforcement of sanitary rules in the watersheds, it is unnecessary to maintain and operate expensive water-purification works. Water supplied to MDC consumers is treated with small amounts of chlorine and ammonia as it enters the distribution system.

The forest resources of the Quabbin watershed yield between 3,000,000 and 4,000,000 board feet of timber a year cut from the 119,000-acre watershed. Areas are cut in accordance with strict conservation principles under the supervision of Bruce Spencer of New Salem, Quabbin forester. Proceeds of sales are used for management of the reservoir. In addition to timber and cordwood sales, there are permits issued to occasional pulp wood operations and to a firm which manufactures guard rail posts.

The MDC has argued for some years that the Quabbin Reservoir and its other existing water resources are inadequate to meet future needs, and it has been promoting diversion of water from the Connecticut River to the Quabbin (via the Northfield Mountain pumped storage powerhouse). Plans to divert water from Millers River or its tributaries to the Quabbin are also being studied, along with other alternatives, including a watershed management program which involves alteration of vegetation in the watershed (which could affect the local landscape). Conservationists and "home rule" activists in western and central Massachusetts, however, are seriously resisting the MDC plans, suggesting instead that people in Boston and environs conserve water, repair leaky water mains, and utilize sources closer to home. (Information for this section was extracted from J.R. Greene's "Atlas of the Quabbin Valley" and "The Creation of Quabbin Reservoir," and from MDC publications.) See also DANA, ENFIELD, GREENWICH, PRESCOTT, QUABBIN FISHERIES, QUABBIN RECREATION, QUABBIN VERSE, QUABBIN WILDLIFE.

Quabbin Verse

The tragedy of the lost Quabbin towns has been an inspiration to poets for several decades. Here are three samples, the first of which is the song written on the occasion of the final graduation from Greenwich High School. Its author is anonymous. The other verses are from writers each of whom has several books of published verse. J.R. Greene, who has spent all his life in Athol, is author of the "Atlas of the Quabbin

Valley" (1975) and "Creation of the Quabbin Reservoir" (1981). Brendan Galvin is a Cape Codder who has taken an interest in the Quabbin for more than two decades.

Greenwich Graduation Song

To our dear Greenwich we leave our love,
Our honor, loyalty and courage too
Our thoughts will linger here, tho' waters flow
O'er all our homes and farms and schoolhouse too.

Quabbin Reservoir

By J.R. Greene

The winds didn't shift but they blow over water,
after wafting the leaves and the birds for all years.
The rain is the joy of the men at the works,
for the herds and the plows are but thoughts in the waves.
No one works or prays or even sits and talks about
the news and the weather, or love, life and politics.
Fish are all who drink this here or those unknowing
and far away who waste and want but don't seem to save.

Roads go under and streams don't flow
in the bed of the sand and the stumps that serve as markers,
for they even pulled out the dead (so those would forget).
And they say some can't come here but others can,
if they have the right reasons five miles long,
or if they want to study the nothing and write all kinds
of nothing, just to leave behind nothing.

Still a few of us know what's beyond the foundations
and the rust in the pines and the endless water;
your home is your castle until everyone wants it,
then they just come in and take it and his and hers
and even theirs, and all the plants and soil and rocks.
A life means nothing to a lot of greed,
no matter that they could end up being handed
the exact sort of thing that they had demanded.

Enfield, Massachusetts
(Under Quabbin Reservoir)

By Brendan Galvin

Water lets nothing mark it. So, if you need
a preconceived direction, you can troll
down the laid-out streets.
7,000 souls transplanted with their stones.
But, in the knowledge that human work
is always partly done, a few bones go
uncollected. One thinks of a clavicle or two,
an ulna, nothing heavily sunken.
In the steady lean of inland tide
they are turning over, slow-motion parodies
of straws in a wind.
Trolling, lures hook and hang
on the snaggled teeth of a fence,
a lunatic bug collection. Bass coming home
won't close the gate, or keep the path
in deference to the lawn, ignore your shadow,
your rowing on the sky.

Quabbin Wildlife

In many ways the Quabbin reservation is ideal for wildlife. Its vast size and relative freedom from human disturbance make it a refuge unequaled by any other in the Commonwealth. Although visitors may walk most of the abandoned roads and trails, motorized vehicles are limited to a few roads at the southern end of the reservoir. The Prescott Peninsula (in New Salem) is closed to visitors; entry to this portion of land is only by special permit.

The Quabbin is particularly attractive to wildlife because of the great variety of habitat within the reservation. Here there are open fields, shrubby areas, moist seeps, wet meadows and woodlands, and all types of forest. And the area is constantly changing. Beaver are the prime engineers of change and there are many on the reservation. In building their dams, the beaver create ponds – many of them in woodlands. The flooded trees die, attracting insects which in turn attract woodpeckers, and which serve as food for many other birds, fish and amphibians. The woodpeckers create cavities which subsequently become nesting places for wood ducks and hooded mergansers, owls, squirrels and raccoons. The pond itself becomes habitat for insects and micro-organisms that require water, and for the animals that feed on those tiny plants and animals. Fish, frogs, salamanders, turtles and snakes are drawn to the area and they, in turn, attract wading birds. In time, the decaying trees fall and the pond gradually changes into a marshy area with open and emergent vegetation. Muskrats move into the area and associated with them, mink that prey on muskrats. Over thousands of years the marsh fills in and eventually the area becomes an open meadow – used by deer, rabbits, field mice and their associated predators, bobcats, foxes and birds of prey.

Elsewhere windstorms or infestations of insects may open pockets within the forest. Fallen trees provide escape cover; standing ones provide nest and den holes. Sunlight reaching the growth encourages growth of small plants and shrubs at a level animals can reach. When food is plentiful, animals are drawn to that area. Natural succession continues and vegetation grows from field to forest and is set back time and again all over the reservation.

In addition to beaver, muskrat and mink, visitors may come across otters along the banks of ponds and at the edges of the reservoir. In dry upland areas there are chipmunks, red and gray squirrels, snowshoe hare and both eastern and New England cottontails. The woods and old stone walls afford protection to a variety of weasels as they stalk their prey. The forest is home to an abundance of raccoons and to tree-gnawing porcupines. Occasionally a visitor may see a red or grey fox or even an eastern coyote. There are fishers, too, a tough-to-spot black and brown animal that attacks and eats porcupines among other prey. Their popular name, "fisher cat," is a misnomer as fishers are not felines but belong to the weasel family; the number of these unusual mammals increases as the forest matures. For the extremely silent and sharp-eyed observer there is the hope of catching sight of one of the Quabbin's secretive bobcats.

The reservoir itself attracts a wide variety of waterfowl, many nesting, others in migratory passage. Wood ducks and black ducks are common, and even the rarely-seen hooded merganser is relatively abundant. Green-winged teal and common mergansers, while not plentiful, also nest in the area. Few Canada geese nest on the reservation but they are plentiful during migration when large flocks of passing birds settle on the man-made lake en route to southern wintering areas. Other

Golden eagle and carrion

common migrants include scaup, goldeneye, ring-necked ducks and snow geese. Loons are rare at the Quabbin but during the last few years there have been successful nestings. They are sensitive to disturbance and may increase in the Quabbin reservation because of the availability of secluded areas. Other birds that seek out Quabbin because of the seclusion it affords include bald and golden eagles.

Bald eagles traditionally nest along the Maine coast and in southern Canada but in recent years a number of birds have been observed wintering at Quabbin. Baby bald eagles from elsewhere have been introduced by state scientists in the hope of boosting the local population. The eagles are easily disturbed and abandon an area readily if they are bothered or approached too closely. These magnificent birds soar over the reservoir where they feed on fish. When the reservoir is frozen they depend heavily on other animals for food but return to fish as soon as open water re-appears. Occasionally observers may see the eagles in flight from the Enfield lookout tower in Quabbin Park at the southern end of the reservoir. Visitors are cautioned, however, not to try to approach the birds as this may cause them to leave the area.

Golden eagles are comparative newcomers to Quabbin. To date there have been few documented sightings but it is known that two golden eagles were present at Quabbin during the last few winters. Like bald eagles, golden eagles may be watched from lookout points but should not be approached.

Other raptors (birds of prey) also find Quabbin to their liking. During the day visitors may observe red-tailed and red-shouldered hawks, broad-winged and rough-legged hawks, goshawks, marsh hawks, ospreys, and gliding turkey vultures. At night their hunting grounds are taken over by owls – great-horned owls, barred owls, saw-whet and screech owls.

Peregrine falcons, once common in Massachusetts but now endangered, pass through Quabbin on their migratory passage and the Commonwealth's only other resident falcon, the kestrel, is found in abundance.

Quabbin has also been the focus of efforts by the state's division of fisheries and wildlife to re-introduce the wild turkey to its erstwhile home. In 1960 division biologists re-introduced turkeys to the Prescott Peninsula, the most secluded section of Quabbin. Since that time the birds have multiplied and spread to other parts of the reservation where they are occasionally seen by visitors. Other upland game birds sharing the area with the turkey are woodcock and ruffed grouse.

Most visitors come to Quabbin to watch the smaller species. Because of Quabbin's vegetational variety there is something for everybody and almost all of the common species of Massachusetts have been recorded here at some time or other. In addition to the most common species, sharp-eyed birders may find red-headed and pileated woodpeckers, Canada jays, black-billed cuckoos, northern shrikes, and eastern bluebirds. Some 16 types of tiny colorful warbler have been recorded in the area. Birds requiring specialized habitat, such as the blue-gray gnatcatcher which nests in dense mature oak woods, or the pine warbler which nests only in large white pines, find suitable habitat on the reservation.

The areas change in plant composition and maturity and at any time the wildlife can find some area that provides suitable food and cover. Most important there is plenty of space and freedom from human disturbance; for wildlife this is the major attraction of Quabbin. (Adapted from "Quabbin Area Sportsman's Guide, second edition," by Ellie Horwitz.) See also BIRDS, QUABBIN RECREATION, QUABBIN RESERVOIR.

Radio

Only one radio station is located within the Mt. Grace Region – WCAT, with offices, studios and transmission tower all at 660 East Main St., Orange. The station broadcasts at 1390 kilocycles on the AM dial only during daylight hours. Its format has changed from time to time. As of this writing, the station plays mostly "oldies" from the 1940s, 1950s and early 1960s. It also plays contemporary country, disco and rock. Also offered are local news and opinion talk shows.

Residents of the region can usually receive AM and FM

radio stations from Fitchburg, Greenfield, Boston, Worcester, Hartford and other points. A National Public Radio affiliate, WFCR-FM, "Five College Radio" located on the campus of the University of Massachusetts, Amherst, broadcasts at 88.5 on the FM dial. Its programming includes educational programs, classical music, folk music and jazz, as well as the unique 90-minute news broadcast, "All Things Considered," aired daily at 5 p.m.

Restaurants

There is an abundance of eating places in the region ranging from early-morning breakfast haunts and busy lunch counters to pizza houses and dining spots. A few restaurants serve all day long, but most are open for only two meals, either breakfast and lunch, or lunch and supper.

For an evening out or a business lunch, most area residents tend to favor one of the following.

Athol Lobster House, 76 Traverse St., Athol, Tel. 249-6236; nautical motif; open for dinners Thursday through Sunday (bar open nightly); seafood, steaks and chops.

Athol Steak House, 14 Grove St., Athol, Tel. 249-8766; opposite the Uptown Common; cocktail lounge; lunch and dinner and Sunday buffet brunch.

Batch's Red Rooster, East Main Street, Orange, Tel. 544-3300; lunch and dinner; popular among senior citizens.

The Cupola, 29 West Main St., Orange, Tel. 544-2526; light, airy dining room in refurbished coach house; upstairs lounge; decor accented by plants and by woodwork crafted by local artisans; open daily at 11:30 a.m. (noon on Sundays).

Fox Run, Ward Hill Road, Phillipston, Tel. 249-8267; April to Thanksgiving; 5-9 weekdays, 5-10 Saturday, 12:30-8 Sunday, closed Tuesday; woodshed lounge; old farm setting.

French King Restaurant, French King Highway, Millers Falls, Erving, Tel. 413-659-3328; function room available.

King Phillip Restaurant, Athol Road, Phillipston, Tel. 249-6300; open for dinners Thursday through Sunday; bar open daily.

J & B Restaurant, 47 Daniel Shays Hwy., Orange, Tel. 544-2202; closed on Monday.

Pearl Island, West Orange Road at Route 78, Orange, Tel. 544-6854; Chinese and Polynesian specialties; located in unusual art deco building (formerly White Drum).

Pete and Henry's Cafe, Blossom Street, South Royalston, Tel. 249-9845; fried foods specialty; Thursdays through Saturdays from 4 p.m., Sunday from 1 p.m.

White Pillars, The Common, Petersham, Tel. 724-6646; somewhat formal.

Other eating places are:

Athol Pizza House, 518 Main St., Athol, Tel. 249-3762.

Auntie's Place, 475 East Main St., Orange, Tel. 544-7737; drive-up snack bar; outdoor tables.

Bald Eagle Motel, Daniel Shays Highway, Orange, Tel. 544-2101; breakfast only.

Box Car Restaurant, Route 2, Erving, Tel. 544-6992; in former railroad station; breakfast and lunch; dinner weekends and during hunting season.

Brothers Pizza, 449 Main St., Athol, Tel. 249-8755.

Cinnamon's Restaurant, 491 Main St., Athol, Tel. 249-6033; all three meals.

The Coffee Shoppe, 24 North Main St., Orange, Tel. 544-6851.

Common Pub, 326 East Main St., Orange, Tel. 544-7875; pizza, grinders, Italian specialties; full liquor license; open daily 11 a.m. to 11 p.m.

Cottage Restaurant, 7 West Main St., Erving, Tel. 544-8567; lunch only.

Country Duffer, Route 122, Petersham.

Dery's Drive-In, 360 East Main St., Orange, Tel. 544-2093; seasonal; outdoor tables.

Larry's Diner, 5 West Main St., Orange; breakfast and lunch; opens at 5 a.m.; adjacent to Mt. Grace Sportsplex.

Liz and John's Place, 567 Main St., Athol, Tel. 249-8400; breakfast and lunch.

Main Street Diner, 311 Main St., Athol, Tel. 249-8529; breakfast and lunch.

Maroni's Restaurant, 99 Hapgood St., Athol, Tel. 249-9847; breakfast, lunch and supper; featuring Italian foods, seafood and steaks; open Monday through Saturday.

Mary's Place, 544 Main St., Athol, Tel. 249-6298; breakfast and lunch.

New Salem Store and Restaurant, Daniel Shays Highway, New Salem, Tel. 544-7393; breakfast and lunch; closed Tuesday; home-made breads and pies and soups.

Norma's Restaurant, 1261 Chestnut St., Athol, Tel. 249-9534.

Omer's Lounge and Restaurant, Exchange Street, Athol.

Orange Bake Shop, 1 South Main St., Orange, Tel. 544-6102.

Orange House of Pizza, 1 East Main St., Orange, Tel. 544-2720.

Quabbin Gateway, Daniel Shays Highway, Orange, Tel. 544-2986.

Silver Front Cafe, 613 Main St., Athol, Tel. 249-4126; lunch specials.

Summit Restaurant, 1493 Main St., Athol, Tel. 249-7154.

Tool-Town Pizza, 246 Exchange St., Athol, Tel. 249-9828.

Village Snack and Dairy Bar, 111 Brookside Rd., Athol, Tel. 249-8005; seasonal; outdoor tables; soft and hard ice cream.

White Cloud, 627 East River St., Orange, Tel. 544-6821; across from airport; serving 6 a.m. to 3 p.m.; closed Monday.

River Rat Race

The River Rat Spectacular, perhaps the world's zaniest canoe race, has been a major annual event in the Mt. Grace Region since 1964.

Now established as a tradition for the first Saturday in April, the race pits pairs of canoeists from near and far competing for prize money as they paddle the five-mile stretch of the fast-moving icy Millers River from Athol to Orange.

More than a canoe race, the spectacular has become the basis of an annual springtime bacchanalia, the biggest party of

South Main Street bridge in Athol moments after the start of race

191

Canoeists paddle past spectators on riverbank off South Athol Road

the year for the citizens of Athol and its downstream neighbor, Orange.

The day begins at 10 a.m. with the River Rat Promenade, a catch-all parade featuring local dignitaries, police, firemen, high school musicians, floats and costumed characters. Canoeists start assembling in late morning and the race begins – usually with a shot from a cannon – at 1 p.m. just upstream from the South Main Street bridge in downtown Athol.

The start of the race is the zaniest moment of all, as the more than 300 canoeists attempt to work their way through the 30-foot-wide opening under the granite bridge. The beer starts to flow early in the day and a carnival mood is apparent on the river as well as on the riverbanks.

As many as a third of the entrants are in it just for the fun, and some of the paddlers hope to win half-serious wagers with their peers – oblivious of the official competition, which includes various categories and classes.

New Yorkers Bob Zaveral of Mt. Upton and Jeff Shultis of Oneonta hold the record for the event, completing the course in 35 minutes, 44 seconds, in 1981.

It all began at the end of winter in 1964 in an Athol barroom, the Silver Front, when two of the saloon's regulars, known as Whip and Sput, argued about who could beat whom in a race down the river. Before long, a race was organized, and in all 12 canoes made it to the river on March 21, 1964. The winners of the first race, Sonny Soucie and Art Forand, took 48 minutes, 45 seconds to make it to Hart's Landing in Orange. That year, as in most of the succeeding years, several of the entrants ended up in the drink! With the Millers River "polluted all to heck," as it says in the "Rat Pack Theme Song" (author anonymous), it has been de rigeur for those who get dunked to see a doctor for a tetanus shot!

The event has become an institution, with upwards of

Scene in Orange: aftermath of the race

10,000 spectators on hand. Viewing the race is an adventure in itself, and spectators crowd every conceivable viewing point – railroad trestles, riverbanks, overhanging trees and rooftops. After the start, many spectators hightail it for their cars to make their way to such good viewing spots as the bridge on Daniel Shays Highway, the grassy riverbank off South Athol road, or the finishing point just upstream from the South Main Street bridge in Orange.

An entry fee is charged, with the prize money coming from those funds. The race is coordinated by River Rat Spectacular, Inc. (c/o Harriet Ellsworth, Mill Road, Barre MA 01005), in cooperation with the Athol Daily News.

Rodney Hunt Co.

Because the treatment of human wastes is a subject matter that is not ordinarily a topic of polite conversation, the inner workings of sewage treatment plants is hardly a matter of general public knowledge. Most people know what a flush toilet is, but how many know what a sluice gate is? Nowadays, you can't have one without the other!

One of this area's most important industries, the Rodney Hunt Co. of Orange, plays a crucial role in the manufacture of equipment for the successful treatment of sewage containing human and industrial waste. For this reason, Rodney Hunt's workers can be proud of the job they are doing in combatting pollution and keeping America healthy.

Sluice gates – the massive sliding doors that somewhat resemble garage doors – are the main product manufactured by Rodney Hunt at its plant on the banks of Millers River. Approximately 600 workers are employed at the company, which has successfully resisted the recent downward turn in the na-

193

tional economy. In fact, the company will be providing equipment for the large new treatment plant being constructed by New York City on the banks of the Hudson River.

Other important Rodney Hunt products are industrial rolls and custom castings. The rolls, made of cast iron, stainless steel, aluminum, brass or bronze, are used in many industries, especially those using web conveyance machinery. Products made of paper, plastic, textile, steel and rubber, for example, use industrial rolls.

The castings are produced at the company's modern gray iron foundry. "Why is that almost every prospective customer who visits our foundry becomes a repeat customer?" asks a company pamphlet. "Maybe it is the difference in dedication to quality that they can sense in our people, or maybe it is the fact that they have never seen such a clean, well-maintained installation." The castings are used in machine tools, paper machines and other industrial equipment.

Rodney Hunt, the company founder, came to Orange in 1840 after spending his early years in Ashburnham and Winchendon. He became a millwright and went into business for himself, initially manufacturing plows for farmers. Because of the existence of a small textile fulling or carding mill in the area, he found a ready market for rolls and fulling mills as well as waterwheels.

During the Civil War, Rodney Hunt manufactured equipment for mills in Athol which were experiencing an upsurge in business because of the Union Army's demand for wool fabric.

Rodney Hunt Co. buildings and railroad tracks in Orange

A year later, he established a machine shop and foundry in Athol along the Millers River, and following the success of the business, the Rodney Hunt Machine Co. was incorporated in 1873. Following a fire in the winter of 1882, the company was relocated in Orange.

During the 1930s, the company pioneered the use of stainless steel in the fabrication of textile machinery, and in the 1940s its Water Control Apparatus Division was formed – an outgrowth of the company's previous involvement with water power. Sluice gates originally were used in facilities that depended on water power. In the early 1950s, Rodney Hunt branched out into the process equipment field with its "turbafilm" processor, a thin film evaporator, used in the production of instant coffee and fruit concentrates, but this division was sold in the 1960s when the company evaluated its markets and opportunities for growth.

Cost-effective water control equipment is Rodney Hunt's main business, with customers in more than 48 countries – both municipal and industrial applications involving water pollution control systems and hydroelectric power plants.

Athol's Lake Rohunta, as the name implies, is owned by Rodney Hunt Co., and the lakeshore Pine Beach there is maintained as a recreation area for employees.

Royalston

Royalston is a sparsely-populated traditional rural community with a significant percentage of "newcomers" who arrived in the 1970s and 1980s. Two population clusters exist – in the center around the common and in South Royalston around the remains of abandoned industrial buildings – but many of the townspeople live in widely-dispersed homes, old and new, along more than 70 miles of curved, hilly country roads.

One of the town's best-known natural features is Doane's Falls, a popular scenic attraction and swimming hole. Less known but equally scenic are Spirit Falls and Royalston Falls.

Royalston is also admired for its unique well-preserved historic common, location of a graceful slate-roofed town hall and the First Congregational Church with its tall steeple (replaced after it was toppled in a storm in the 1938 hurricane), along with many handsome residences exhibiting the classical beauty of Federal and Greek Revival architecture.

Royalston is located in Worcester County, bordered on the

north by Richmond and Fitzwilliam, N.H., on the east by Winchendon, on the south by Templeton, Phillipston and Athol and on the west by Orange and Warwick.

The town's land area is 41.99 square miles – placing it 29th in size among the state's 351 cities and towns. Its population is 955 and the population density is 23 persons per square

Royalston barn-raisers use time-tested timber-frame method

Aerial view of historic Royalston Common including town hall

mile. Royalston is one of some 40 towns in the state with a population under 1,000. The town's population jumped by 18 percent in the 1970s, and continual gradual growth is expected.

Royalston's terrain is rugged, with elevations running to 1,361 atop White Hill in the west and 1,015 feet at the Common, dropping to about 800 feet at the edge of Millers River in South Royalston. Royalston's soil is mostly rough and stony with some areas of loam.

Many residents have gardens and keep small amounts of livestock. There are a few commercial farms, including one large dairy farm on Athol-Richmond Road, owned by Bert Bartlett. Small subsistence farming was important throughout the town's history and considerable effort has been made recently by newcomers to revive old farms or carve new farms out of woodland. Royalston's agricultural heritage is reflected in active Grange and Junior Grange organizations.

The town is mostly forested, including Royalston State Forest, part of Otter River State Forest, flood control land controlled by the U.S. Army Corps of Engineers, part of the Birch Hill Wildlife Management Area controlled by the Division of Fisheries and Wildlife of the Massachusetts Department of Environmental Management as well as many tracts owned by conservation trusts, corporations and non-residents. Cutting of trees for lumber and cordwood is a factor in the economic life of the community, and an active town Conservation Commission is attempting to monitor the logging so that restrictive laws are not flouted. Permanent sawmill operations include the Walter Hubbard Lumberyard on Athol-Richmond Road and the Putney Mill on North Fitzwilliam Road near the state line.

Aside from the Millers River, major streams in town include the east branch of Tully River, Lawrence Brook and Priest Brook.

Royal-shire, as the town was initially called, was settled by six families in 1762 and was incorporated as the town of Royalston on Feb. 19, 1765. The town was named after the Hon. Isaac Royal, a Tory who donated money and land for the settling of the town and whose portrait is displayed in the town hall (though he did not reside in Royalston). Royal lived in Charlestown, later moving to Medford, and served those communities in public office before sailing off to England in 1776 when the Revolution broke out. Royalston, unlike some other towns in the state, did not change its name despite its patriotism and revolutionary fervor.

Royalston experienced growth in the late 1700s and early 1800s as a result of the harnessing of water power, leading to the establishment of local tanneries, grist and saw mills and potash works. The population grew from 617 in 1776 to 1,243 in 1880. Agriculture, including the raising of sheep, was the chief means of livelihood for the town's early settlers.

In the early 1800s, industries began to develop in the area of the Common, including grist mills, brickyards, tanneries, a hattery and cabinet shops. The waters of Little Pond, west of the Common, were diverted from their natural outlet and carried around by a canal through a hollow north of the Common, furnishing water power for several shops, the most important being a cabinet shop owned by Joseph Sawyer.

Among Royalston's most famous sons were two who became state governors in the latter half of the 19th century – Alexander Bullock who served as governor of Massachusetts and Asabel Peck who served as governor of Vermont. The two lived near one another as small children, but Peck's family moved to Vermont.

Alexander Bullock was the son of Rufus Bullock, who had become the wealthiest man in the town and had built one of the grandest houses on the common. This house later became known as the home of Gov. Bullock. In the early 20th century, the Bullock residence was purchased by the Donald Hill family, which used it as a weekend and summer home. Indeed, the grand houses of the Common became used primarily as summer homes for much of this century, with some of them eventually falling into a state of disrepair. In recent years, several of the houses changed hands, and their new owners have pursued a program of preservation and restoration, bolstered by the creation of historic district by-laws in 1980.

The village of South Royalston was established from parts of Athol and Gerry (now called Phillipston). By 1812, South Royalston had its own mills and small businesses, creating a community (sometimes called South Village) somewhat separate from the rest of the town – a division that has endured even to this day. Among South Royalston's industries were a cotton and woolen mill, furniture shops and a company that made shoe pegs. South Royalston had two advantages which influenced both business and population – its natural water power and the railroad line – creating a natural opportunity for growth. (In 1982, the town appropriated funds to further a study of hydropower on Millers River in South Royalston through possible refurbishing of an old dam.) During the turn of the century, many immigrants came and settled in the village, among them a large segment of Finnish people, some of whom still make their homes in the South Village. Irish immigrants were also among the newcomers, leading to the establishment of a Catholic church in the community – the church remains today under the jurisdiction of the Athol parish.

Although there were several small industrial concerns, only one large manufacturing business figures in the town's economic history. That was the American Woolen Co., located in South Royalston on the same site as the first Royalston Cot-

Lane traversing pine woods off Turnpike Road in Royalston

199

Grange Youth member awaits start of soapbox derby at village fair

ton & Wool Manufacturing Co. established in 1812. The textile manufacturing operation on that site was the basis for the fortune of Royalston's most successful businessman, Rufus Bullock, who worked as a schoolteacher and farmer before becoming a country merchant. Along with Silas Coffin, Bullock owned the Royalston Cotton & Wool Manufacturing Co., but when the textile mile burned in 1833, Bullock became the sole proprietor. He then built what became known as the stone mill, with four sets of woolen looms, and continued to operate the place until his death in 1858, building up a large fortune and becoming active as well in public affairs and philanthropy. His wealth and status paved the way for the political success of

The Dillon-Durant homestead in West Royalston

his son, Alexander Bullock.

After Rufus Bullock's death, the mill changed hands several times and eventually became the property of the Whitney family, but fire struck again in 1892. In the early 1900s, the facility, then known as the American Woolen Co., was expanded on both sides of the Millers River to a total of 82 looms and 150 workers. Its main line was bed blankets "of a fine quality," according to Lilley Caswell's history of the town.

In 1928 the Great Depression closed the mill, which was subsequently bought by Mason and Parker Co. of Winchendon, engaging in the manufacture of toys, beach chairs and other products. Then fire struck again, on March 25, 1939, destroying the mill and putting the company out of business. All that remains is a tall chimney surrounded by foundation ruins overgrown with brush. Saved from the original set of buildings was a storage shed, now part of Pete and Henry's Cafe, Royalston's only eating establishment, which specializes in fried foods and is one of the few restaurants in Massachusetts that serves frogs legs.

Royalston's population peaked at 1,667 in 1840, but by the late 1800s, its decline as an industrial center had begun and today virtually no manufacturing takes place in Royalston. Currently, the occupations of the town's populace, as surveyed in 1980 on the basis of the town street list, showed over a third of the adults working as laborers or service-providers ("blue collar"). About one-third of the adults are homemakers or are retired. Approximately 14 percent are professionals or students in higher education.

Zoning was established in the mid-1970s, emphasizing protection of the town's rural character. The "Residential District" covers the South Village, where 40 percent of the population resides. The town's few businesses are located here, including Pete and Henry's and White's General Store. The "Historic Residential District" includes Royalston Center, and this zone is subject to regulation by the Historic District Commission. The "Rural, Residential and Agricultural District" includes the remainder of Royalston's territory. Except for some home businesses, construction trades, logging and farming, Royalston has little economic activity of its own; most of its residents work in other towns, especially Athol and Gardner, with a few commuting considerable distances to Boston and other eastern Massachusetts communities. See also ANGEL GABRIEL, BIRCH HILL DAM, CHASE MEMORIAL, DOANE'S FALLS, JACOB HILL, OLD ROYALSTON SCHOOLHOUSE, SPIRIT FALLS, ROYALSTON FALLS, TULLY DAM AND LAKE and ZITA.

Royalston Falls

Royalston Falls, located in a remote part of West Royalston off a poorly-maintained dirt road (Falls Road) near the New Hampshire border, is contained in a 205-acre tract owned by Trustees of Reservations, the Milton-based conservation group chartered in 1891 to preserve for the public "beautiful and historic places and tracts of land" within Massachusetts.

Prof. Edward Hitchcock, in his "Geology of Massachusetts" published in 1841, described the falls, then located on the farm of Calvin Forbes and popularly known for many years as Forbes Falls, as "one of the finest indeed in the state." Hitchcock wrote: "The stream is not more than ten feet wide at the spot, but it descends 45 feet at a single leap into a large basin, which from its top had been excavated by the erosion of the water. The sides, to the height of 50 or 60 feet, are formed of solid rocks; now retreating; now projecting; crowned at their summits by trees. Many of these lean over the gulf, or have fallen across it; so that upon the whole, the scene is one of great wildness and interest."

At one time, the owner of the property "improved" the surroundings by building a railing around the falls, with a flight of stairs to go below them, and seats, tables and swings in the grove adjoining. The place was visited by thousands every

Royalston Falls in winter is a massive ice sculpture

season, and for many years, an annual town picnic was held there with musical entertainment, attracting residents of several surrounding towns.

Today, the old staircase is gone, although the Trustees of Reservations recently installed a cable railing on one edge of the precipitous chasm. Access to the very bottom of the falls requires a roundabout hike and a wade or swim upstream a short distance.

The rock formations, smooth and rounded, are dramatic

and interesting, and the moss and ferns growing on the sides of the precipice add to the attraction. The Falls is reached by a relatively easy hike of approximately 15 minutes from the parking area near the top of a steep hill, approximately three miles from the intersection of Falls Road and Route 68. This road is poorly maintained. Visitors without the appropriate vehicle may find it advisable to drive no more than two miles up Falls Road, walking the remaining distance. A trail to the falls starts at the small parking area (on the left), which is designated by a sign posted by the Trustees of Reservations. Access is also possible from the Newton Cemetery on Route 32 along the Metacomet-Monadnock Trail, a hike of approximately 30 minutes each way. This is not an outing for small children. See also METACOMET-MONADNOCK TRAIL.

Royalston State Forest

Royalston State Forest consists of two undeveloped tracts of land covering 776 acres of rugged terrain in the western part of Royalston. The larger of the two parcels lies on either side of Falls Road, running in an "L" shape southwesterly from the New Hampshire border. The other portion is on either side of Route 32 near Butterworth Road.

The Falls Road tract includes trails for hiking, cross-country skiing and snowmobiling. Royalston Falls is nearby. The Royalston quadrant topographical map indicates this forest's boundaries. See also ROYALSTON FALLS.

Sentinel Elm

The site in Orange near the Athol line of the old Sentinel Elm, also called Indian Signal Elm, is marked with a plaque on a boulder on what is now the Julius Gordon farm, Moore Hill Road. A roadside sign, part of the Athol History Trail, is nearby. As described by Beatrice M. Miner in her "History of Orange," a fort erected on this hilltop was "a safety haven for them if attacked by Indians who called it West Payquage Hill, on which stood the Sentinel Elm for over 200 years until October 1931 when it gave up to the elements, having been struck by lightning, enduring many terrific windstorms and gradual decay. Mr. Frank McManamy helped Grandpa Moore saw off the tree following the lightning bolt."

The plaque states: "Site of Sentinel Elm. Lookout of Nipmuck Indians and settlers, located on Pequoiag Hill, Orange,

downed by high winds Oct. 26, 1931. We, the Margery Morton
Chapter of the Daughters of the American Revolution with the
Orange and Athol Historical Societies set this boulder in
memory of its contribution to history. October 26, 1969."

The D.A.R. published a book about the landmark, and it
was the subject of a J.F. Gilman painting once available in a
popular post card reproduction. Some residents of the area
own relics of wood from the fallen elm.

Services

Many specialized services are available in each of the
towns of the region – not only the commercial centers of Athol
and Orange but in the smaller towns as well. The range of
skills and talents is impressive.

Some of these services are provided by professionals whose
places of businesses are well-advertised, while others are self-
employed or part-time workers who depend on word of mouth
or the casual distribution of their business cards in order to obtain customers. For the purposes of this guidebook, newspaper
advertisements were placed to invite individuals to place a
listing here, free of charge, but response was limited. In order
to ensure a more complete listing in future editions of this
guidebook, the publisher invites written submissions to be
sent to Millers River Publishing Co., Box 159, Athol MA 01331.

For access to services not listed here, the reader is advised
to consult such sources as newspaper classified advertisements, telephone "yellow pages" listings and bulletin
boards that can be found in various business establishments
such as country stores, diners and agricultural supply
outlets. The Millers River Trade Service, listed below under
"Barter," is another excellent source of information about
available services. The reader is also advised to check listings
under ARTS AND CRAFTS and FARM PRODUCTS and other
categories in this guidebook. In any case, it should be
understood that the following is a partial listing:

BAIT – Lake Mattawa Bait Shack, Steve and Helen
Holmes, proprietors; 350 Holtshire Rd., Orange MA 01364;
Tel. 544-6377.

BARTER – Millers River Trade Service, a project of the
Millers River Center for Regional Self-Reliance, Mark Shoul,
New Boston Road, South Royalston MA 01331, Tel. 249-9222;
skills and goods exchanges, apprenticeship program, garden
exchange, tutor-learning exchange, share-a-home; more than

100 items listed; "founded on the belief that the economic development of our region does not depend entirely on politicians and big government, but rather is closely related to our own abilities to discover and extract, in the most efficient way possible, the greatest amount of value from the resources that exist right in front of us."

BUFFET CATERING – Katherine Whittier, 83 Union St., Athol, Tel. 249-8250; everything homemade; also pickles, jams, jellies, pastry, fudge.

BUILDERS – Skip Ciccarelli, Athol-Richmond Road, Royalston, mail to RFD 2, Athol MA 01331, Tel. 249-2605; woodworking and ceramic tile specialties; Dibble and Imhoff, carpenters, Box 77, Wendell MA 01380, Tel. 544-2663; Tom Musco, timber framing, Royalston MA 01368, Tel. 249-9633.

CARPENTRY AND DESIGN – Corey Jones, Moosehorn Road, New Salem, Tel. 544-2696; new homes, remodeling, additions, sunspaces, masonry.

CLOWN – "The Waffle Clown," Joshua J. Dostis, Neilson Rd., New Salem, mail to RFD #1, Orange MA 01364, Tel. 544-2822; parties, performances, promotion and workshops; topics include theater, musical instruction, waffle-making, cartoons and lettering, solar tree house design and construction, movement games, model building, clowning; free brochure on request.

GUNS – Buck's Gun Shop, Wendell Road, Warwick Star Route, Orange MA 01364, Tel. 544-3513, Floyd Foster, proprietor; new and used guns, ammunition, accessories, antique guns.

LUMBER – Steve Kurkoski, Hard To Find Lumber, Wendell Road, HCR W177, Warwick MA 01364; extra-wide or extra-long hard and soft lumber; specializing in table tops.

PLANING – Petersham Lumber Co., William E. Pajak, proprietor, East St., Petersham , Tel. 724-6647.

RESTORATION CARPENTRY – Timber Frame Co., Robert Gravley and Jerry Marcanio, proprietors, Butterworth Road, Royalston, mail via RFD 2, Orange MA 01364, Tel. 249-4643; specialists in restoration and reproduction of period architecture including colonial, Federal, Greek Revival and Victorian; exterior and interior work; consultations.

SHARPENING – Putnam's Saw Shop, R.H. Putnam, proprietor, 86 High St., Orange MA 01364, Tel. 544-6970; saws and tools, carbide work, complete sharpening service, tooth replacement.

SIGNS – Sunset Signs, Kathy Rice, proprietor, 35 Creamery Hill Rd., Orange, Tel. 249-6797; specializing in interior signs, showcards, banners, catering to the smaller businesses, also magnetic signs and license plates.

SILK-SCREENING – Shoul-Suyenaga Designs, New Boston Road, South Royalston MA 01331, Tel. 249-9222; hand silk-screened canvas bags, stationery and cards, T-shirts, other gift items.

TIBETAN RUG SALES – Tashi Ling Tibetan Rugs, Dan and Esther Shepardson, 115 Templeton Rd., Athol, Tel. 249-4469; and Bill and Sally Shepardson, Blake Corner Road, Phillipston, Tel. 249-6351; Oriental rugs from the Himalayas handknotted by Tibetans in Nepal; 100 percent wool with cotton warp; stock of 3 ' by 6 ' rugs plus special orders.

WOOD HEAT – Clean Sweep Chimney Cleaning Co., Tim Fisk, proprietor, Orange, Tel. 544-2655; chimney inspections and cleaning, stove installations and repairs; White and Blue Cloud #1, Joseph St. Hilaire, proprietor, 140 Mt. Pleasant St., Athol, Tel. 249-9145; chimney building, repairs and cleaning; stainless steel and fire clay liner installations.

Shays Rebellion

The name of Capt. Daniel Shays of Pelham is known to most area residents in connection with the highway (Route 202) that runs along the western edge of the Quabbin Reservoir. In fact, Daniel Shays Highway runs near the very birthplace of the man who gave his name to an important though often-neglected event in early American history: the Shays Rebellion of 1786-87.

The peace of 1783 let the American army disband, but the troops were paid in paper money of little value. At the close of the Revolutionary War, the state of Massachusetts had accumulated debts and thus imposed taxes upon people who did not have the means to pay them or their rising debts. Commercial and banking interests supported by the state government headquartered in Boston began closing in on the region's small farmers, using judicial process. Widespread foreclosures and jailings were a result.

Discontent mounted until in 1786 approximately 12,000 men, many of whom had fought British tyranny, rose up to oppose their new oppressors. In search of armaments, approximately 2,000 insurgents led by Shays marched to the federal arsenal at Springfield which was filled with muskets, cannons and ammunition. (The Springfield Armory is now a U.S. historic park and is open to visitors.)

The attack failed and the insurgents withdrew, with government troops under Gen. Benjamin Lincoln in pursuit. The Shaysites, as they were called, traveled through Amherst and Pelham across land that now lies under Quabbin Reservoir, stopping in Petersham to set up camp as a raging winter storm ensued. On that night (Feb. 3, 1787), Lincoln and his men departed Hadley and traveled 30 miles through the storm to arrive in Petersham Sunday morning to surprise the embattled farmer-soldiers at breakfast.

Shays and about 150 of his men were taken prisoner; the others fled northward through Orange, Warwick and West Royalston and across the line into New Hampshire. Warwick historian Charles Morse has researched a specific local angle, as recorded in Beatrice Miner's "History of Orange":

"About 300 of Shays' followers fled down the hill to Athol, and on through Orange to Warwick, until they reached the old 'Goldsbury Tavern' kept by Col. James Goldsbury, where they were given food and shelter, as many as he could house. The others were sent to Asa Conant's about a mile farther north. Soon after the men left Warwick, Col. Goldsbury was arrested by the government for high treason and charged with conspiring with others to overthrow the government. There are no authentic records of the trial, but testimony showed that while Col. Goldsbury sympathized with Shays' men, he was paid for everything and for hay and grain the horses had. Because he was paid for service rendered, he gained acquittal and continued as innkeeper."

Though some men from area towns participated in the insurgency, many townspeople were only sympathizers and did not agree with the taking up of arms. Voters showed their sympathy in 1787 when the incumbent Gov. James Bowdoin was defeated by John Hancock, who was expected to show clemency and issue pardons. All the accused men who gave the oath of allegiance were taken back into citizenship; among them were numerous residents of area communities whose oaths were found in the state archives by Athol historian William Lord. Rebellion leaders who had been convicted and sentenced to be hanged were pardoned after a few months' probation.

Many historians believe that the Shays rebellion was a factor leading to the more conservative mood when the U.S. Constitution was written, as indicated in various provisions protecting the new American government from what was seen as "the rabble." The Shays Rebellion became a post-Revolutionary symbol of the ongoing rebellious American spirit while simultaneously its suppression became a symbol of the commitment of the American government to protecting and maintaining its authority. It's no wonder, then, that the naming of the highway after Shays engendered minor controversy. (Quabbin Highway was another suggested name, but in the end there was no vocal objection to naming the roadway after local upstart/hero Shays.)

Shays Rebellion also serves as a reminder of the independent spirit of small farmers and of the long history of mistrust of residents of central and western Massachusetts of the Boston-based state government.

Sheep and Wool

Sheep became an important part of New England agriculture in the mid-1800s. Wool was the reason. With the invention of the power loom in 1824, U.S. mills competed successfully with their British counterparts and the industry flourished. There were hundreds of thousands of sheep being raised in Massachusetts, but the sheep business began to fall apart soon thereafter as the midwest was opened up to migration.

In recent years sheep raising ceased being an important part of the region's agriculture and became a peculiar, picturesque and generally unprofitable farm activity.

The raising of sheep seems to be on the rise again around Massachusetts. Purebred sheep can be sold for breeding stock, weavers appreciate natural yarns, and lambs are sold anytime but especially at Easter for traditional ethnic dinners. There is a New England Wool Pool located in nearby Northampton. Some money can be earned from selling the sheepskins of slaughtered animals and from selling manure.

Following are some area farms that raise sheep:

Karl Bittenbender, 110 Athol Rd., North Orange, Tel. 249-3026.

Jason's Fleece, Fred and Sue Hellen, proprietors, Turnpike Road, Petersham, Tel. 249-4238; natural yarns, including heathers and tweeds; tanned hides, carseats, bicycle seats, lambs for freezers, fleece for spinning.

George Northrop and Kathleen Collins, Ward Road, Royalston, Tel. 249-4407, registered Romney ram at stud, Romney and Romney cross fleece.

Tom and Paula Duston, Tully Road, Orange, Tel. 249-6242; natural wool yarn, raw wool, blankets, sheepskins.

Victor's Farm, Victor and Sandy Superchi, proprietors, Daniel Shays Highway, New Salem, Tel. 544-6679.

Shopping

The downtown shopping districts of Athol and Orange, like those of many New England communities, have been struggling to survive in recent years as customers are won away (helped by the convenience of automobile travel) to distant shopping districts and especially the ubiquitous malls.

Owners of the stores on main shopping streets of the two communities work hard to please their customers, who come from throughout the region. These owners of small businesses, against increasingly difficult odds, strive to play an important role in the life of the community (which suffers each time a storefront becomes empty). Local merchants offer personalized service, a willingness to fill special orders for merchandise not on their shelves and a smalltown amiability that cannot be matched at any cavernous mall store.

In 1982 a new Greater Athol-Orange Chamber of Commerce was formed with a growing membership of merchants, professionals and industrialists. The Chamber has a professional executive vice president and is striving to promote area business and industry. Its office is located at 465 Main St., Athol MA 01331, Tel. 249-3849.

In addition to the typical collection of stores carrying basic merchandise – hardware, clothing, stationery, drugs and so on – Athol and Orange have several supermarkets (all locally-owned) as well as numerous neighborhood food stores and convenience stores, some of which successfully compete with the supermarkets in terms of price and quality. These "mom and pop" outlets offer their customers the convenience of neighborhood shopping and personal attention plus late-night and Sunday hours.

A portion of the area's residents favor cooperative buying for food. Two small coops or buying clubs are:

New Salem Food Coop; information available from Ellie Voutselas, Tel. 544-7535.

Flower Hill Coop, Warwick; information available from Nancy Kamerer, Tel. 544-2919.

Country stores, offering local residents friendly convenient service, can be found in Petersham, Wendell, Wendell Depot, South Royalston, Phillipston, Warwick and Erving. For the visitor or Sunday joy-rider, a country store can be a pleasant oasis. See also ARTS AND CRAFTS, TRADITIONS.

Solar Greenhouse

The experimental Wintergreen Cooperative Solar Greenhouse, 58 Logan Ave., Orange, is one of the largest solar greenhouses in the northeast and is one of the most unusual buildings in the area. The structure is 124-ft. by 24-ft. and was built with the goal of providing organically-grown vegetables for sale year-round to members and the community at large.

Members of this non-profit corporation range from elderly local gardeners to "New Age" solar energy enthusiasts who travel an hour or more to participate in volunteer activities. In comments made at the 1979 groundbreaking, State Rep. Bill Benson called the project a "wise use of taxpayers' money." Former education/outreach coordinator Richard Asinof described the greenhouse as "a wonderful example of how appropriate solar technology works." Wintertime temperatures on sunny days reach into the 80s while it is freezing outside. However, there have been various problems with the construction from the outset and only some of these have been solved. Funding is a critical issue, although the greenhouse has already received tens of thousands of dollars in grants from the National Center for Appropriate Technology and other agencies.

For a few years, seedlings were raised for sale to the public and hundreds of area residents, young and old, attended educational programs. However, in 1983, waning interest on the part of members and the public along with lack of funds (as federal largesse ended) led to the closing of the facility.

Spirit Falls

Spirit Falls, owned by Harvard Forest, flows down Jacob Hill about one mile west of the Royalston Common. Its water, cascading along steep cliffs through a densely wooded area and finally into Long Pond on the east branch of the Tully River, comes from Little Pond at the edge of the Common.

The falls and 68 acres of surrounding land was given to Harvard Forest in 1963 by Mrs. Charles T. Brues in memory of Dr. Charles T. Brues, a Harvard University entomologist.

Easiest access to Spirit Falls is by means of a mile-long forest roadway (no vehicles allowed) that runs north from Doane's Hill Road, Royalston, just east of the little bridge crossing the east branch of the Tully River at the base of the

Doane's Hill. There is a gate across the road at this point, which is near the place in the river where canoeists launch their craft to paddle upstream to Long Pond. The forest roadway narrows into a footpath leading to a brook; it is a steep hike following the brook upstream along the hillside to the falls. There are several smaller cascades below the high falls. The falls can also be reached along a forest road from Route 68 near the bottom of "Jacob's Ladder." The falls is indicated on the Royalston quadrant topographical map. See also HARVARD FOREST, JACOB HILL and TULLY DAM AND LAKE.

Sports

Dozens of team and individual sports are enjoyed by residents of the region. The best-attended and most talked-about athletic events include the River Rat Spectacular canoe race from Athol to Orange on the first Saturday in April and the "Turkey Day" football competition between Athol High School and Ralph C. Mahar Regional School on Thanksgiving Day.

Interscholastic sports competition includes the following: football, field hockey, volleyball, soccer, cross country, basketball, baseball, softball, track and field, golf and tennis. "Boosters" groups in area towns support high school athletics.

The Mt. Grace Sportsplex (7 West Main St., Orange, Tel. 544-7844) offers Nautilus physical fitness equipment, racquetball and aerobic dance.

At the YMCA, athletic activites include league sports: youth basketball, youth soccer and men's basketball. The Y also sponsors a youth swim team, a girls' gymnastic team, a running club and a girls' synchronized swimming club. The Y also provides tennis and karate instruction; basketball, tennis, racquetball and squash tournaments; exercise, weight training and girls' gymnastic classes and non-league volleyball and basketball competition for men over 30. Special features include physical fitness testing and "The Y's Way to a Heathy Back" course.

The Orange Recreational Association sponsors seasonal sports for boys and girls, including soccer, basketball, softball and baseball.

There is Little League and Babe Ruth team competition in Athol and Orange, and for adult men there are teams in the Starrett League and Pequoig League. The Pequoig Softball

League has eight 18-player teams which compete the first week of May through mid-July, with playoffs in August. In addition, teams participate in an invitational Labor Day tournament. One representative per team forms the league's board of directors.

The Pequoig Bowmen's Club has a clubhouse and archery

Athol High School athlete shows his determination

range off South Athol Road.

Snowmobile enthusiasts are organized in two different groups, Quabbin Snowmen, Inc. (secretary: Frances O'Brien, Tel. 724-3308) and the Sno-Snoopers Snowmobile Club, Inc. (secretary: Lunette Prue, Tel. 544-3144).

Founded in 1955, the Twin County Horseshoe League has 10 teams from Athol, Orange, Shelburne Falls, Leyden, Erving, Winchendon, Turners Falls and Gardner. The league, which is sanctioned by the National Horseshoes Pitchers' Association, is open to the public. Participants compete one night a week May through September. Bernard Barnes of Orange, a member of the Orange Peels team, is league vice president.

The Orange Gun Club, Inc., was founded in 1884. Its headquarters is the former Kellogg Pasture, about 80 acres, off West River Street, with a clubhouse built in 1958. Facilities include rifle and pistol ranges. Activities include fishing and target and trap shooting. Other clubs dedicated to hunting and fishing include the Athol Rod and Gun Club (secretary-treasurer: Ralph Lundquist, Hardwick Road, Petersham, Tel. 724-3476), which has a clubhouse off Pinedale Avenue, and the Royalston Road and Gun Club, with facilities in South Royalston. The North Worcester County Quabbin Anglers Association (P.O. Box 79, Athol MA 01331) is one of the largest organizations in the area, with more than 400 members. The Millers River Beagle Club, Inc., (president: Leslie Barnes, 544-6081) maintains a clubhouse and fenced-in woodland area in Orange for training and periodic field trials of rabbit-hunting dogs. Large amounts of acreage in state-owned forest land and wildlife management is open to hunting. There is state-sponsored stocking of pheasants in the area as well as stocking of trout in lakes and streams.

Public tennis courts are available in Orange at Butterfield Park and in Athol at Fish Park and Silver Lake Park. Information on these facilities is available in each town from the town clerk.

Lessons in scuba diving are given at the YMCA, and this sport is practiced by the Athol Frogmen (Valmore Willhite, president, Tel. 249-2033). Brendon Crumb, an accomplished scuba-diving instructor and underwater photographer, operates Cap'n Crumb's Scuba Center, 535 South Main St., Orange, Tels. 544-2070 or 544-2678, listed as an International Training Facility of the Professsional Association of Diving Instructors.

There are two golf courses in the area, both privately owned but open to the public. Ellinwood Country Club, 1928 Pleasant St., Athol, Tel. 249-9836, with an 18-hole course, is operated by an elected board of governors for more than 200 members. In 1981, the cost of a family membership was $465 while the cost for a single membership was $330. There are moderate green fees for visiting golfers (higher on weekends). The course rating, or what a good player could average on the course, is 69 for men and 68 for women. Facilities include a snack bar, lounge, pro shop for sales and repairs, and a banquet hall frequently used for wedding receptions and other occasions. Club pro Ivan Bourque offers golf lessons.

The Petersham Country Club, North Main Street, Petersham, Tel. 724-3388, has a nine-hole course, built in 1922. It is 2,938 yards length-wise and is a par 35. Its course rating is 33.2. The greens are short which make the course a challenge, according to Don Cross, club pro. The club, which has memberships and is open to the public, is run by a 12-member board of directors. The average membership costs $300 a year; the public pays $5 for one round of play. Robert Wood of Hardwick is president and Michael Staiti of Barre is vice president.

Curling is one of the more unusual sports found in the region. The Petersham Curling Club (724-3210), built in 1962 and located on North Main Street, has two playing areas and offers family and individual memberships (price range, $150-$210). The season goes from November through March. Viewing of curling competition is open to the public. Facilities include a bar and function room. Play runs Monday through Saturday with approximately 120 persons participating in men's, women's and mixed leagues. The club is run by a board of governors headed by president Rick Robinson of Winchendon and vice president William Ellis of Athol.

Canoeing is one of the area's popular sports, with Millers River offering both flatwater and whitewater canoeing. Various other area lakes and streams are popular with canoeists. Lawrence Brook and Priest Brook in Royalston, smaller winding streams, offer an interesting and challenging environment for the canoeist. The River Rat Spectacular in early April and the Merchant's Canoe Race each summer (Tully Lake to Long Pond in Royalston) are the principal competitive events. Northfield Mountain recreation area offers canoe instruction. Kayaks are sometimes seen hereabouts.

Road-running and jogging are popular in this region as interest locally has increased along with the national trend. The YMCA sponsors the Orange to Athol Millers River Road Race in conjunction with July 4 festivities.

For bicyclists, area roadways offer a combination of flatland and hills, with mostly light automobile traffic. Old paved roads inside the Quabbin watershed are of particular interest, especially in the former center of Dana (now Petersham). There are no bicycle paths as such in the region. Some area residents participate in Franklin-Hampshire Freewheelers Bicycling Club, P.O. Box 9, So. Deerfield MA 01373.

A well-run cross-country ski area with rentals available and trails extending into Erving is located at Northfield Mountain off Route 63 north of Millers Falls. Other opportunities for cross country skiing abound, as many unplowed roads wind their way through public lands in state forests and other conservation areas. Logging roads and jeep roads along power lines provide other access to wooded and scenic areas for the adventuresome cross-county skier. Geodetic maps are helpful and skiers must share some roadways with snowmobilers. As for downhill skiing, the Snow Hill ski area in Phillipston closed recently, and is for sale. The state's Department of Environmental Management is revamping the downhill ski area at Mt. Wachusett in nearby Princeton. Mt. Watatic Ski Area in Ashby and Berkshire East in Charlemont are only an hour from here, and various ski areas in Vermont and New Hampshire are also within easy reach.

Volleyball is played informally in area towns. Regular Sunday games can be found, weather permitting, in the centers of Royalston and Warwick, for example. See also CURLING, FISHING, NORTHFIELD MOUNTAIN, RIVER RAT RACE, QUABBIN FISHING and YMCA.

Stacy Memorial

A granite stone with a metal plaque attached to it stands on the green in the center of New Salem in homage to a Revolutionary War patriot. In large letters are printed the name and dates: "Lt. Col. William Stacy, 1733-1804," followed by this explanation:

"Alarm bells called the citizens to this green Apr. 20, 1775, to learn of the battle at Lexington. There was indecision until First Lieutenant Stacy stepped forward and said, 'Fellow soldiers, I don't know how it is with you, but for me I will no longer serve a king that murders my own countrymen.' Pulling out his commission from the crown, he tore it to bits and trod it underfoot. Amid wild cheers a militia company of patriots was

formed and under the gallant Stacy as captain marched off to
Cambridge. May such patriotism ever be with us."

Starrett's

The L.S. Starrett Co. of Athol, which employs more people
than any other company in the Mount Grace Region – approximately 1,500 men and women – is an internationally-known
tool manufacturer. The total number of industrial products
made and sold by the company exceeds 3,000. Among the
items produced are precision tools, steel tapes, electronic
gauges, dial indicators, gauge blocks, digital readout measuring tools, granite surface plates, vises, hacksaws, hole saws,
band saws and precision ground flat stock.

Much of the company's production is concentrated in hand
measuring tools (including such items as micrometers, steel
rules, combination squares and many other items for the individual craftsman), and precision instruments (such as vernier calipers, height gages, depth gages and measuring instruments which manufacturing companies buy for the use of
their employees).

These tools and instruments are sold throughout the U.S.
and Canada and over 100 foreign countries through industrial
distributors. By far the largest consumer of these products is
the metalworking industry, but other consumers are
automotive, aviation, marine and farm equipment shops and
tradesmen such as builders, carpenters, plumbers and electri-
cians.

The company's principal plant is in Athol. There are other
manufacturing plants in Cleveland, Ohio, and Mt. Airy, N.C.,
with foreign manufacturing subsidiaries in Brazil and
Scotland.

Net sales in recent years have topped $100 million annual-
ly, and the company's net working capital is listed at approximately $50 million. Current and former employees own ap-
proximately one-half of the company's outstanding stock,
which is listed on the New York Stock Exchange.

Starrett's was founded in 1880 by Laroy S. Starrett, great-
grandfather of the company's current president, Douglas R.
Starrett. The company's evolution over the years is told in the
1980 edition of "The Starrett Story," subtitled "A brief account
of the origin and development of the L.S. Starrett Co., Athol,
Mass., and how it became the 'World's Greatest Toolmaker.'"

"L.S. Starrett, like so many of the early captains of industry, had his roots in the soil. His boyhood in China, Maine, was typical of American farm life one hundred years ago" – so starts the story. Eventually Starrett moved to Massachusetts and owned his own farm, but he had an "invention on the brain." He invented a meatchopper or "hasher," acquired a "silent partner," and by chance met a man who recommended Athol as a likely place for manufacturing his invention.

He moved here, became associated with the Athol Machine Co. (which he bought in 1905), and soon had the meat chopper business running "and turned his inventive genius to other products." The official account continues: "Among the patents taken out by Mr. Starrett (eventually about one hundred) was a line of bench vises which are still manufactured in Athol and a shoe hook-fastener which later was universally used."

A combination square with a sliding blade was an important Starrett product, first made in Athol in 1877 at the old Richardson shop where the YMCA now stands. Steel rules and tapes, Fay calipers and dividers and micrometers came next, followed by improved cutting blades and dial indicator gauges. During World War II, the company boosted production by 800 percent and received the Army-Navy "E" Production Award as a result.

Careful hand work contributes to the accuracy of Starrett products. In the machinists square room, for example, workers today use a tall ribbon of light to adjust tools by hand so that over the distance of one foot they are perfectly square within one-tenth of one-thousandth of an inch. The Starrett standard for accuracy is equivalent to "inspection grade" in the English system and is well above all U.S. government requirements.

In the company's own tool room, workers design many machines for use in the manufacture of tools. The company makes its own screws, with special threading, as a means to protect the quality of the brand name.

One of the hottest items in Starrett's new catalog is the new "bear cat tooth" for its band saws. Developed by John Grant, Richard Newton and Tom Neumeyer, the company claims its new saw "will outlast any blade."

Energy-conscious, the company recently invested $130,000 in a new incinerator that burns paper and wood waste to manufacture steam.

New and old machinery work side by side at Starrett's. A computerized screw machine does its job near an older model. An old General Electric generator attached to a water wheel, using Millers River water, has manufactured some of the plant's electricity.

The company's products are listed in the Starrett Catalog, more than 500 pages long, which lists and describes the tools and explains their uses. Another useful publication is the Starrett Book for Student Machinists and a new classroom aid, "How to Read, Use, Care For Micrometers and Vernier Gages."

Competition for products of the type made by Starrett's comes from several domestic and Japanese companies, but the company remains optimistic that its tools "will continue to set the world's standard of accuracy."

Stonemasonry

Some of the most beautiful structures in the region are made of stone, including bridges, granite foundations, retaining walls, road and railroad bridges and abutments and a few houses. Here and there, small sections of cobblestone streets can be observed though most of these have been paved over. Large granite quarries in nearby Fitzwilliam, N.H., provided much of this raw material, though other smaller quarries were opened closer to area towns. With the development of inexpensive concrete in the 1930s, stone construction has become increasingly uneconomical and rare.

James Dowd of Glasheen Road, Petersham, Tel. 724-3239, is one of the area's most accomplished and respected stonemasons. Dowd works with some old tools (and perhaps a

Granite puzzle: stone wall on North Main Street in Orange

knack as well) inherited from his maternal grandfather, Gustave Cloutier, a Canadian, who also worked with stone. The stone barn that Dowd constructed on the premises of Harry Buell, Oliver Street, Petersham, readily visible from the roadway, is a work of art and a tribute to this ancient craft. See also KEYSTONE BRIDGE.

Synagogue

Temple Israel at the corner of Walnut and Union streets in Athol is the spiritual home of the area's Jewish community. Dedicated in 1950, the brick building replaced the old wooden Agudas Achim synagogue on Pine Street built in 1910 when the immigrant Jewish community formed an association and decided a "shule" was needed.

Temple Israel is affiliated with the Conservative branch of American Judaism; its traditions and practices fall somewhere in between those of the stricter Orthodox and the more liberal Reform movements.

The roots of the Jewish community in the Athol-Orange area go back to the first itinerant Jewish peddlars who sold hardware from packs on their backs and horse-drawn carts. Following worsening of persecution of Jews in Eastern Europe at the turn of the century, there was a surge of immigration to the United States. While most of these immigrants remained in the large cities of the East Coast, a few came to rural areas such as this one. Those who settled in Orange and Athol (rarely in outlying towns, except in recent years) worked in retail trade, developed movie theaters and other real estate, and served in various professions.

The local Jewish community remained small, not even reaching the national average of three percent, and no Jewish cemetery was ever established here.

Television

Residents of the region normally receive television signals from stations in Boston, Hartford, Worcester and Springfield. Cable service offered by the Warner Cable Co., 359 Main St., Athol, is available to almost all sections of Athol and to much of Orange, with expansion projected into the Tully section of Orange. Under new licensing agreements with selectmen in both towns, expanded cable service includes optional extra programming such as "Home Box Office" and "The Movie Channel," as well as sports, news and religious offerings.

Town Pound

During the 1700s, New England farmers allowed their livestock to roam free, and often the animals would trample another farmer's crops, leading to hassles. Therefore stone or wooden corrals were built to confine the animals until the owner claimed them and paid a fine.

In North Orange, the remains of an old pound made of large stones can be seen on Wheeler Avenue just north of its intersection with East Road.

The first Orange pound was located in the center of North Orange in the yard of Benjamin Mayo, a farmer elected pound keeper in 1784. The keeper had to make sure the animals were fed and watered; he collected fees and damages from the owners and his salary was a portion of fines collected.

The pound that stands on Wheeler Avenue was constructed after the Mayo pound, it seems, perhaps to house larger numbers of animals as the settlement grew. The first pound has entirely disappeared and the one on Wheeler Avenue has not been used since 1920. According to a roadside plaque placed near the pound in 1976 by the Orange Bicentennial Commission, this is one of the very few pounds still standing in Massachusetts although most colonial towns had one or more.

Traditions

Many of the traditions associated with smalltown New England can be found thriving in this region. There are fairs, reunions, banquets and balls, affirming a sense of community year after year. Parades or other commemorations are held each year on Memorial Day, Independence Day and Veteran's Day. Shopping streets are decorated for Christmas. High schools have homecoming parades and celebrations in conjunction with traditional gridiron rivalry. Local high school girls vie for scholarships and accolades in several "queen" contests held during the year. Community bands offer old-fashioned concerts on octagonal bandstands on town commons.

The change of the seasons is apparent not only by the obvious change in the weather but by the perennial reminders of the persistence of local agriculture – maple sap boiling off in the spring, fresh garden products from the rhubarb of early spring to the displays of pumpkins around Halloween and

Thanskgiving, apple harvest in local orchards. Traditional crafts from chair caning to quilting are preserved by men and women throughout the region. Burning cordwood to keep warm, although dramatically increased in the late 1970s, never really ceased being part of the area's way of life. Area residents can hire chimney sweeps dressed up in a top hat.

Clown and friend at July 4 festivities

Old Home Day in Wendell

Vintage cars and even horse-drawn carriages can occasionally be seen on area byways.

Area residents live up to the ancient maxim "Waste not, want not," as is evident by the love of flea markets and other opportunities for purchasing used merchandise at bargain prices. The largest flea markets frequented by area residents are located nearby – the Rietta Flea Market on Route 68 in Hubbardston and the Ken Miller Flea Market on Warwick Road in Northfield. Each weekend when the weather is favorable, especially in spring and fall, area residents sell their unwanted treasures and junk at events known variously as yard sales, tag sales, garage sales, barn sales and porch sales. The best way to find out about the location of such sales – sometimes involving several households at once – is to check the classified ads in the Friday and Saturday editions of local newspapers.

Village fairs and "Old Home" days are popular annual events; these are often held in the summer in conjunction with flea markets and special events such as a pinewood derby for children. Churches and other groups often sponsor bingo, card parties and suppers featuring home-made food. While a complete schedule of such events is not available in advance, newspaper advertisements and posters displayed in area businesses can lead the visitor to one of these traditional gatherings virtually every weekend except in the dead of winter, when things show down for the area's people as well as for the trees and the bears. See also ENGINE SHOW AND FLY-IN, HATCHET HUNT and RIVER RAT RACE.

Tully Dam and Lake

Located in the southwestern part of Royalston, Tully Lake State Recreation Area is part of the U.S. Army Corps of Engineers 1,130-acre Tully flood control area. The recreation area is leased to the state's Department of Environmental Management by the federal government, which owns and controls the land.

The recreation area offers wilderness camping (with special facilities for canoeists) and fishing. Doane's Falls, Spirit Falls and Long Pond are nearby. Facilities include a boat launch. The 300-acre lake is stocked with trout. The water is dark with tannin but its water quality is rated "good." Swimming is not permitted in Tully Lake. There is a picnic area with barbecue grilles and a comfort station. An overlook area at the south end of the dam, just north of the Athol line on Route 32, offers a scenic vista of Tully Mountain and other hills to the west, and of Tully Lake itself with its many pine-covered islands.

Wildlife species that have been observed in the area include fisher cat, bobcat, coyote, deer, black bear, ruffed grouse, raccoon, beaver, mink, otter, rabbit and snowshoe hare.

The story of the creation of Tully Lake goes back to the hurricane of September 1938 which devastated the region. Under flood control legislation a plan was developed soon after the flood to build the Tully Dam on the east branch of the Tully River and, further east, the Birch Hill Dam on the Millers River (the larger of the two projects) to hold back flood waters and thereby protect downstream communities, including Athol and Orange. Between them, the two dams would control 225 square miles of the 392 square miles of the total Millers River watershed drainage area.

Tully Dam is located 3.9 miles above the junction of the Tully and Millers rivers in Athol. It is a rolled-earth type of dam, with a rock slope protection and impervious core. It has a top width of 30 feet and a top length of 1,570 feet. Route 32 runs right across the top of the dam, which contains 185,000 cubic yards of material. The top of the dam is 62 feet above the riverbed, and 684 feet above sea level. The drainage area of the dam is 50 square miles, with a spillway crest of 1,130 acres. The spillway is about 800 feet southeast of the left abutment of the dam; it was blasted through rocks and is spanned by Route 32; part of this spillway is located in Athol. Outlet of

Tully Lake as seen from overlook at south end of flood control dam

the dam is a circular tunnel, with an electrically operated gear-driven slide gate and for emergency purposes a crane-operated slide gate.

Work on the project began in 1947 and was completed in 1949. Creation of a restricted flood control area involved land acquisition to an elevation of 668 feet above sea level; amounts taken by the government were 1,300 acres for fee and four acres under easement. Total cost of the project was $1,551,600.

In addition to the Tully Dam staff, the U.S. Army Corps of Engineers Lower Connecticut River Basin is headquartered here. This office covers the two dams in Royalston, plus Barre Falls dam in Barre and Knightville and Littleville dams in Huntington. As part of its maintenance of the dams for flood control purposes, the local staffs regularly gather weather data, including testing of snow to determine its water content to predict spring runoff.

According to calculations by the Corps, the existence of Tully Dam prevented an estimated $5,400,000 in damages that would have occurred in 1955 had there been no dam.

The origin of the name Tully, given not only to the dam, lake and river but to the village in Orange (called Tulleyville on some old maps), is obscure. L.B. Caswell's history of Athol contends the river, often called Tully Brook (especially the west branch), derived its name from an Indian's dog. The story goes that the dog was following a deer and pursued it across meadows into the waters of the brook, but the deer fought back and succeeded in holding the dog under the water, drowning it. In her history of Orange, Mrs. Beatrice Miner notes, "Later this story was discounted as Tully was found to be a good English name, not Indian. But some contend the family name of Tully was a Massachusetts, or New England name of early settlers, possibly a man who surveyed lands in the area." See also BIRCH HILL DAM, CAMPING, DOANE'S FALLS, SPIRIT FALLS.

Twenty-Four Hours

Two business establishments in the area serve the public around the clock:

Cullen's Sunoco, Daniel Shays Highway (intersection of Routes 2 and 202), Orange, Tel. 544-8565; gasoline, vending machines, some groceries.

Xtra Mart, 270 South Main St., Orange, Tel. 544-7998; gasoline, groceries, coffee, fast food.

Union Twist Drill

Union Twist Drill is nationally known as a manufacturer of fine cutting tools. Although residents of the area generally refer to the factory as "UTD," the correct current name is Union/Butterfield Division of Litton Industrial Products. Litton Industries, headquartered in Beverly Hills, Calif., acquired the UTD Corp. in 1968.

The roots of the firm go back to 1890 in Providence, R.I., where Frank Gay began a manufacturing endeavor. The company, known as Gay and Flint, moved to Athol in 1894, at which time the L.S. Starrett Co. bought a one-third interest. Starrett sold his interest to Edgar T. Ward and the company became known as Gay and Ward.

In 1905, Gay and Ward sold the company to John A. McGregor and Associates. The new owners included John Boynton, John MacSkimmon, John Drury and Simon MacKay, who provided the right combination of business and technical skills. This was the start of the Union Twist Drill company. UTD grew quickly and produced a line of drills, reamers, end mills, milling cutters and hobs. Through a program of expansion, the company acquired other manufacturing firms and increased its output of new products including taps and dies. One of the companies purchased was the the Butterfield Company, whose plant at Derby Line, Vt., straddling the U.S.-

Canadian border, is now a part of Union/Butterfield.

In 1919, high speed steel was developed and Union Twist Drill secured national recognition when it successfully developed cutting tools using the new material while competitors were left behind. Other companies were acquired and the firm continued to grow. Under Litton, the management of the Athol and Derby Line plants has been consolidated in the name of efficiency. The president of Union/Butterfield is Ronald E. Quigley.

An organization for employees, the Twisters' Fun Club, was established in 1954 to promote athletic, recreational, educational and social activities. The club sponsors a scholarship program and owns a lakeside property with a beach, pavilion and camp in New Salem.

There are approximately 600 employees at UTD, although economic problems in 1982 led to lay-offs of a large portion of the work force. Employees are represented by United Electrical Radio & Machine Workers of America, Local 276.

Unusual Mammal

There is a predator few people have ever seen that roams the Massachusetts hill country, including the towns of the North Quabbin region, climbing trees, swimming lakes and streams, hunting and killing with the speed and cunning of a cat. This fox-sized mammal, weighing between five and twenty pounds, looks something like an overgrown mink with long legs and a bushy tail. The broad head and neck, usually greyish-brown, tapers gracefully into a black-footed, brownish black body that sports a jet black tail. Adult males tend to be twice as large as females and have a coarse, grizzled fur, while females tend to be darker and possess a silky fur that is in demand for coats and stoles.

The animal is the fisher (Latin name: Martes pennanti), also known as the fisher-cat, tree-fox and blackcat. It is actually a member of the Mustelidae (weasel family), but considering some of its feline habits and physical traits, it's no wonder the word "cat" appears in a number of its colloquial names. Even the name "fisher" is inappropriate since the animal rarely catches fish like its aquatic cousin the otter. It probably got the name fisher from the early trappers who noted its fondness for traps baited with fish, although they called it the fisher-marten to distinguish it from the pine marten. There is also the possiblity that early settlers thought it looked like the

227

European pole cat, called the fitche or fitchet, and the name evolved into "fisher."

The fisher is an alert, energetic mammal that leads a solitary life. Ever-active, it may be found hunting year-round in the daytime or at night (its preference). A typical fisher home range is 8-15 miles in diameter and is criss-crossed with dozens of fairly straight fisher trails. Often as not it overlaps the ranges of other individual fishers. When the fisher finds itself in need of sleep, or if a severe winter storm strikes, the animal dens up for a short time in one of several convenient hollow trees, logs or crevices located along its trails. A fisher rarely digs a den, preferring instead to appropriate the work of other animals while hiding these hideouts with leaves.

The fisher breeding season runs from February to April and is the only time fishers seek out the company of their own kind. This is also the time when the young are born. Shortly after a female bears a litter she goes into heat and breeds again. The fertilized ova develop only slightly, however, and then go into a 9- to 10-month period of dormancy before attaching themselves to the walls of the uterus and resuming normal embryonic growth. This process, called delayed implantation, is a common trait of all weasel family members and the result is that nearly all adult females are pregnant throughout their lives!

The young fishers are usually born in a warm den located 30 or more feet up in a hollow tree, although rock crevices and hollow logs may also be commandeered as nurseries. Litter size varies from one to four and the young are born blind, deaf and helpless. They develop rapidly, however, and are completely weaned in four months. Male fishers take no part in rearing the young. Both sexes become sexually mature within their first year, and they may live for as long as ten years.

Fishers hunt in a haphazard manner, searching holes and crevices, going up and down trees snuffling through bird and squirrel nests. They don't stalk prey or chase it down. Instead, they rely on surprising unsuspecting prey sleeping in one of the many hollows fishers are constantly darting in and out of. Fishers will kill and eat almost anything they can overpower, including rabbits, mice, squirrels, shrews, birds, reptiles and amphibians. Occasionally they eat insects, beechnuts, apples and carrion. Most prey is dispatched with a quick bite to the base of the skull. Fishers can hunt in the trees almost as well as they do on the ground, and using their long, powerful legs they often bound between trees like squirrels. The fisher's cat-like retractable claws are well adaped for arboreal work and

Fisher photographed in Worcester Science Center

the animal can move up and down tree trunks head first.

The size disparity between male and female fishers is especially noticeable in the region of the head, neck and shoulders. The average outdoorsman, coming upon the skulls of a female and male fisher, would almost certainly conclude the remains belonged to two different species of carnivores. Biologists speculate that this differential reduces competition between the sexes for food. Females can utilize prey species in small holes where male fishers are unable to enter, while males, with their powerful jaws and muscular necks, may overcome larger prey.

Perhaps the fisher's most famous trait is its marked preference for dining on porcupines – a fact that has endeared the fisher to foresters (as porcupines do so much damage to trees). Few predators will attempt to kill porcupines, having learned through bitter experience that the "knight of a thousand lances" is virtually invincible. Fishers will go out of their way to get porcupines, usually driving them from trees so they can be dealt with on the ground. Porkys are attacked repeatedly about the head, the fisher darting in and delivering quick slashes to the rodent's face and neck until it succumbs due to loss of blood. Another common method of attack is to burrow under a porcupine in deep snow and slash upward into the unprotected belly.

Once dispatched, the porcupine is eaten from the inside out, the fisher consuming flesh, innards and smaller bones and leaving a neat, hollowed-out skin behind. Fishers have no problems in passing quills, feathers and bones through their digestive systems. Even more amazing is the fact that many fishers are carrying horrendous numbers of quills in their hides – yet they show no signs of infection or other ill effects! Most other animals, including dogs, who have tangled with a porcupine will suffer considerable agony and infection and may even die. No one knows how fishers are able to absorb quills with impunity. In areas where porcupine populations have become over-abundant, fishers have been introduced and have proven themselves to be excellent natural limiting agents that keep the tree-munching rodents in check.

At present, fishers are found from Alaska to Rhode Island and north throughout much of Canada. When the first settlers arrived fishers were found as far south as North Carolina, but the destruction of the dense forests the fisher prefers for habitat combined with unregulated trapping pressure gradually drove the southern edge of the population northward. The fisher was considered extirpated from Massachusetts by the mid-1800s when nearly 70 percent of Massachusetts was cleared land, but the forests gradually returned beginning shortly after the Civil War, and today they are mature enough to support fishers once again. The handsome mammals began moving back in only 15 years ago, but today they are found in northern Essex, Middlesex, Worcester, Franklin, Hampshire and Berkshire counties, and they have already expanded their range past Massachusetts and into Connecticut and Rhode Island.

The fisher is managed as a renewable fur resource by the state's Division of Fisheries and Wildlife. The animal has few natural enemies other than an occasional bobcat, although kits may perish due to chills, fighting among themselves or in the talons of hawks and owls. Fishers may not be hunted in Massachusetts but a small percentage is trapped each year. The first trapping season on fisher opened in 1972 and until

230

1977 was 121 days long. Fur prices during that period were low (average pelt price in 1973 was $17), but as they began to climb again many trappers began to concentrate their efforts on this lucrative catch, and the season was reduced to 61 days in 1978. When the "harvest" jumped from 45 animals in 1978 to 169 in 1979 in response to increasing fur prices (well over $100 by late 1982), the season was further reduced to only 30 days, and the number of trapped animals decreased to approximately 115 animals.

Mandatory tagging of fisher pelts was established in 1976 and mandatory carcass returns in 1978. This tagging takes place at the Birch Hill Wildlife Management Area and similar state outposts where fishers are caught. To ensure that the resource is not over-exploited, state wildlife biologists analyze the fisher carcasses which are turned in each year. (This is hazardous duty – remember the porcupine quills!) A canine tooth is removed from each animal, and after a long series of acid baths, stain dips and microsections, it yields a clear series of tree-like growth rings which give the animal's age. Analysis of the age structure of the trapped animal sample gives biologists a representation of the age structure of the population as a whole. Reproductive tracts are also analyzed. Division officials report that the age and reproductive data look good at present, and with rigorous trapping limitations now in effect, the fisher population is thriving and producing a harvestable surplus. Yet, because the animal is known to be vulnerable to overtrapping, Division biologists will continue to monitor the population structure closely and if the data should ever indicate that the population is being over-harvested, more stringent limitations on trapping would be instituted. It is expected for now that the population will continue to expand into all available habitat.

Because of their secretive habits fishers are extremely difficult to study in the wild, and many people who spend a good deal of time in the woods have never seen a fisher. Even the Divison's own wildlife photographers, among the best in the nation, have been largely frustrated in their efforts to capture a fisher on film. If you want to try your hand at spotting a fisher in the wild, however, keep the following items in mind: 1. Fishers are more active in the summer than they are in the winter; 2. Fishers seem to thrive wherever trees and prey are availale. 3. Fishers are particularly fond of forested swampland. 4. Fishers tend to avoid areas where there is no overhead cover. 5. Fishers love porcupines. Given that information, you are likely to be successful in placing yourself within the home range of a fisher, but don't be too disappointed if you never see the animal – you're in good company.

The forests are returning, trapping pressure has been regulated, and the fishers have moved back in. Once considered strictly a wildnerness species, the fisher is now appearing occasionally in populated areas, although it always carries a certain aura of the wilderness about itself. Much is still to be learned about the habits of these interesting predators, but now that a good resident population is well-established, more will be available for monitoring and observation. Alert, secretive and never found in high concentrations, fishers are difficult to study, but it is certain that they have returned to the Commonwealth, and they are here to stay. Given the large amount of public conservation land in the nine towns of the North Quabbin region, the fisher is assured a permanent home here. (From an article by Peter Mirick in Massachusetts Wildlife. Reprinted with permission.)

Warwick

This is a town of "hills and hills upon hills," as Charles Morse noted in his book "Warwick, Massachusetts: Biography of a Town," published in 1963 during the town's bicentennial. In addition to being hilly the land is primarily forested, and nearly half of it is owned by the state – as Warwick State Forest and Mt. Grace State Forest.

Mt. Grace, at 1,617 above sea level, is the highest point in the region and the name of this hill is sometimes used to describe the entire nine-town area, as in "The Mt. Grace Region." Bennett's Knob, part of Mt. Grace, is 1,475 above sea level, and the peak of Little Mt. Grace to the south is at 1,225 feet. Warwick's lowest elevation is 606 feet at Moss Brook at the town's southern end.

Warwick, with a population of 603, is the least populous of the region's nine towns. Even so, it experienced an increase of 23 percent in the decade from 1970-80. Warwick is spacious, with 37.64 square miles, ranking it 45th in the state in size. It has 16 persons per square mile, ranking it 340th in population density.

Warwick is bordered on the east by Royalston, on the southeast and south by Orange, on the southwest and west by Erving and Northfield and on the north by the New Hampshire towns of Winchester and Richmond.

Smalltown amiability is characteristic of this community.

Detail of fountain in Warwick center

The Warwick Woman's Guild, for example, founded in 1921, carries on numerous activities of a social and charitable nature. Membership is extended automatically to all women in the town and thus the Guild unites all the town's women in a single organization. Warwick has a truly volunteer fire department – one of the few in which firefighters are not paid for their time – and the town's firefighters are well-known for their self-sufficiency, including the construction of a fire engine.

The territory that was to become Warwick was given by the Province of Massachusetts to descendants of soldiers who died during the disastrous expedition to Canada under Sir William

Phipps in 1690. When war broke out between England and France in 1690, Phipps, a native of Maine, was dispatched at the command of 36 ships and some 2,500 men with the object of capturing Quebec. Heavy casualites on the battlefield and from smallpox resulted.

The towns of Roxbury and Brookline had sent a company of 60 men under the command of Captain Andrew Gardner, and it was their descendants (and one survivor, Samuel Newell) who petitioned the state for recompense. In 1735-36, four tracts were laid out and awarded, establishing four townships (places that eventually became known as Warwick, Ashburnham and Winchendon, and Guilford, Vt.).

Warwick was part of the parcel initially referred to as "Gardner's Canada" or "Roxbury Canada." Settling the land was a struggle involving the making of roads, building houses and setting up sawmills and grist mills. (Millstones from an 18th century grist mill were saved and placed in the town park in front of the library in 1927 and can still be seen there.) On Nov. 12, 1761, the proprietors recorded the names of 37 settlers who were occupying 44 "rights." Only six of the settlers owned the lots on which they resided. Settlers and proprietors were involved in the process by which the General Court (state legislature) established the town of Warwick on Feb. 17, 1763.

"How Warwick received its name cannot be definitely stated," according to Morse. "It is generally believed that the intent was to honor Guy, Earl of Warwick, who played a prominent role in the early colonization of New England. It is well known that the city of Warwick, R.I., was named in this manner. Another possiblity might be found in the fact that Elisha Rich, a leading proprietor as early as 1753, was supposed to be descended from Lord Robert Rich, Earl of Warwick."

With its rugged terrain and no major source of water power, Warwick never developed large-scale agriculture or industry. By 1830, however, the town had numerous small industries closely related to the small farms and forests that made up the town – using hydropower from dams on small streams. The town's population was 1,150 in 1830, already dropping off from its peak of 1,256 in 1820. As Moore reports, "Among the industries then functioning we find 12 sawmills and two more equipped to manufacture shingles, clapboard and pail staves; four grist mills to grind grain to flour; two tanneries to cure the hides of animals; two cabinet shops, three blacksmith shops and two more equipped with trip hammers for the manufacture of scythes, axes and cutting tools; one potash plant, an industry once quite prevalent in the area; two clothing shops where cloth was woven and prepared for local use."

One of the these industries was a sawmill where Daniel N. Smith developed a kind of revolving planing machine, described by local historian Morse as an invention that "was to revolutionize the planing of lumber."

Railroad construction brought progress to nearby towns, but no iron horse wended its way through these hills, and with the building of the railroads, the stagecoach lines that had run through Warwick from Brattleboro to Worcester were abandoned. Industries moved away from Warwick to be closer to means of transportation. Notations in the diary of William Cobb – a document much-quoted by Morse – indicate the decline of industries in town in the years just prior to the Civil War.

This decline was by no means total, and in the years following the war, sawmills, a tannery and a shoe-manufacturing shop were among the town's major employers. One attempt to establish a glass industry was a fiasco, however.

Many of the old industrial dams are gone, but the mountain streams are part of the town's landscape, traveling in various directions toward three different rivers (all within the Connecticut watershed). Kidder and Mountain brooks drain the north central part of the town to merge into Mirey Brook and flow through Sunny Valley north to the Ashuelot River in New Hampshire. The Northfield Brook and its tributaries drain most of the northwest part of town, becoming Mill Brook as it crosses Northfield to enter the Connecticut. The west branch of the Tully River rises in the northeastern corner of Warwick and flows southward, passing through Sheomet Pond (Clubhouse Pond) continuing through Orange to meet the east branch in Athol where it empties into the Millers River. Gale Brook wends its way through Brush Valley to Wheelers Pond where it changes its name to Orcutt Brook and flows south through West Orange into the Millers. The overflow of Moores Pond creates Darling Brook which joins Moss Brook and continues through Erving State Forest and enters the Millers at Wendell Depot.

What Morse described as an "orgy of timber-cutting" at the turn of the century led to widespread conservationist concern in Warwick as throughout the nation. Locally, Dr. Paul W. Goldsbury, a descendant of a pioneer family of Warwick, promoted a plan to establish a state park or forestry reserve at Mt. Grace. Eventually the state bought most of this mountain and gradually took over much more land. During the Great Depression, the federal government established two Civilian Conservation Corps camps in Warwick.

Some timber-cutting and work related to forest products remained part of the town's economic life. The effort of Fred Lincoln and other woodsmen to deal with the thousands of trees that blew over during the hurricane devastation of 1938 is chronicled by Morse. At present, one of the few functioning places of business in Warwick is the sawmill and chain saw business of Stephen Clark on the Athol Road.

Warwick's center includes its town hall, the Unitarian Church, library, historical association building, the Warwick Inn, the Warwick Country Store, the Center School with its adjacent Fellows Memorial Field (named in honor of Sgt. Winifred Fellows of Warwick who died as the result of wounds received on a World War II battlefield in Germany), the Metcalf Memorial Chapel, the fire station and numerous residences. The only other population cluster in Warwick is at Moores Pond, where there is a mixture of year-round residences and summer camps.

Warwick could be described today as a "bedroom community," in that most of the economic activity of its citizens takes place outside the municipal limits. There is nonetheless a significant portion of the citizenry that is self-employed, including farmers, carpenters, woodsmen, artists and homemakers. Home gardening and raising of livestock is common. The Bowers Farm at Mayo Corners, east of the town center, has the picturesque look of a traditional farm, but its main agricultural activity is the raising of young stock for resale. Oliver Fellows of Chase Hill Road has the only commerical farm in town.

In addition to the state forests, another state-owned institution is the Warwick Forestry Camp, officially known as MCI-Warwick (Massachusetts Correctional Institution-Warwick).

Warwick experienced a bit of turmoil in the late 1960s and early 1970s when a commune with more than 200 members, the Brotherhood of the Spirit, was established here. Controversy surrounded the group and the town indicated its displeasure with the commune's alleged failure to comply with health codes and its attempt to intervene in local politics. However, a few Warwick residents went out of their way to befriend the unusual newcomers to the town, a few of whom became permanent residents after the commune relocated.

Because of the large amount of public land and the lack of

economic opportunity here, population growth has been minimal. Here and there where pieces of land have changed hands, however, newcomers are growing roots in this ancient, rocky New England soil, joining in community life. More than any other area town, perhaps, Warwick retains the mood, customs and imagery of Yankee New England. Old-time residents and newcomers alike seem to want it that way. See also COMMUNES, FOUNTAINS, LAUREL LAKE, LEONARD MONUMENT, MT. GRACE STATE FOREST, PRISON CAMP, WARWICK STATE FOREST, WAWBEEK ROCK.

Warwick State Forest

Initial land purchases for Warwick State Forest were made in the 1920s; there are now 7,100 acres of land traversed by 27 miles of dirt road open to the public for motorcycling, smowmobiling and horseback riding. Camping is not permitted. The terrain is forested and hilly, ranging from 700-1,200 feet above sea level. The forest covers a large portion of the town in five tracts of land and includes two bodies of water.

Within the forest near the Orange and Royalston town lines is found Sheomet Lake, fed by the west branch of the Tully River and known locally as Clubhouse Pond. The 31-acre lake, stocked each spring with trout, was created around the time of the Civil War when a dam was built by Augustus Bliss. It is called Clubhouse Pond because it was formerly owned by a private club that maintained a large building on its shore, but when the club dissolved the state obtained the land and the pond. There is a boat-launch ramp on the northern end of the lake; motorboats are not permitted and there are no rentals available.

Richards Reservoir, 17 acres in size, is located off Richmond Road. Also in this area is the Warwick Forestry Camp, a minimum-security state correctional facility.

Warwick State Forest's boundaries are shown on two topographical maps, the Mt. Grace and Northfield quadrants. See also WARWICK.

Water

Water is one of the abundant natural resources of this region, although as with many places in the world, it is often taken for granted. Few people, unfortunately, have an adequate understanding about where their water comes from and about the various problems associated with the protection of water supplies from pollution, lowering of the water table and other dangers.

The pure and plentiful water of western and central Massachusetts is coveted by the more populous area in Eastern Massachusetts, and local officials and citizens are becoming increasingly wary of this.

Conservationists throughout the state are actively criticizing the water-grabbing policies of metropolitan Boston and are urging top-level state policies promoting economic growth in the less-populated part of the state rather than the removal of water to the Boston area. Specifically, the Millers River Watershed Council has gone on record opposing a current plan by the Metropolitan District Commission to divert water from the Millers and tributaries to the Quabbin Reservoir.

The Millers is the area's principal waterway. It flows from east to west and is fed by various streams, mostly from the north. The largest Millers River tributaries are the Tully River (east and west branches) and Priest Brook. The Swift River (east, west and middle branches) is another major waterway; all branches flow into the Quabbin Reservoir, the area's principal water resource. Quabbin water is currently not available to any area community.

There are numerous lakes and ponds which assist with water for drinking, fire protection, and recreation – not to mention enjoyment of their natural (or man-made) beauty.

Athol has a municipal water supply that serves most of its residents from three major sources – the Newton Reservoir (on the dammed up Buckman Brook), the Phillipston Reservoir and a deep well off South Street. The Phillipston Reservoir, adjacent to two busy roadways, has become polluted with excessive road salt runoff in recent years and it has been necessary to dilute it with water from the other sources. However, the town is satisfied that its current water sources are adequate for the foreseeable future. Athol supplies municipal water to homes in the Packard Heights section of Orange.

The town of Orange recently upgraded its municipal water system, used by residents of the town center, with expenditure of more than $1 million for new storage tanks on the north and south sides of the town center and a new productive gravel-pack well off Daniel Shays Highway.

Villagers in South Royalston have a private corporation to provide well water. There are some other collective arrangements for water where there are clusters of population,

238

but in outlying areas, residents depend on gravity fed springs, shallow dug wells and drilled wells (sometimes called artesian wells).

Here and there throughout the region are natural springs, some of which have been outfitted with pipes to serve residents who are dissatisfied with drinking chlorinated municipal water or who for whatever reason desire pure spring water. Rather than publish the precise location of such springs here – as most of them are on private property – those who wish to find them will have to depend on word of mouth.

Pure water is cherished, enjoyed and needed; many people in the region have been learning about the importance of this resource and are doing more to protect and conserve it. See also FOUNTAINS, LAKES AND PONDS, MILLERS RIVER, QUABBIN RESERVOIR.

Wawbeek Rock

"In the Beginning – God." Thus reads the inscription (from Genesis I) on a huge boulder at the side of Hastings Pond Road at the edge of woodlands just south of Warwick Center.

Wawbeek Rock was dedicated in 1916 as a unique monument to God's work on earth. The Athol Young Men's Christian Association had a summer camp for boys in the vicinity of the rock; in 1916 the rock and the camp were dedicated "Wawbeek," from the Algonquin Indian word for "big rock."

Fred Bergquist of Warwick, an expert stonecutter in the Quincy Granite Works for 20 years, and R.N. Berry, then general secretary of the YMCA, spent considerable time in marking and cutting the Biblical quotation on the side of the rock and the name "Wawbeek" near the top.

Geologists estimate that this boulder was carried here 12,000 years ago through a natural cataclysm called the Wisconsin glaciation. The Rev. George T. Jones, pastor of the Warwick Unitarian Church, in comments at the dedication, cast a religious light on the piece of granite. He said, "It was born in the center of the earth. Out of the depths it has come in some terrific explosion. It fell into the deep snow and ice and it floated here to a strange land. It leads us back to its Maker; He who is greater than all His works. It tells us that in the beginning was God, its Maker, who created Heaven and the Earth."

Wayside Cross

A unique Christian cross of rust-colored steel stands on a small lawn between St. Francis of Assisi Church and its rectory at 105 Main St., Athol. The story of this attractive metalwork is told on a plaque on the nearby brick church wall:

"Lithuania is called 'land of crosses' and there are more than 300 different styles of wooden wayside crosses throughout the country. Our cross of stylized tulips is inspired by these wooden shrines but is not characteristic of any specific area of Lithuania. Under the Communist regime the crosses are not tolerated and many are disappearing. So we carry on the tradition here in the U.S.A. where we now live and worship.

"The architect Ramojus Mozoliauskas, using four and one half tons of Corten steel, designed this 13½-ft. high cross. This is an original work of art blending the modern and traditional spirits of the original wayside cross. Corten steel is maintenance free and the rust cover gives it protection and a soft appearance.

"Blessed and dedicated Oct. 14, 1979."

A religious relic is buried at the foot of the cross under a stone. According to Father Justin Steponaitis, pastor of the Lithuanian congregation, the original display of this relic under glass had to be altered due to technical problems.

A plaque at the foot of the cross states: "In memory of Walter J. Micuta, Ladish and Micuta families. Bendonis and Pralinsky families."

Wendell

A member of the Wendell Bicentennial Committee, Broadus Mitchell, characterized his town for the occasion of its 200th anniversary in 1981. Writing in the Wendell Post, a community paper (Box 113, Wendell MA 01379), Mitchell noted:

"Wendell has never been exclusive. The original church was Congregational without question, but when the Baptists were not welcome in Shutesbury, they were happily received here. And Methodists and Mormons equally. Wendell slaughtered nobody, not witches nor redmen nor Shaysites. We have no buildings that proclaim themselves; there is not a column in the place, nor do school and church, town hall and library appear less serviceable with their plain entrances.

Wendell Center farmstead

"The town fathers chose a notable hilltop that may be called unique. The Wendell green, affectionately tended, overlooks the countryside, for the landscape falls away to the north, east, south and if not to the west, it ought to do so for the sake of symmetry. Wendell is airy. Not in the sense of putting on airs, but in the sense that it is free-breathing, independent, unobtrusively content with itself, not envious of others."

Wendell has the distinction among the nine towns in the region of experiencing the most dramatic population change in recent years – from 292 in 1960 and 405 in 1970 to a 1980 census figure of 694. The increase in the last decade was 71 percent. The census showed 305 residences in 1970 compared to 145 in 1970, an increase of 110 percent. The figures don't show it, but many of these new structures are owner-built homes.

This shift is due in good measure to the creation and growth during those years of the University of Massachusetts in nearby Amherst. Many of Wendell's newer residents can trace their decision to move to the town to some involvement with the university.

The relatively stable population of Wendell was rocked by this sudden influx of newcomers in the late 1960s and early 1970s. Previously, the inhabitants of the town had aligned themselves largely in terms of family loyalties. The arrival of people from the outside introduced different values and lifestyles.

Wendell has been characterized as containing a mix of "old-timers" and "hippies." While out-of-towners may retain this perception, inside Wendell such distinctions have become somewhat blurred. Because few founding families remain, many of the "old-timers" are not natives but people who moved here several decades ago, such as the older members of the Diemand family, whose poultry farm is one of the few businesses to export a product (eggs) from Wendell to the outside world. As for the "hips," as they are sometimes called, few choose to maintain an in-group identity. Most newer residents are more broadly classified as "new people," ranging broadly in lifestyle and values.

In addition, Wendell's population swells seasonally with the regular return of "the summer people," families who have summered in town for many years. Indeed, some summer homes are found in all area towns. These people are generally regarded and awaited with genuine affection.

More than any other area town, nonetheless, Wendell has made a mark for itself as having a significant number of newcomers with different ideas. Residents of Wendell have played an important role in such alternative institutions as the Our Daily Bread Food Cooperative (now defunct) and the Wintergreen Cooperative Solar Greenhouse, both in nearby Orange. Wendell's unique personage, Charles Thompson Smith, bearded eccentric, Biblical scholar and political activist, is known in anti-nuclear circles throughout New England as "Father Clam" for his work on behalf of the Clamshell Alliance. At election time, a high percentage of Wendell voters choose third party candidates. Conservationists in Wendell have played a role in preventing construction of a new Route 2 through the town on the southern bank of the Millers River. Wendell made news statewide a few years ago when late-staying town meeting voters passed an article instructing the police chief not to enforce laws against cultivation of marijuana. A subsequent special town meeting rescinded the first vote, and there are those who look upon the whole episode as an embarrassment.

Lack of communication between the newcomers and oldtimers, noticeable in the late 1960s and early 1970s, is mostly a thing of the past. Town government participants include a cross-section of the current population, and a community spirit is apparent. Some of the feeling of community is shared with residents of adjacent New Salem, which has undergone a similar shift in population. Elementary schoolchildren from the two towns attend the modern Swift

242

River School, located purposefully right on the New Salem-Wendell town line and run by a school committee with residents from both places.

Wendell is the archetypical "hilltown" referred to by residents of the Connecticut Valley, a term describing topography but in some subtle way saying something as well about the people. It is one of the hilliest towns in the eastern part of Franklin County, with an elevation at the town center of approximately 1,164 feet above sea level.

The Millers River forms the entire northern boundary of the town, separating it from Erving. About half of this northern border is traversed by the Boston and Maine Railroad. The only numbered state highway in Wendell is Route 2 – only a few hundred yards of the artery as it crosses the Millers River from Orange and then returns across it again into Erving. Wendell is about six and a half miles long and about five and a half miles wide, hilly and forested, with a large portion of the land area taken up by Wendell State Forest. The town has 31.91 square miles; it ranks 76th in the state in area. Its population density is 20 persons per square mile (about the same as nearby Royalston and Petersham), ranking it 330th in the state in density. Wendell is bordered on the north by Erving, on the west by Montague, on the south by Leverett and Shutesbury and on the east by Orange and New Salem.

The top of Orcutt Hill, 1,306 feet above sea level, in the southeastern part of town, is Wendell's highest point. A close second is Bear Mountain, 1,281 feet above sea level; this hill is

Ballou's sawmill

243

seen by motorists traveling on Route 2 along the edge of Millers River in Erving. The lowest elevation, approximately 300 feet, is beyond Mormon Hollow at the point in the Millers River where Lyons Brook ends its northbound course – at the point where Wendell's boundary intersects with those of Montague and Erving.

The earliest settlers of Wendell came to the northern part of the town as early as 1754. The act of incorporation was passed May 8, 1781, and provided for the northerly part of the town of Shutesbury and part of a tract of land called Ervingshire lying on the south side of Miller's River, to be formed into the town of Wendell. The town was named in honor of Judge Oliver Wendell of Boston, who owned much land in and around the town. One historian wrote that Judge Wendell "is said to have been a great patron of the town, which he frequently visited," but the historian added that the "only donations he made, as far as records show, were a christening-basin and pulpit Bible to the Congregational Church."

Wendell Center, the locality of the earliest settlement, is located in an elevated region four miles from Wendell Depot, where the river and railroad are found. The Depot was once a populated industrial area, but the community dwindled after railroad service declined and a power-generating dam was washed away in 1936. Locks Village, near the Shutesbury line, was another population center; the remains of many of its people rest in the picturesque old cemetery on Jennison Road.

Wendell's population survived for most of its history on agriculture with a smattering of industry including lumber milling and the braiding of palm-leaf hats. Sawmills have been important throughout the town's history, but the last one ceased operation in 1982 and was put up for sale by its proprietor, Robert Ballou. At present, there is much backyard gardening in town, and some raising of livestock for home use, but the only agricultural endeavor of any proportion is the family-run Diemand Egg Farm. Joseph Diemand's Mormon Hollow Auto, specializing in used Ford parts and offering tow service, is one of the few Wendell businesses serving the public. There are two country stores (Wendell Country Store in the center and Gibbs Store in the Depot), and a private alternative school, the Maple Valley School.

Many of the people in town travel to nearby communities, including Amherst and Greenfield, for employment, but there are numerous self-employed artists and tradesmen. Wendell has been the home for several years of "Loose Caboose," a successful rock-reggae band that frequently performs in local and

Two generations at Wendell Old Home Day

distant nightspots and has recorded an album in Jamaica. Other bands associated with Wendell now or in the past are the Wendell Rangers, the Magic Music Band and Outerspace Band – the latter band resurfaces occasionally for its high-energy rock and roll gatherings at the Warwick Inn. Outerspace member John "Klondike" Koehler, provider of professional sound systems to nationally-known performers, makes his home in Wendell on Bear Mountain. Former Magic Music Band members Jeffrey Bauman and Judith Ann-Marie are involved with the Wendell Recording Studio and the independent Ra record label. There is a newsletter, Wendell Music Scene, Box 184, Wendell MA 01379. Beginning in the late 1970s, there has been an annual women's music festival in the town hall featuring women performers from Wendell and other Connecticut River valley and hilltown communities.

Wendell's Congregational Church, closed for some years, has been saved from gradual decay by a town-wide effort, and services were reinstated in 1982. The modest public library has had successful film showings. A popular event is the annual fall supper held at the town hall under the sponsorship of the Quabbin Coon and Turkey Club. Wendell Old Home Day, held each summer on the common, is well-known for smalltown sociability and amiability across the barriers of age and background. See also WENDELL STATE FOREST.

Wendell State Forest

Located south of Millers River in Wendell, the Wendell State Forest covers 7,566 acres of rolling forested hills. It includes two ponds, several streams, hiking trails and miles of gravel and dirt roadways. Laurel and blueberries abound, and the area is open to hunting of large and small game. Within the area are cellar hole sites, school and factory sites and a portion of a charcoal kiln.

Initially purchased in the 1920s, some of the park development and road systems are attributable to the Civilian Conservation Corps' work in the 1930s. Much of the land was burned early in the century and in more recent years the forest has suffered damage from fires started by sparks from railroad brakes and from the gypsy moth caterpillar plague. A cordwood program supervised by state foresters to enable homeowners to cut their own firewood has been in existence for several years.

At the Ruggles Pond recreation area, just over the Montague line, facilities include a parking area, swimming beach, picnic area (54 tables and 34 grills), ballfield with pavilion and pit type sanitary facilities. Ruggles Pond is a manmade ten-acre lake, and although weedy in parts it offers a bucolic site for swimming and fishing. The forest headquarters is at the entrance to the Ruggles Pond area, and maps can be obtained there.

There is a boat launching ramp at the northern end of Wickett Pond, off Wickett Pond Road. The pond, which covers 29 acres, is stocked with trout. Motorboats are not permitted and rentals are not available.

The elevation ranges from 800 to 1,100 feet above sea level. There are two lookouts off Jerusalem Road. A state information sheet indicates 20 miles of unpaved car roads, 28 miles designated as motorcycle roads, 32 miles as snowmobile roads, five miles of horse trails, and six miles of hiking trails (including a portion of the Metacomet-Monadnock Trail with a trailside Adirondack shelter).

Wendell State Forest is accessible from Wendell Center, Wendell Depot, Farley, Montague and Millers Falls. Additional information about the forest, its facilities and the woodcutting program may be obtained from the supervisor, Tel. 413-659-3797. See also METACOMET-MONADNOCK TRAIL.

Whitaker-Clary House

The Swift River Valley Historical Society was founded in 1940 for the purpose of preserving memories of the pre-Quabbin days. The Society includes the four flooded Quabbin towns – Dana, Enfield, Greenwich and Prescott – plus the town where the building now stands, New Salem.

Large amounts of memorabilia (not to say ghosts!) can be found in the Whitaker-Clary House on Elm Street, North New Salem. This house was built by Capt. and Mrs. William Whitaker in 1816. The last owner was Harriet Bridges Clary.

Five-corner signpost from New Salem Center at Whitaker-Clary House

The building was acquired by the society from the Metropolitan District Commission in 1962 for use as its museum.

There is some information here about the creation of the huge reservoir, but the emphasis is on remembering the people and places from the towns that lie beneath the water. Included are genealogical data, letters, clothing, furnishings and artifacts. In the house's entry room are samplers made by Quabbin-area women more than a century ago. A closet is filled with old kitchen utensils. Paintings of houses and scenes from the once-busy farming and manufacturing towns fill the walls. In the dining room, everything is from Prescott.

The New Salem room (one of the bedrooms), contains the home-made "triplets' cradle" once slept in by Mary, Marie and Mahala Goodnow, born in 1845. In the Enfield-Greenwich room, a painting of Greenwich village is on display; it was willed to the Society after being in Martha's Vineyard for many years. Other paintings of merit are on display.

Letters with the final day of mailing from the flooded towns, Jan. 14, 1939, are exhibited. In the North Dana Room, the straw hats and bonnets and boxes made in the small mills along the Swift River have been collected and preserved in cases. Dominating the room is a stained glass window from the Dana Universalist Church.

Some of the memorabilia is stored in a shed and barn behind the house. The shed has old tools, and the barn contains the old Dana fire truck, a 1929 Model A Ford, still seen in parades, and large machinery such as old washing machines and a honey extractor. Huge train station signs from the old "rabbit run" between Athol and Bondsville are here.

Outside on a side lawn is a unique roadside sign to some places that no longer exist: Millington, Dana, North Prescott and others. This "five corners directory," which once stood in the center of New Salem, curiously includes Indianapolis. The story goes that one time when the sign was being restored, a relative of Ward Hunting was on hand and asked why his town wasn't on there. They asked what his town was and he answered, "Indianapolis," and so that was included in the directions west. A plaque on the sign explains it was made by Porter Eaton in 1886 and restored by George Fisher in 1906, Herman Hanson in 1951 and William O'Brien in 1981. Also outside are veterans' honor rolls from Enfield and Greenwich.

Members in the society come not only from the inundated Quabbin towns and nearby communities but from all across the country. In 1983, enrollment was more than 600, and membership is welcome from individuals anywhere who can appreciate what it means to remember the land, houses, people and a way of life passing into history.

The Whitaker-Clary House is listed in the National Register of Historic Places. It is open to visitors regularly each summer and by appointment. The society has its annual meeting in the summer and schedules special events. Information about membership and visiting hours is available from the Swift River Valley Historical Society, Box 24, New Salem MA 01355, and from Priscilla Spencer, Tel. 544-6807.

Y.M.C.A.

The Athol Area Y.M.C.A., describing itself as a "purposeful community center," offers many programs to residents of all ages, male and female.

Offered are courses in physical fitness, swimming, gymnastics, jogging, scuba diving, life saving, dancing, cross-country skiing, first aid and self-defense.

The Y sponsors workshops and discussion groups, trips to athletic events, an annual foot race, the annual Washington's Birthday Hatchet Hunt for children, and a Boy Scout troop. Facilities include gymnasium, swimming pool, racquetball courts, weight and exercise room, lounge, game room, office rentals and a men's dormitory.

The Y has a professional staff and charges membership and day use fees, raising additional funds through various projects. The Y has a stated policy that "no child is refused membership due to a family's financial difficulty."

Detailed information about facilities, programs and fees are available at the Y.M.C.A., 545 Main St., Athol MA 01331, phone 249-3305. See also HATCHET HUNT, SPORTS, WAWBEEK ROCK

Zita

The former Empress Zita of the Austro-Hungarian empire first came in July 1940 to reside in the "Bastille," the two-story home of her host, Calvin Bullock, on Royalston Common. At that time, the widowed monarch was in exile from the Nazi advance in central Europe.

Zita was born an Italian princess in 1892 and by dint of her marriage to Archduke Charles of Augsburg in 1911 she became empress and queen of Austria and Hungary. Deposed during the turmoil of World War I, the Hapsburg monarchs refused to accept republican rule of their homeland and carried their courtly lifestyle to exile. They lived on the Portuguese island of Madeira, where Charles died in 1922. After his death the royal family settled in Spain and later moved to Belgium. The Nazi invasion of Belgium prompted flight across the ocean. They lived in Canada and the U.S. for a decade.

The royal family eventually returned to Europe from North America but their extended presence in Royalston and Athol made local history and is remembered by many. Richard Chaisson recalled Empress Zita's sojourn in a 1972 newspaper column:

"When the nobility crowded into Royalston, so did the curiosity-seekers and news reporters. But the family preferred seclusion. Athol State Police, on orders from headquarters, kept a trooper stationed at the mansion every night during the Empress' stay. A line of private guards also stood at attention inside the fence at times. She got police escort during most of her local travels, but in her simple life she also enjoyed private walks around the common.

"Once situated here, they found a more permanent home near Quebec, but Zita returned every summer, through September. Rev. Wilfrid A. Tisdell of Immaculate Heart of Mary Church, Winchendon, was her private chaplain during these stays. She revisited him in 1964.

"Her children were frequent visitors in those first years. Then there was her secretary, two maids and a chauffeur.

"For nine summers, until 1949, the empress could be seen entering Our Lady Immaculate Church in Athol, attending early Sunday Mass in her favorite pew near the front."

Zita, who turned 90 in 1982, remains on the social scene of Europe's royalty. She attended her grandson's wedding in Luxembourg in 1982.

Illustration Credits

Explanatory note: Any photograph not listed below was taken by the author. Aerial photographs, by the author, were taken from an Athol-Orange Aero Club plane with Gerald Brousseau as pilot. Prints of most of the photographs in this book are available: for information, write to Millers River Publishing Co., Box 159, Athol MA 01331.

Acknowledgements

Valuable assistance in the preparation of "North of Quabbin" was provided by many individuals, to whom I wish to express my gratitude.

Richard Chaisson of Athol, journalist and historian, provided full access to his voluminous files of written materials about his home town and surrounding communities.

Arthur H. Platt, president of the Greater Athol Orange Chamber of Commerce, provided encouragement at various phases in the preparation of this book.

Richard J. Chase, publisher of the Athol Daily News; Ted

Chase, manager of Highland Press; Harley Smith, production superintendent of the Daily News; and the staffs of both firms cooperated in every possible manner.

"North of Quabbin" was typeset by the author in Tiffany type style on the Compugraphic photo-typesetting equipment at the Daily News with the help of Robert Perkins, foreman, and computer operators Rebecca Henry and Marie Coleman. The book was printed using the photo-offset process on the newspaper's Goss Community press by pressmen Richard Roy and James Boudreau. Binding was done at the facilities of the Highland Press.

Other employees of the Athol Daily News have helped with the project in small and large ways. They include Elizabeth Lincoln, Alice Smith, Kathleen Johnson, Joyce O'Lari, Cheryl Archibald, Melissa Gallagher and Randy Chase.

A limited amount of advertising has been published in this book to provide some financing and lower the price. The support of these businesses has been essential.

Encouragement and assistance was provided by several state officials, including Tod Lafleur and Michael Pelletier of the Division of Forests and Parks, Richard Cronin and Ellie Horwitz of the Division of Fisheries and Wildlife, and Ernest Lucci, Irene Otis and Randy Maxson of the Department of Commerce and Development.

Among those who helped with information, photographs, words of encouragement or in other ways were Irmarie Jones, Catherine Danahar, Gerald Brousseau, Linda Smith, Olive Taylor, Virginia Frye, Les Campbell, J. R. Greene, Mary King Cross, Debbie Blanchard, Jean Fuller, Kathy Olson, Don Pugh, Leo Parent Jr., Pearl Care, Mark Goldstein, Charles Morse, Beatrice Miner, Ina ("Reliable Jane") Underwood, Donald Schlicke, Kent Dumas, Alan Bowers, M. Dexter Gleason, Mark Shoul, Robert Gray, Myron Becker, Kathy Becker, Kathleen Collins, George Northrop and Dave Malinoski.

While the assistance of these various individuals is acknowledged, they are in no way responsible for any of the shortcomings, omissions and errors that may be contained in this work.

Some of the material in this book originally appeared in slightly different form in various publications, including local histories, newspaper articles, and publicity pamphlets published by public or private agencies, and due to lack of resources most of the information obtained from such sources has not been independently verified. Some of the photographs were previously published in the Athol Daily News and other periodicals. Among the particularly useful sources were articles published in the Athol Daily News, Orange Enterprise and Journal and Worcester Telegram, and the following works: "The Athol Area Library and Community Analysis" (1981); "Overall Economic Development Program Plan for the Orange-Athol Labor Market Area of Western Massachusetts" (1979); William Lord's "History of Athol" (1953); Beatrice Miner's "History of Orange, 1753-1976"; Lilley B. Caswell's "History of the Town of Royalston" (1917); "Portraits of History" by David Belcher and Robert Kelly; and J.R. Greene's "Atlas of the Quabbin Valley" (1975) and "Creation of the Quabbin Reservoir" (1981).

The Millers River Publishing Co. was established by the author for the purpose of publishing this book and is not affiliated with the Athol Daily News or the Highland Press. Information concerning errors and omissions, and any other comments on the material herein, should be sent to the author at Millers River Publishing Co., Box 159, Athol MA 01331. Corrections will be made in future editions.

About the Author

Allen Young has lived for the past ten years in Royalston, where his favorite pastime is gardening. He was born in 1941 in Liberty, N.Y., and grew up on a poultry farm in the foothills of the Catskill Mountains. He has a master's degree from the Columbia University Graduate School of Journalism. He began his writing career covering sports for a hometown weekly while a student at Fallsburgh Central High School, and has worked ever since as a journalist, editor and author. His articles have appeared in The New York Times, Christian Science Monitor, Boston Globe, Washington Post, Preservation News and many other periodicals. He is assistant editor of the Athol Daily News.

Allen Young

This cow gives cream for the author's coffee

Farmer and lambs on a Royalston homestead

256